Peer Mentoring in Music Education

Peer Mentoring in Music Education: Developing Effective Student Leadership offers a practical guide to peer mentoring in music education, enabling music teachers to implement and benefit from this technique with their students.

Drawing on extensive and current research in education and music education, the core focus of this book is on the instructional practice of peer mentoring and how students can become effective leaders. Through case studies and examples focused on music education, the author shows how peer mentoring can transform learning for all students and foster student leadership as part of a student-centered instructional approach. Part I explores the foundations of these instructional practices, the role of the music teacher, the role of the student, and how socializing and student leadership contribute to meaningful learning. Part II portrays stories of four exemplary music teachers who use peer mentoring and student leadership in their music programs across a wide array of age levels and music classes and ensembles. Music teachers will benefit from learning about the transformative power of peer mentoring and student leadership, and how these instructional practices aid with diversity, equity, inclusion, and access so that all students are valued in the music class and ensemble.

Peer Mentoring in Music Education: Developing Effective Student Leadership provides a comprehensive guide for in-service and preservice music teachers seeking to understand peer mentoring and incorporate this technique in teaching.

Andrew Goodrich is Assistant Professor of Music Education at Boston University.

Peer Mentoring in Music Education
Developing Effective Student Leadership

Andrew Goodrich

NEW YORK AND LONDON

Designed cover image: s_maria/Shutterstock

First published 2023
by Routledge
605 Third Avenue, New York, NY 10158

and by Routledge
4 Park Square, Milton Park, Abingdon, Oxon, OX14 4RN

Routledge is an imprint of the Taylor & Francis Group, an informa business

© 2023 Andrew Goodrich

The right of Andrew Goodrich to be identified as author of this work has been asserted in accordance with sections 77 and 78 of the Copyright, Designs and Patents Act 1988.

All rights reserved. No part of this book may be reprinted or reproduced or utilised in any form or by any electronic, mechanical, or other means, now known or hereafter invented, including photocopying and recording, or in any information storage or retrieval system, without permission in writing from the publishers.

Trademark notice: Product or corporate names may be trademarks or registered trademarks, and are used only for identification and explanation without intent to infringe.

ISBN: 9781032153223 (hbk)
ISBN: 9781032153216 (pbk)
ISBN: 9781003243618 (ebk)

DOI: 10.4324/9781003243618

Typeset in Sabon
by Apex CoVantage, LLC

This book is dedicated to music teachers everywhere, who believe in the transformative power of students leading the learning that occurs in music classrooms.

Contents

Preface   xiii
Acknowledgments   xvi

Introduction: The multi-faceted nature of peer mentoring and student leadership   1
Student leadership 2
Meaningful learning 3
Diversity, equity, inclusion, and access 4
How this book is organized 4
Benefits of this book 8
Summary 9

PART I
Foundations of peer mentoring and student leadership   15

1. Peer mentoring and sharing knowledge   17
  Snapshot 1: Mrs. Jackson's jazz ensemble 17
  Foundations of peer mentoring 20
    Meaningful learning 20
    Characteristics of peer mentoring 22
    Foundations of peer mentoring summary 24
  Other types of student-centered learning 24
    Cooperative learning 24
    Collaborative learning 25
    Peer tutoring 26
    Peer-assisted learning 27
  The nature of knowledge 27
    Foundational knowledge 28
    Non-foundational knowledge 28
    Tacit knowledge 29

      Explicit knowledge 29
      Knowledge summary 29
   Questions for discussion 30
   Reflection 30

2   **The role of the music teacher**   35
   Snapshot 2: Ms. San Pedro's summer choir meeting 36
   Getting started: Creating a supportive learning environment 38
      Diversity, equity, inclusion, and access 40
      Co-creating brave spaces for learning 41
      Power relationships 44
      Othering students 45
      Diversity, equity, inclusion, and access summary 46
   Constructing the peer mentoring system 46
      Selection of mentors and mentees 47
      Meeting with mentors and mentees 48
      Mentor modeling 51
      Constructing the peer mentoring system summary 52
   Instruction options for peer mentoring 53
      Individualized instruction 53
      Differentiated instruction 54
   Teacher authority and peer mentoring 55
   Questions for discussion 56
   Reflection 56

3   **The role of the student**   63
   Snapshot 3: Mr. Gardner's youth orchestra rehearsal 63
   Prior knowledge in the peer knowledge exchange 65
   Student roles in peer mentoring 66
      Fixed role 67
      Reciprocal role 67
      Student roles summary 68
   Levels of engagement in peer mentoring 68
   Online peer mentoring 69
      Asynchronous and synchronous structures 69
      Engaging with peers at other institutions 70
      Providing resources beyond the music classroom 70
      Online peer mentoring and learning 70
      Issues with online access 71
   Peer mentoring outside of school 72
   Student reflection 72

Contents ix

    Types of reflection 73
    Ways to reflect 73
    Reflection summary 75
  Questions for discussion 75
  Reflection 75

4 **Socializing and leadership**   80
  Snapshot 4: Mr. Ramirez's fourth-grade general music class 80
  Socializing as springboard for student interaction in peer mentoring 83
    Socializing 83
    Benefits of socializing 84
    Interruptions, peer pressure, sarcasm, and disparate abilities 85
    Role of the music teacher with socializing 86
    The many dimensions of socializing 86
    Socializing summary 87
  Verbal and nonverbal interactions 87
    Verbal interactions 88
    Nonverbal interactions 88
      Modeling 88
      Imitation 89
    Verbal and nonverbal interactions summary 89
  Socializing: The building blocks of leadership 89
    Leadership for musical reasons 91
    Leadership for nonmusical reasons 91
    Effective traits of student leadership 91
    Leadership summary 94
  Preparing student leaders 94
    Sharing leadership with students 96
    Preparing student leaders summary 97
  Questions for discussion 97
  Reflection 98

PART II
Narrative portraits of four music teachers   107

5 **Dana Monteiro 109**
  Introducing Dana 109
  Discovering samba 112

x   Contents

  Genesis of student leadership and peer mentoring 113
  Teacher as facilitator 114
  Peer mentoring and samba 115
  Student leadership 115
    Strength in numbers 116
    Students modeling behavior and commitment 117
    Student directors 118
    Diversity and inclusion 118
    Preparing student directors 119
    Leading warm-ups 120
    Leading the samba class 120
    Alumni leadership 122
  Questions for discussion 124
  Reflection 124
    Roles of teacher and facilitator 124
    Peer mentoring and learning a musical style 125
    Preparing student leaders 126
    Modeling and imitation 127

6 Kara Ireland D'Ambrosio   132
  Introducing Kara 132
  Early experiences using peer mentoring as a music teacher 135
  Using peer mentoring 136
  Preparing students for peer mentoring 137
    Student interactions 138
    Student initiative 140
    Rotating peer mentoring roles 141
  Questions for discussion 142
  Reflection 142
    Sharing knowledge 143
    Using school resources for peer mentoring 144
    Structuring peer mentoring 145
    Modeling and monitoring peer mentoring 145

7 Sharon Phipps   148
  Introducing Sharon 148
  Philosophy of peer mentoring 151
  Mentoring the student mentors 152
    Preparing mentors and mentees 152
    Setting objectives 154

Pairing students together 155
　　　Continual monitoring of peer mentoring 156
　　　Student initiative with peer mentoring 157
　Peer mentoring and students with disabilities 158
　Questions for discussion 159
　Reflection 160
　　　*Creating peer mentoring and student leadership
　　　　opportunities 160*
　　　Setting goals and objectives 162
　　　Stepping up to leadership: Student initiative 162

8　**Vince Cee**　　　　　　　　　　　　　　　　　　　　　164
　Introducing Vince 164
　　　Noticing students helping each other learn 166
　　　Beginning to develop student leadership 166
　　　Refining his ideas about teaching 167
　　　*Allowing students to take the initiative with their
　　　　learning 168*
　　　Current teaching position 169
　Student leadership 170
　　　Qualities of effective student leadership 171
　　　Eating lunch together 172
　　　Orchestra council 174
　　　Expanding leadership 175
　　　Student reflection 176
　　　Student identity 177
　　　Peer mentoring for lifelong participation in music 178
　Questions for discussion 178
　Reflection 179
　　　Creating opportunities for student leadership 179
　　　Leadership and reflection 180

Blended progression: Peer mentoring and student leadership　182
The organic processes of peer mentoring and student
　leadership 182
Peer mentoring is student leadership 183
　Developing a community of learners 185
Looking forward 186
Appendix: Methods　　　　　　　　　　　　　　　　　　188
Methods 188
Narrative portraits 188

    Participant selection 189
    Participants 189
    Interviews 190
    Data analysis 190
    Reliability 191
  Quick tips 191
    Participant selection 192
    Participants 192
    Interviews 193
    Data analysis 193
    Reliability 193

Bibliography   195
Index   208

Preface

Throughout my formative years as a trumpet player in school music ensembles, I often found that my peers who shared their knowledge with me helped to elevate my performance skills. Not only did their advice help me to play the trumpet at a higher level, but hearing them play the trumpet motivated me to spend more time practicing. I continued to be motivated by my peers when I pursued my undergraduate degree as a music education major at the University of Montana. I distinctly remember trumpet players who were recent graduates of the program and went on to make a living playing on cruise ships sharing their knowledge and experiences with me when they returned home on break. This knowledge included musical tips, such as what it takes to perform at a high level on a daily basis, and how to listen to other musicians in the band. At the time, though, I was most interested in what they learned in their trumpet lessons with studio musicians in Los Angeles when their boats docked. I was eager for this information, and after they shared their newfound knowledge with me, I would run to the practice room and work on what they had just explained and modeled for me.

Upon completion of my undergraduate degree, I taught K–8 general music, choir, and band for one year and was then offered a job as a high school band director. When I began teaching at the high school, I was well aware that I was a recently licensed music teacher who needed help with managing the band rehearsal. Many students engaged in behavior for which I did not have a prepared response, including talking out of turn while I rehearsed the band. As I pondered how to improve my classroom management skills, I noticed the primary culprits engaging in unacceptable behavior were a group of sophomores. They disrupted rehearsals more frequently than their peers, especially when they tried to generate laughs from everyone. They would also play their instruments when they were not supposed to. As I considered their behavior, I realized they were actually exhibiting leadership skills in that they easily commanded attention from their peers but not in a positive way. I quickly dubbed this *negative leadership* and contemplated how I could help improve their behavior toward *positive leadership*.

I also realized this group of sophomores were some of the most musically talented students in the ensemble. Even as a novice music teacher, I was intuitive enough to figure out that by meeting with them one-on-one, I could help them develop their leadership and get them to help with promoting positive behavior among their peers. I began meeting with them in brief, informal meetings immediately before rehearsals. I reinforced my expectations for proper rehearsal behavior, such as not talking when I was rehearing the band or when their peers asked questions. I emphasized that proper behavior began with them and that they could lead by example for their peers.

An ideal classroom management situation did not occur overnight; we still experienced many speed bumps during my first year at the high school. But, throughout the school year, these sophomores began to demonstrate positive leadership skills by modeling proper behavior. Once their behavior improved, I started to encourage them to use their leadership skills to mentor their peers and help elevate the musical performance level of the ensemble. I also began debriefing with them after each rehearsal. I identified moments when they did a wonderful job providing musical directives to their peers and pointed out musical issues that still needed improvement. I began setting goals for the student mentors to focus on for the next day's rehearsal, such as intonation. I gradually began to realize that they knew what the ensemble's musical issues were and started asking them for their insights on how we could elevate our performance level. This helped to further establish mutual trust between us, and I felt like they were taking on more ownership in the ensemble via their mentoring of their peers. Their negative leadership was turning into positive leadership, and the band began making wonderful improvement due in large part to the leadership exhibited by these student mentors.

After some trial and error, my first peer mentoring system was up and running, and I felt like I could focus my attention less on classroom management and actually engage in meaningful musical experiences with the students! But, when this group of student mentors graduated two years later, the peer mentoring system fell apart. I did not yet understand the importance of guiding *all* students through the process of peer mentoring to help with continuity in the program. I had focused primarily on these student mentors, thinking that the other students—the mentees—would ultimately become mentors on their own volition. What I did not comprehend is that I needed to actively guide all students through the process of being a mentor *and* a mentee. I did not quite yet grasp that in addition to the informal meetings. I needed to hold formal, structured meetings and devote rehearsal time to help guide all the students through the process of peer mentoring.

What I also did not realize at that time is that peer mentoring is actually a common instructional technique used in many school music programs. Music teachers use peer mentoring with their students to aid with both musical goals (e.g., learning music) and nonmusical goals (e.g., classroom management).[1] Researchers have found that the music teacher plays an active role with maintaining peer mentoring systems,[2] including meeting frequently with student mentors and mentees, working with them to develop their leadership skills, reinforcing expectations, modeling peer mentoring practices, and helping students to reflect on what they learned and what they did not learn during peer mentoring. When students mentor each other, they are engaging in leadership as they share their knowledge and experiences with their peers. Peer mentoring and student leadership can be used with students at all grade levels in general music classes[3] and any type of music ensemble (e.g., concert choir and jazz combo).[4] Peer mentoring is an effective instructional technique in any music class and ensemble; in fact, students often retain more of what they learn from each other than what they learn from their teachers.[5] It then follows that students would find music making more meaningful if they had some input in the content and format of learning in music classes and ensemble rehearsals. Peer mentoring is a multi-faceted instructional technique that provides opportunities for students to become leaders to contribute their knowledge for meaningful learning in music classes and ensembles.[6]

Acknowledgments

This book is a culmination of my passion for peer mentoring and student leadership. I developed a keen interest in peer mentoring during my years as an undergraduate music education major and trumpet player at the University of Montana. These formative experiences instilled in me a desire to use peer mentoring and student leadership in my teaching practice, and later as a researcher. Over time, I realized I had learned enough through my varied teaching and research experiences with peer mentoring and student leadership to begin writing a book about these instructional techniques.

Writing a book obviously takes an enormous amount of time and effort, and I received help from many people throughout the process. Acknowledging people is a risky endeavor, for I fear that I may neglect to mention someone. Yet, I would be remiss if I did not recognize the people who were instrumental in helping this book become a reality. I am appreciative of the support from the editor at Routledge, Genevieve Aoki, who facilitated the review of the book proposal and promptly answered all my questions, and the editorial team who helped this book come to fruition. I am also indebted to the anonymous reviewers of the proposal, whose feedback provided me with new insights into thinking about key concepts presented in this book. Their attention to detail vastly improved the breadth and depth of how peer mentoring and student leadership are presented throughout this book.

To ensure that the content of this book is presented in a research-to-practice approach and is relevant to school music teachers, I sought the expertise of two alumni from the doctoral program in music education at Boston University to review the proposal. David Doke, an orchestra teacher in Atlanta, Georgia, and Troy Davis, a concert band and jazz band director in Saratoga, California, are highly knowledgeable about peer mentoring and student leadership. David and Troy provided valuable insights as researchers and, more importantly, as music teachers who use these instructional techniques in their music classrooms and ensembles on a daily basis. I tasked them with making sure the content was applicable to K–12 music teachers, and that ideas were based in scholarship on peer mentoring and student leadership. Their critique provided

Acknowledgments xvii

valuable suggestions for me in the writing process and ensured that the content presented throughout this book was relevant to school music teachers.

A large portion of this book comprised new research. I conducted interviews of music teachers to help make the content relatable to the reader and to contribute new knowledge to the research on peer mentoring and student leadership. I am thus indebted to the generosity of the music teachers who graciously gave up their time to be interviewed for this book. Not only did they respond immediately to my request for an interview, but their enthusiasm for peer mentoring, student leadership, and this book provided me with great inspiration and motivation as I engaged in the writing process. For the "quick tips" in Chapters 1–4, I am thankful to Esteban Adame, Tiffany Unarce Barry, David Cosby, Troy Davis, Gary Gillett, Warren Gramm, Helene Grotans, Terri Knight, Alley Lacasse, and Lieven Smart. I am extremely humbled by their expertise. Their vast array of knowledge and experiences make wonderful contributions to this book. I am also deeply indebted to the four music teachers who are portrayed in the narrative portraits in Chapters 5–8: Dana Monteiro, Kara Ireland D'Ambrosio, Sharon Phipps, and Vince Cee. Together, they encompass a holistic portrait of the many ways music teachers can use peer mentoring and student leadership in their music programs. Their generosity with their time for the interview, reviewing drafts of their respective chapters, and their willingness to share their successes and struggles with peer mentoring and student leadership comprise a highly important part of this book. This book would, quite literally, not exist without the participation of these music teachers.

I owe an immense amount of gratitude to Karin Hendricks, my colleague in the music education department at Boston University. Karin was selfless with her time and was always willing to let me bounce ideas off her with regard to the content of this book. In addition to content, she continuously shared her insights about the book writing process, from crafting a proposal to writing the actual book. Karin generously offered to read the proposal and, later, portions of this book. I am constantly amazed at her depth of knowledge, and I am extremely thankful for her critique and support. A special shout out to my colleague, Kinh Vu, who proclaimed in a hallway one day in the School of Music, "You are THE person to write a book on peer mentoring." That bit of encouragement motivated me to move forward with crafting my ideas into a book proposal. I am also thankful to Tawnya Smith, another colleague in the music education department. Tawnya was always willing to listen to my latest progress with the book and graciously devoted time for me to bounce ideas off her about writing the narratives in Chapters 5–8, including reading an excerpt from Chapter 5. I am also grateful for my colleagues in the music education department at Boston University, whose skills with conducting research combined with their intellect, sense of humor, and teaching inspire me every day.

I am thankful for the tireless efforts of Grace Bybell, my research assistant at Boston University. Grace was extremely busy during my time writing this book. She pursued her M.M. in music education, held a full-time job, and maintained a private flute studio. Grace was always willing to help at a moment's notice, and she contributed a significant amount of time to this project. She transcribed all the interviews, reviewed formatting, double-checked the endnotes to make sure they aligned with the bibliography and vice versa, and drafted the table of contents. Her attention to even the most minute detail significantly enhanced the quality of this book.

Finally, while I wrote this book, I often thought of how Duke Ellington titled his autobiography, "Music Is My Mistress." For my wife, Mary Cicconetti, this book was my mistress for the past couple of years, and for that I owe her tremendous gratitude. Mary showed a great deal of patience with me as I placed the writing of this book at the top of my priority list. She was always willing to hear about my latest ideas for the book and how chapters were developing, and she listened intently as I shared all of the wonderful information I was learning from the interviews. Even though she has not read the book at the time of this writing, I suspect she practically knows every word in it due to my constant talking about it during morning coffee, lunches, dinners, walks, and playing tennis. Her patience with me and this book knows no limitations. And for that, I owe her the biggest thanks of all. I could not have written this book without her insights, love, compassion, and support.

Notes

1. Andrew Goodrich, "Peer Mentoring and Peer Tutoring among K-12 Students: A Literature Review," *Update: Applications of Research in Music Education* 36, no. 2 (2018): 13–21, https://doi.org/10.1177/8755123317708765.
2. Clifford K. Madsen, David S. Smith, and Charles C. Feeman Jr., "The Use of Music in Cross-Age Tutoring within Special Education Settings," *Journal of Music Therapy* 25, no. 3 (Fall 1988): 135–144, https://doi.org/10.1093/jmt/25.3.135.
3. Alice Ann Darrow, Pamela Gibbs, and Sarah Wedel, "Use of Classwide Peer Tutoring in the General Music Classroom," *Update: Applications of Research in Music Education* 24, no. 1 (Fall-Winter 2005): 15–26, https://doi.org/10.1177/87551233050240010103.
4. Warren Gramm, "Peer Mentoring in a Modern Band" (DMA dissertation, Boston University, 2021), ProQuest (AAT 28317250).
5. Darrow, Gibbs, and Wedel, "Classwide Peer Tutoring"; Andrew Goodrich, "Peer Mentoring in a High School Jazz Ensemble," *Journal of Research in Music Education* 55, no. 2 (July 2007): 94–114, https://doi.org/10.1177/002242940705500202; Bernadette Butler Scruggs, "Learning Outcomes in Two Divergent Middle School String Orchestra Classroom Environments: A Comparison of a Learner-Centered and a Teacher-Centered Approach" (PhD dissertation, Georgia State University, 2009), ProQuest (AAT 3371516).
6. Goodrich, "Peer Mentoring and Peer Tutoring."

Introduction
The multi-faceted nature of peer mentoring and student leadership

Student-centered learning is becoming prevalent in music education in the 21st century. Organizations emphasize the importance of student-centered learning practices, such as Comprehensive Musicianship through Performance (CMP), Arts PROPEL, and Partnership for 21st Century Learning,[1] and the National Core Arts Standards include components of student-centered learning and recommend that music teachers utilize student self-assessment and self-regulation.[2] In addition, many school districts now implement policies based in social–emotional learning (SEL) that create learning opportunities for students that go beyond subject matter, such as the development of social–emotional skills that help students with "understanding and management of life tasks, such as . . . relationship building and adaptation to the current demands of contemporary society."[3] These tasks include self-awareness, social awareness, self-management, relationship skills, and responsible decision-making.[4] Thus, student-centered learning plays an important role in helping teachers and students with SEL.[5]

Peer mentoring is a powerful instructional tool to use with your students. Researchers and music teachers have discovered its benefits and how it contributes to *meaningful learning*. Peer mentoring allows for increased student autonomy and places greater responsibility on students to contribute to their learning. It can help students increase their knowledge about music and motivate them toward learning.[6] When students share their knowledge, they play a more active role in their learning[7] that can elevate their ownership in the music class and ensemble.[8] Throughout the peer mentoring process, students take part in the highest levels of learning,[9] where mentors and mentees develop problem-solving skills and enhance their decision-making skills.[10]

Peer mentoring applications are flexible: You can determine how many students engage in mentoring; whether it occurs in dyads, in groups, or as an entire class; and how often and when to use it in classes and rehearsals. Peer mentoring structures are also flexible. They include hierarchical structures, where a more-knowledgeable peer mentors a less-knowledgeable peer,[11] and nonhierarchical structures, where peers considered to be of equal ability engage in roles of mentor and mentee concurrently.[12] Your role as the music teacher is also flexible:[13] You can deliver instruction and lead ensemble rehearsals but can also serve as a facilitator where you share the delivery of instruction with your students, allowing them to contribute to meaningful learning.[14] With peer mentoring, then, there is no one-size-fits-all approach; you might even use it differently in different classes and ensembles in the same music program.[15]

All students have the potential—with your guidance and encouragement—to learn how to engage in peer mentoring. In collaborating with parents, family members, private teachers, and instructors in other disciplines, you can guide students through the process of learning how to present and share their knowledge.[16] Peer mentoring is a rewarding investment of time and energy, for you also learn from students as they mentor each other. Enabling students to contribute what they know can be a valuable opportunity for you to expand your own perspectives and help students to reinforce their knowledge, build their self-esteem, and develop their confidence.[17] Peer mentoring is a music teacher's instrument for creating and nurturing a learning environment where holistic, meaningful, and all-inclusive music education can take place for every student.

Student leadership

Researchers have found that peer mentoring and leadership are intertwined; one of the main benefits of peer mentoring is it helps students to develop their leadership skills.[18] Student leadership is an important part of any music class or ensemble, and you likely use student leaders already, including section leaders, upper grade level students who are respected due to being leaders in other organizations. Student leaders can help you with making musical and nonmusical decisions.[19] Research indicates that peer mentoring allows every student to engage in leadership roles.[20] Through peer mentoring, you can have numerous students engage in leadership at the same time[21] or rotate leadership responsibilities among the students.[22] Being a student leader is not merely a title or a position but an opportunity for students to help their peers become better at what they do.[23]

As leaders, students can share their knowledge and experiences with each other and lead by example, contributing to elevated learning in the music class and ensemble rehearsals.[24] When students engage as leaders during peer mentoring, they can help each other with musical concepts such as improvisation and composition,[25] work together to better understand music fundamentals,[26] share their knowledge about technique,[27] and simply share their musical interests.[28] Student leaders can also help prepare their peers for class and rehearsals by showing them how to engage in proper warm-ups prior to rehearsal, and they can emphasize the importance of performing at a high level.[29] During peer mentoring, student leaders can help their peers with problem-solving when encountering musical performance issues, and they help to increase participation via contribution to learning objectives.[30] Despite the numerous benefits of student leadership, it is important for you to play an active role with monitoring what student leaders say to their peers, for researchers have found that issues with peer pressure and sarcasm can emerge during peer mentoring.[31]

Ultimately, though, under your guidance, the benefits of peer mentoring and leadership go beyond elevating musical knowledge and performance level in the music class and ensemble. Classroom management can improve when students model appropriate behaviors, such as interacting respectfully with their peers and talking only when it is appropriate.[32] Student leaders can pass on group expectations and program traditions to their peers.[33] A wonderful aspect of student leadership during peer mentoring is that students can assist you with making musical decisions,[34] selecting repertoire,[35] and assigning parts.[36] These interactions between you and the students help to create an environment where you and your students share in the learning process, and ultimately, all students have a voice in their learning.[37]

In developing leadership skills, students gain confidence and increase their self-esteem.[38] Insofar as it calls for student interaction, peer mentoring also helps socializing within the group. Through peer mentoring, students learn how to work with others and both lead and accept advice from their peers. These interactions build trust among students, who can then experience the friendships and sense of community that grow out of that trust.[39] Leadership, then, is an essential component of peer mentoring, and student leaders can help their peers and you, the music teacher, to create meaningful learning experiences.[40]

Meaningful learning

Peer mentoring provides opportunities for students to contribute to what knowledge is shared during learning, and when they learn from each other it improves their achievement with learning subject matter.[41] Not only do student mentees learn as a result of peer mentoring, but student mentors learn as well.[42] Student mentors reinforce their knowledge when they "giv[e] elaborated explanations."[43] This can include explaining musical concepts, such as music fundamentals.[44] Both mentors and mentees can reinforce musical concepts during peer mentoring,[45] and both also learn how to organize material for instruction,[46] learn to stay on task,[47] develop problem-solving skills,[48] and elevate their comprehension of what they are learning.[49] In addition, sharing in the shaping of what they learn helps students express their ideas about music and understand how to give and receive advice from their peers. Critical reflection on learning is also an important part of the meaningful learning process for students, and peer mentoring provides you with the opportunity to guide mentors and mentees through the process of reflecting on what and how they are learning.[50] Reflection, then, depends upon the particular learning needs identified by you at any given time.[51] Regardless of whether the student is the mentor or the mentee, learning becomes more meaningful with the increased engagement that takes place in peer mentoring.

Diversity, equity, inclusion, and access

Peer mentoring provides an opportunity for creating learning opportunities that can aid with issues of diversity, equity, inclusion, and access in the music ensemble. Researchers have revealed the inequalities that exist in school learning environments; they are not always safe spaces for marginalized students. School boards and administration are also implementing new standards in teaching, such as the Social Justice Standards from the Southern Poverty Law Center that address identity, diversity, justice, and action (IDJA).[52] For example, students with disabilities encounter negative stereotypes and are often not included in school music activities,[53] students who identify within LGBTQ+ identities can face peer harassment[54] and violence,[55] and minoritized students (e.g., Asian, Black, and Hispanic) encounter racism.[56] As a music teacher, you and your students can use peer mentoring to co-create brave spaces for learning for all students.[57] However, you need to be aware of potential issues when using this instructional technique with your students. For example, the hierarchical structure of peer mentoring holds potential to create issues with othering of students,[58] in addition to hierarchical structures where some students "may be dominant such that it may limit mutual learning and contributions from other parties."[59]

Under your careful guidance and supervision, though, peer mentoring holds great potential for marginalized students to develop leadership skills via peer mentoring. Subsequently, previously marginalized students can become leaders in their school and surrounding communities. Peer mentoring practices promote acceptance of all students, regardless of race, ethnicity, cultural background, gender identity, or sexual identity.

How this book is organized

This book encompasses a comprehensive overview of the myriad ways you can use peer mentoring and leadership with your students. It is divided into two parts. Part I: Foundations of peer mentoring and student leadership explores the foundations of these instructional techniques. The first chapter defines peer mentoring and meaningful learning and includes an explanation of the different types of mentoring and other student-centered learning instructional practices—like peer tutoring and cooperative learning—that are sometimes confused with the term *peer mentoring*.

You will then learn about the characteristics of peer mentoring that help to distinguish it from these other student-centered instructional practices. The chapter then outlines the different types of knowledge shared and constructed by students during peer mentoring.

Chapter 2 reviews your role as the music teacher with setting up and maintaining peer mentoring in detail. It discusses how you can create an atmosphere conducive to peer mentoring, and how peer mentoring aids in promoting diversity, equity, inclusion, and access to create a sense of belonging for all students. This includes co-creating brave spaces for learning during peer mentoring with marginalized students, so all students have a voice to contribute toward meaningful learning. You will learn how to select mentors and mentees, model peer mentoring for your students, and how to continually monitor their behavior and learning. You will also learn how to structure peer mentoring for students in dyads, groups, and all students at the same time. Throughout this discussion, you will learn how to avoid creating learning situations that hold potential for abusing power, such as othering of students. Finally, you will learn how to maintain your authority as the music teacher and provide opportunities for students to assume authority when peer mentoring.

Chapter 3 examines the role of the student in peer mentoring. Research indicates that students come to music classes and ensemble rehearsals with prior knowledge,[60] and you play a pivotal role in helping them share what they know with each other. In addition, this chapter describes how students construct new knowledge. It provides an overview of fixed-role peer mentoring, where more-knowledgeable peers share knowledge with less-knowledgeable peers, and reciprocal peer mentoring, where peers with similar knowledge and abilities share what they know concurrently as mentor and mentee. Online peer mentoring is also explored, and you will learn ways to effectively create peer mentoring opportunities for student engagement and learning in both fully remote and hybrid learning environments. Finally, the chapter ends with a discussion of how peers can reflect upon what they are learning from each other, how they depend on each other in peer mentoring, and how both the mentor and mentee learn during the activity.

Chapter 4 embodies leadership presented through the concept of socializing. Nearly all of the research on peer mentoring highlights socializing as one of the main elements of peer mentoring. Through the concept of socializing, this chapter builds upon the contents of the first three chapters to explain how peer mentoring helps to develop leadership skills among students for both musical and nonmusical reasons. Verbal and nonverbal interactions during socializing are explored, including how students engage in modeling and imitation during peer mentoring. You will also learn how peer mentoring helps to develop leaderships skills for marginalized students and how student leaders can help you to create safe and welcoming learning environments. In addition, you will learn how peer mentoring helps students with making musical decisions in rehearsals and how students can effectively socialize with each other during peer mentoring through verbal and nonverbal interactions. Helpful tips are also provided to help you identify and monitor peer pressure, sarcasm, and exclusionary language or behavior.

Part II: Narrative portraits of four music teachers portrays stories of four exemplary music teachers who use peer mentoring and student leadership in their music programs.[61] These music teachers illustrate different ways to use peer mentoring and student leadership across a wide array of age levels and music classes and ensembles. Each chapter focuses on a single music teacher, and they share their successes and struggles with peer mentoring and student leadership in their respective music programs. Together, these music teachers in Part II provide a holistic portrait of the multi-dimensional nature of peer mentoring and student leadership. In each chapter, you will learn about the music teacher's background, including their early experiences with peer mentoring and leadership, and when they first began using these instructional techniques. You will then learn about their current use of peer mentoring and student leadership with their students. Next, questions for discussion will help guide your thinking about salient aspects of each music teacher's story. Finally, each chapter concludes with a reflection to highlight the salient parts of the music teacher's story contextualized with content from Chapters 1–4 to help you reflect upon and to consider new approaches for how you use peer mentoring and student leadership with your students.

Chapter 5 focuses on Dana Monteiro, who directs the samba program at the Frederick Douglass Academy in Harlem, New York. In this chapter, you will learn about Dana's journey from being a music teacher who served as the sole authority of knowledge to becoming a facilitator who guides peer mentoring and student leadership. Dana discovered that peer mentoring and student leadership are intertwined with learning samba, and he designed the samba program at Frederick Douglass based on the samba schools in Rio de Janeiro, Brazil. In his role as a music teacher, Dana serves as a facilitator who guides students through the process of how to mentor and how to lead the ensembles. You will learn how peer mentoring and student leadership help to elevate performance levels in the samba ensembles. Peer mentoring and student leadership also aid with heightened student ownership and commitment, including students coming in during their lunch periods to play in the ensembles in addition to alumni returning to campus to play on a regular basis. Ultimately, peer mentoring and student leadership nurture student enthusiasm for lifelong participation in music.

In Chapter 6, you will learn about how Kara Ireland D'Ambrosio uses peer mentoring with her transitional kindergarten (TK) through eighth-grade students in the west side of Bay Area Peninsula, California. Kara's early experiences with being a mentor and being mentored instilled in her the notion that students can play a major role in meaningful learning in the music classroom. Kara considers learning a partnership between herself and the students, and the students share their knowledge and musical interests with each other to help lead the learning. Kara begins using peer mentoring with TK students to help develop a community of learners, and she plays an active role creating, guiding, and monitoring peer mentoring. She also develops leadership in her students to help lead the learning in the music classroom. In Kara's classes, peer mentoring and student leadership contribute to holistic and multi-dimensional learning, where the students contribute their voices to learning, and thus contribute to meaningful learning in the music classroom.

Chapter 7 explores how Sharon Phipps, a middle school band director in Boxford, Massachusetts, uses peer mentoring and student leadership based in individualized and differentiated instruction to provide meaningful learning experiences for her students. For Sharon, getting to know what her students know, and do not know, is an important first step for successful peer mentoring. Sharon spends a significant amount of time preparing students for peer mentoring, including how to mentor and be mentored. Sharon works with the students to create objectives for peer mentoring on a daily basis, and she continually monitors their progress. Although peer mentoring takes time out of her busy schedule, you will learn how it ultimately saves her time when students begin mentoring on their own accord. For Sharon, peer mentoring helps to prepare the next generation of leaders in society, in addition to giving students important life skills on how to interact with people throughout their lives. You will also learn about Sharon's experiences with typically developing students and students with disabilities engaged in peer mentoring. Not only does peer mentoring aid with in-depth learning and comprehension of subject matter, but ultimately Sharon considers it to make learning more enjoyable for her and her students.

In Chapter 8, you will learn about how Vince Cee, director of the orchestra program at the International School of Kuala Lumpur (ISKL), Kuala Lumpur, Malaysia, uses student leadership as a gateway to peer mentoring in orchestra rehearsals. Vince shares his story with how he observed the power of student-led learning in his formative years of teaching and how this led to him learning everything he could about student leadership. Vince realized that creating an orchestra council of student leaders in tandem with creating a welcoming atmosphere conducive to student input in learning were the first steps toward creating meaningful learning opportunities, where student contributions to learning were valued. Throughout this chapter, Vince shares his struggles and ultimate successes with guiding students through the process of sharing their knowledge and experiences with each other, and how peer mentoring became an important part of his orchestra program. Ultimately, student leadership is about service, and for Vince, student leadership is of primary importance to the success of peer mentoring. He instills in his students the values of integrity, energy, and the importance of doing what you say you are going to do when you are in a leadership position.

8 Introduction

Finally, the book concludes with Blended progression: Peer mentoring and student leadership. This reflection disseminates the salient aspects of peer mentoring and student leadership shared by all four of the music teachers in Chapters 5–8 to provide further opportunities for you to reflect on your own teaching practice. The similarities and differences between how these music teachers use peer mentoring and student leadership are explored for you to digest, and these will provide additional opportunities for you to reflect upon and synthesize the content not only from their stories but from information presented throughout the entire book.

Benefits of this book

Peer Mentoring in Music Education: Developing Effective Student Leadership offers a comprehensive overview of peer mentoring for music teachers. It is designed to accommodate a broad audience of teachers, whether you have never used peer mentoring with students (e.g., preservice teachers and teachers in their first teaching position) or you are an experienced music teacher seeking additional information to refine and enhance how you use this instructional technique with your students. The contents of this book encompass all of the different ways peer mentoring can be used in music classes and ensembles, and the book highlights its power as a transformative instructional practice for meaningful learning, diversity, equity, inclusion, and access.

In a research-to-practice approach, this book includes theoretical ideas based on the current research in education and music education, and its core focus is on the instructional practices of peer mentoring and how students can become effective leaders in music programs. The information presented throughout this book can be used in any music class and ensemble, whether it is a TK class, a concert choir of 100 students, or a popular music ensemble of six students. Although teaching methods are included throughout the book, each chapter also contains five practical elements designed specifically for the busy in-service and preservice music teacher. These elements will serve as quick and easy-to-locate reference points. They include:

- **Snapshots:** The peer mentoring snapshots in each chapter provide examples inspired by current research in peer mentoring and student leadership. These narrative vignettes bring peer mentoring and student leadership to life and help you to understand and reflect on the ways in which you can use them in your music classes and ensembles. These snapshots are topical and set up the main components of peer mentoring and student leadership presented in the chapter. Throughout the chapter, the discussions on peer mentoring and student leadership are connected back to the snapshot.

- **Quick tips:** Quick tips are helpful bits of advice from actual practicing music teachers, who use peer mentoring and student leadership in their school music classes and ensembles.[62] They are intended to help contextualize the content as you reflect on how these teachers use peer mentoring and student leadership with their students.

  > **Quick tip:** Quick tips are helpful suggestions from practicing music teachers. Scattered in boxes in appropriate spots in the chapter, these tips are easy to find and apply when needed.

- **Mini-summaries:** Mini-summaries appear throughout each chapter and provide summarizing information after major sections. These mini-summaries are provided as a quick and easy-to-access resource and reference for in-service music teachers who are implementing peer mentoring and student leadership.
- **Questions for discussion:** These questions are designed to help you think about and synthesize the material in each chapter for your own use. Preservice music teachers in licensure programs, for instance, will find these questions helpful for class discussions.
- **Chapter reflections:** Chapter reflections included at the end of each chapter provide opportunities for further thought. They are meant to help you synthesize the content in each chapter, reflect upon how you use (or would use) peer mentoring and student leadership, and consider how to best use these instructional techniques in different music classes and ensembles. Reflections in Chapters 1–4 focus on the content of the chapter. Reflections in Chapters 5–8 focus on the content of each chapter combined with content from Chapters 1–4 to provide you with further opportunities for reflection on your own teaching practice.

Summary

Peer mentoring and student leadership are multi-faceted instructional techniques that can benefit *all students* with creating meaningful learning opportunities in music classes and ensembles. Under your guidance, students can learn how to share their knowledge with their peers, and through this process vastly improve learning. Not only do student mentees learn, but student mentors also learn and can reinforce their knowledge through the process of explaining musical concepts to their peers. As a result, all students can elevate their performance levels, gain a feeling of belonging to a group, and be more open to sharing and receiving knowledge from their peers.

Student leadership is a salient part of peer mentoring, and under your guidance you can help students with learning how to become effective leaders. In addition to sharing their knowledge, student leaders can model proper behavior, help with establishing and maintaining group expectations, and aid with continuing program traditions. Throughout this process, students can help you in delivering effective and meaningful instruction for everyone in the music class and ensemble.

Peer mentoring and student leadership extend beyond helping students to improve their musical performance levels and can assist with nonmusical details, such as classroom management. Together, the musical and nonmusical objectives of peer mentoring and student leadership serve as a foundation for you and your students with creating safe learning environments where the backgrounds and perspectives of marginalized students are valued. In turn, all students can engage in transformative and meaningful learning in music ensembles.

As you read this book, you will learn about the wide-ranging approaches to peer mentoring and student leadership that can help you refine how you currently use these practices with your students. If you are considering using peer mentoring and student leadership for the first time, the comprehensive information throughout the book is presented in a sequential manner to help guide you through the process of how to implement and sustain these practices with your students. Whether you are an in-service or preservice music teacher, you will discover new ways of understanding how the *processes* of peer mentoring and student leadership contribute to meaningful learning for all students.

Notes

1. Dee Hansen and Leslie A. Imse, "Student-Centered Classrooms: Past Initiatives, Future Practices," *Music Educators Journal* 103, no. 2 (2016): 20–26, http://doi.org/10.1177/0027432116671785.
2. "National Core Arts Standards," www.nationalartsstandards.org; Hansen and Imse, "Student-Centered."
3. Nádia Salgado Pereira and Alexandra Marques-Pinto, "Including Educational Dance in an After-School Socio-Emotional Learning Program Significantly Improves Pupils' Self-Management and Relationship Skills? A Quasi-Experimental Study," *The Arts in Psychotherapy* 53 (2017): 36, https://doi.org/10.1016/j.aip.2017.01.004.
4. Pereira and Marques-Pinto, "Socio-Emotional Learning."
5. Scott N. Edgar, *Music Education and Social Emotional Learning: The Heart of Teaching Music* (Chicago, IL: GIA Publications, 2017); Keith Topping, "Trends in Peer Learning," *Educational Psychology* 25, no. 6 (2005): 631–645, https://doi.org/10.1080/01443410500345172.
6. Andrew Goodrich, "Peer Mentoring and Peer Tutoring among K–12 Students: A Literature Review," *Update: Applications of Research in Music Education* 36, no. 2 (2018): 13–21, https://doi.org/10.1177/8755123317708765.
7. Warren Gramm, "Peer Mentoring in a Modern Band" DMA dissertation, Boston University, 2021), ProQuest (AAT 28317250); Keith J. Topping and Stewart Ehly, "Peer Assisted Learning: A Framework for Consultation," *Journal of Educational and Psychological Consultation* 12, no. 2 (2001): 113–132, https://doi.org/10.1207/S1532768XJEPC1202_03.
8. Goodrich, "Peer Mentoring and Peer Tutoring."

9. Alice Ann Darrow, Pamela Gibbs, and Sarah Wedel, "Use of Classwide Peer Tutoring in the General Music Classroom," *Update: Applications of Research in Music Education* 24, no. 1 (2005): 15–26, https://doi.org/10.1177/87551233050240010103; Andrew Goodrich, "High School Jazz Ensemble," *Journal of Research in Music Education* 55, no. 2 (2007): 94–114, https://doi.org/10.1177/002242940705500202; Erik Johnson, "Peer Teaching in the Secondary Music Ensemble," *Journal of Education Training Studies* 3, no. 5 (2015): 35–42, https://doi.org/10.11114/jets.v3i5.906; Bernadette Butler Scruggs, "Learning Outcomes in Two Divergent Middle School String Orchestra Classroom Environments: A Comparison of a Learner-Centered and a Teacher-Centered Approach" (PhD dissertation, Georgia State University, 2009), ProQuest (AAT 3371516).
10. Scruggs, "Learning Outcomes."
11. Barry Bozeman and Mary Kay Feeney, "Toward a Useful Theory of Mentoring: A Conceptual Analysis and Critique," *Administration and Society* 39, no. 6 (2007): 719–739, https://doi.org/10.1177/0095399707304119.
12. Johnson, "Secondary Music Ensemble."
13. Gramm, "Modern Band."
14. Andrew Goodrich, "Peer Mentoring in an Extracurricular Music Class," *International Journal of Music Education* 39, no. 4 (2021): 410–423, https://doi.org/10.1177/0255761420988922; Gramm, "Modern Band."
15. Goodrich, "Peer Mentoring and Peer Tutoring."
16. Richard S. Webb, "An Exploration of Three Peer Tutoring Cases in the School Orchestra Program," *Bulletin of the Council for Research in Music Education*, no. 203 (2015): 63–80, https://doi.org/10.5406/bulcouresmusedu.203.0063.
17. Karin S. Hendricks, *Compassionate Music Teaching: A Framework for Motivation and Engagement in the 21st Century* (Lanham, MD: Rowman & Littlefield, 2018).
18. Darrow, Gibbs, and Wedel, "Classwide Peer Tutoring"; Goodrich, "High School Jazz Ensemble"; Scruggs, "Learning Outcomes"; Jeff Taylor, "Peer Mentoring within the Middle and High School Music Department of the International School of Kuala Lumpur: A Case Study" (DMA dissertation, Boston University, 2016), ProQuest (AAT10135020).
19. Johnson, "Secondary Music Ensemble."
20. Darrow, Gibbs, and Wedel, "Classwide Peer Tutoring"; Goodrich, "High School Jazz Ensemble"; James M. Kouzes and Barry Z. Posner, *The Student Leadership Challenge: Five Practices for Becoming an Exemplary Leader* (Hoboken, NJ: John Wiley & Sons, 2018); Scruggs, "Learning Outcomes."
21. Scruggs, "Learning Outcomes."
22. Lucy Green, *Music, Informal Learning, and the School: A New Classroom Pedagogy* (Burlington, VT: Ashgate, 2008).
23. Kouzes and Posner, "Student Leadership Challenge."
24. Goodrich, "Extracurricular Music Class."
25. Lucy Green, *How Popular Musicians Learn: A Way Ahead for Music Education* (Burlington, VT: Ashgate, 2002); Katherine Strand, "Nurturing Young Composers: Exploring the Relationship between Instruction and Transfer in 9–12 Year-Old Students," *Bulletin of the Council for Research in Music Education*, no. 165 (2005): 17–36, www.jstor.org/stable/40319268.
26. Goodrich, "Extracurricular Music Class."
27. Goodrich, "Extracurricular Music Class"; Lucy Green, *Music, Informal Learning, and the School: A New Classroom Pedagogy* (Burlington, VT: Ashgate, 2008).
28. Goodrich, "High School Jazz Ensemble"; Green, *How Popular Musicians Learn*.

29. Tamara T. Thies, "Student Leaders as Change Agents: Benefits Emerging from a Curricular Change," *Visions of Research in Music Education* 23 (2013): 1–25, http://www-usr.rider.edu/~vrme/v23n1/visions/Thies_Student_Leaders_as_Change_Agents.pdf.
30. Scruggs, "Learning Outcomes."
31. Johnson, "Secondary Music Ensemble."
32. Thies, "Student Leaders."
33. Goodrich, "Peer Mentoring and Peer Tutoring"; Goodrich, "High School Jazz Ensemble"; Andrew Goodrich, "Counterpoint in the Music Classroom: Creating an Environment of Resilience with Peer Mentoring and LGBTQIA+ Students," *International Journal of Music Education* 38, no. 4 (2020): 582–592, https://doi.org/10.1177/0255761420949373.
34. Goodrich, "High School Jazz Ensemble"; Goodrich, "Extracurricular Music Class."
35. David Hebert, "Music Competition, Cooperation and Community: An Ethnography of a Japanese School Band" (PhD dissertation, University of Washington, 2005), ProQuest (AAT 3163382).
36. Hebert, "Music Competition."
37. Johnson, "Secondary Music Ensemble."
38. David Reed Doke, "Collaborative Learning among High School Students in an Alternative Styles Strings Ensemble" (DMA dissertation, Boston University, 2020), ProQuest (AAT 27955823).
39. Goodrich, "High School Jazz Ensemble"; Johnson, "Secondary Music Ensemble."
40. Green, *How Popular Musicians Learn*; Scruggs, "Learning Outcomes."
41. Darrow, Gibbs, and Wedel, "Classwide Peer Tutoring"; Goodrich, "High School Jazz Ensemble"; Scruggs, "Learning Outcomes."
42. Goodrich, "High School Jazz Ensemble"; Green, *How Popular Musicians Learn*; Green, *New Classroom Pedagogy*; Hebert, "Music Competition"; Scruggs, "Learning Outcomes."
43. Christine Howe, *Peer Groups and Children's Development* (Hoboken, NJ: John Wiley & Sons, 2009).
44. Goodrich, "Extracurricular Music Class."
45. Darrow, Gibbs, and Wedel, "Classwide Peer Tutoring."
46. Darrow, Gibbs, and Wedel, "Classwide Peer Tutoring"; Goodrich, "High School Jazz Ensemble"; Hebert, "Music Competition."
47. Darrow, Gibbs, and Wedel, "Classwide Peer Tutoring"; Scruggs, "Learning Outcomes."
48. Richard Mayer, "Rote Versus Meaningful Learning," *Theory into Practice* 41, no. 4 (2002): 226–232, https://doi.org/10.1207/s15430421tip4104_4.
49. Goodrich, "High School Jazz Ensemble"; Jeff Taylor, "Peer Mentoring within the Middle and High School Music Department of the International School of Kuala Lumpur: A Case Study" (DMA dissertation, Boston University, 2016), ProQuest (AAT 10135020).
50. Goodrich, "Extracurricular Music Class"; Howe, *Peer Groups*.
51. Scruggs, "Learning Outcomes."
52. "Social Justice Issues." Southern Poverty Law Center. Accessed January 16, 2021. http://tolerance.org/frameworks/social-justice-standards.
53. Judith Jellison, *Including Everyone: Creating Music Classrooms Where All Children Learn* (New York: Oxford University Press, 2015).
54. Benjamin J. Corbitt, "A Qualitative Exploration of Schools with Gay-Straight Alliances as Learning Environments for LGBTQ Students" (PhD dissertation, California State University, Long Beach, 2016), ProQuest (AAT 10076450).

55. Catherine Taylor and Tracey Peter, *Every Class in Every School: Final Report on the First National Climate Survey on Homophobia, Biphobia, and Transphobia in Canadian Schools* (Toronto, ON: Egale Canada Human Rights Trust, 2011).
56. Juliet Hess, "Equity and Music Education. Euphemisms, Terminal Naivety, and Whiteness," *Action, Criticism, and Theory for Music Education* 16, no. 3 (2017): 15–47, https://doi.org/10.22176/act16.3.15; Jennifer Good, Glennelle Halpin, and Gerald Halpin, "A Promising Prospect for Minority Retention: Students Becoming Peer Mentors," *The Journal of Negro Education* 69, no. 4 (2000): 375–383, https://doi.org/10.2307/2696252.
57. Brian Arao and Kristi Clemens, "From Safe Spaces to Brave Spaces: A New Way to Frame Dialogue Around Diversity and Social Justice," in *The Art of Effective Facilitation: Reflections from Social Justice Educators*, ed. Lisa M. Landreman (Sterling: Stylus Publishing, 2013).
58. Lisa Jones et al., "'We Are the Same as Everyone Else Just with a Different and Unique Backstory': Identity, Belonging, and 'Othering' within Education for Young People Who Are 'Looked After,'" *Children & Society* 34, no. 6 (2020): 492–506, https://doi.org/10.1111/chso.12382.
59. Semiyu Aderibigbe, Djonde Frega Antiado, and Annaliza Sta Anna, "Issues in Peer Mentoring for Undergraduate Students in a Private University in the United Arab Emirates," *International Journal of Evidence Based Coaching and Mentoring* 13, no. 2 (2015): 6580, https://doi.org/10.24384/IJEBCM/13/2.
60. Webb, "Exploration."
61. The data for these narrative portraits in chapters 5–8 were generated from conducting interviews of the participants. For a detailed description of methods, please refer to Appendix.
62. The quick tips are based upon interviews I conducted with the music teachers for this book. For a detailed description of methods, please refer to Appendix.

Part I
Foundations of peer mentoring and student leadership

1 Peer mentoring and sharing knowledge

In this chapter, peer mentoring is explored and how it serves as a platform for sharing knowledge and developing student leadership. To begin this process, it is important to understand the foundations of peer mentoring. These foundations include learning about its historical roots and how peer mentoring aids with meaningful learning to aid with developing critical thinking skills in your students and enhance their comprehension of subject matter. Your role as the music teacher in decentralized learning is also discussed, including how you and your students share knowledge for heightened learning in the music class and ensemble. Understanding these characteristics of peer mentoring can help you fully realize the multi-faceted nature of this instructional technique and to help contextualize how it is defined throughout this book. Exploring the differences between peer mentoring and other types of student-centered learning will also help you to learn what peer mentoring is and what it is not, which will clarify how to use peer mentoring. Sharing knowledge and experiences is a central component of peer mentoring, and you will learn about the different types of knowledge that students can share and construct with each other when they engage in peer mentoring. With this information, you can begin to discover how peer mentoring provides a platform for student leadership. As a point of departure, we look at Mrs. Jackson and her students in one of their jazz band rehearsals.

Snapshot 1: Mrs. Jackson's jazz ensemble[1]

Sunbeam High School is a public high school located in a large school district in the Southwest United States. The top jazz band, the "Sunbeam Jazz Band I," is an auditioned ensemble that rehearses four times every week on Monday, Tuesday, Wednesday, and Thursday from 7:00 to 7:50 a.m.

It is early in the morning in the Sunbeam High School band room, and a few sleepy-eyed students have already arrived for jazz band rehearsal. Some saxophonists and brass players take their instruments out of their cases and begin soaking reeds or buzzing on mouthpieces while the drummer warms up on a drum pad. Travaurus, a freshman trumpet player, begins playing long tones, while Diego, a junior trumpet player, plays licks from a Miles Davis solo. Soon, most of the students are in the band room. Travaurus stops playing long tones and watches Diego intently, concentrating on what he hears.

Diego then plays mixolydian scales in a circle of fifths progression. Mrs. Jackson, the director, walks into the band room and exchanges a few words with Beth, a jazz major from the local university who is helping. Mrs. Jackson then walks to the center of the band room to a music stand with her scores laid out in rehearsal order and says, "Let's get rehearsal started!" The students are now silent and ready to begin rehearsing. Mrs. Jackson cautions, "I need your full attention."

The students sit quietly. The mood in the room is serious; the ensemble has a concert the following week.

Mrs. Jackson looks over to Luis, second alto and a sophomore, and asks him to lead the initial tuning for the rehearsal. He stands up and looks at Gayna, the pianist, who plays a concert B-flat on the piano. The students tune to the note, and Luis cuts them off and asks Gayna to play a concert E for Marla, the bassist. Marla tunes her low E string to the E played by Gayna. Luis then rewards her with a thumbs-up when the string's pitch matches the piano's E. Marla continues tuning her bass, and Luis asks Gayna to play the concert B-flat again, and the students tune. The students finish tuning, and Mrs. Jackson says, "Thank you Luis for leading us through the tuning process."

"You got it!" responds Luis.

"Today," adds Mrs. Jackson, "I want your input with how to fix any musical issues, should we have any. As we've discussed before, please raise your hand before you speak." Mrs. Jackson looks around and counts off the band. They begin the Duke Ellington chart "In a Mellow Tone" arranged by Frank Foster.

Almost immediately, Mrs. Jackson looks at her score, stops the band, looks up, and asks, "Any ideas about how we can get this to sound better?"

Beth, who is standing off to the side of the band, raises her hand. After a nod of approval from Mrs. Jackson, Beth quickly speaks up and says, "Mrs. Jackson, I have an idea to help the trombone players with their sound."

"Fantastic," remarks Mrs. Jackson. "Let's hear it."

Beth looks in the direction of the trombone players and says, "Trombones, you need to really support your sound, like we talked about in sectionals. What'll help is doing some wind patterns. A reminder that you need to wind pattern the phrase on the back of your hand." She holds her right hand out in front of her body to demonstrate. "This helps with your air." Rodrigo, lead trombonist and section leader, nods his head in agreement, and he and Beth have the trombone section place their right hands in front of their mouths so the students can feel the movement of air as they wind pattern the phrase. "Now, play the phrase," says Beth. "I'll count you in." She counts off the trombones, and they play the phrase. "That's more like it," Beth encourages. Rodrigo again nods in agreement, as does Mrs. Jackson, who says, "Thank you, Beth. And trombones, that sounds much better!"

Mrs. Jackson adds, "Be sure you do the wind patterns when you practice on your own. They are so helpful. Oh, and it also really helps to have your bells up over your stands or even to the side of the music stand. Doing so can help to improve your posture and helps to support your sound." She counts off the band again. They play through the shout chorus of "In a Mellow Tone" before she stops.

"Trumpets," she remarks, "your sound is solid, but you're not releasing the note together."

Pam, lead trumpet player, takes the cue from Mrs. Jackson and raises her hand. Mrs. Jackson tells her, "Go ahead, watcha got for us?" and Pam makes a point to the trumpet section, "It would help if we could start the note together, too."

Mrs. Jackson remarks, "Good! I'm glad you're listening to each other. Pam, that's exactly right! Everyone, as we've talked about before, starting and releasing notes at the same time not only helps with us playing together, but it adds an important level of intensity to our sound and helps us swing."

She counts them off once again.

After they play several measures, Mrs. Jackson stops and addresses the band again. "We need to work on our sound, especially the dynamics. How do we fix this?"

Pam raises her hand and enthusiastically says to everyone in the brass and saxophone sections, "Hey! When you see *fortepiano* in the music, you need to keep using your air!"

Mrs. Jackson briefly glances up from the score and says, "That's right, Pam." Before Mrs. Jackson counts off the band again, Pam asks Mrs. Jackson, "Can I take care of something really fast?"

"You bet," responds Mrs. Jackson.

"Trumpets," says Pam. "We need to play the *forte* dynamic at the right level. You keep playing this passage too loud, like it's *forte fortissimo*. You need to play this softer so it's only *forte*. Please mark it with your pencils so you don't forget.

The trumpet players mark their parts.

Mrs. Jackson nods her head and adds a few suggestions of her own before starting the band again. They begin with the shout chorus of "In a Mellow Tone." Mrs. Jackson begins smiling as they play and does not stop the band. They play through the end of the song, and Mrs. Jackson remarks, "Yes! Now that's more like it."

Foundations of peer mentoring

Peer mentoring takes on many forms and has many benefits for music teachers and students. In Snapshot 1, students demonstrated leadership when they helped each other rehearse musical details under the guidance of Mrs. Jackson, who encouraged them to contribute musical ideas to the rehearsal. Diego engaged in nonverbal mentoring by modeling his sound and musical ideas, Luis led the initial tuning process, Pam helped the trumpet players with playing the correct dynamics, and Beth engaged in cross-age mentoring with the trombone section. To help contextualize the different ways that peer mentoring occurred in Mrs. Jackson's jazz ensemble, it is important to understand what peer mentoring is and what it is not.

Mentoring has a long history; its roots are found in classic Greek literature.[2] One of the earliest references is Homer's *Odyssey*. The term *mentoring* is derived from the name of a character in the story. When Odysseus, the King of Ithaca, was away for ten years fighting the Trojans, Mentor guided and taught his son Telemachus. Mentor shared knowledge with Telemachus and facilitated experiences that contributed to his learning. The concept of sharing knowledge and experiences and the teacher as facilitator are key aspects of John Dewey's work, which serves as a theoretical foundation for this book.[3]

From Dewey's writings emerged the term *constructivism*, an approach to education, in which learning is student centered, and the sharing and construction of knowledge are an active learning process for the students rather than a passive one, in which they receive all their knowledge from the teacher.[4] Active learning involves students paying attention to new knowledge they are learning, comprehending it, and then reflecting on their prior knowledge and experiences to help them establish more meaningful and relevant connections to the new knowledge they are learning from their peers.[5] By sharing and constructing knowledge with your students, you can guide them through the process of more thoroughly understanding what they are trying to learn. That aids in meaningful learning, which in turn can help them achieve a higher level of success in learning music.

Meaningful learning

Meaningful learning comprises a holistic learning environment that involves all students engaging in active learning. An important part of meaningful learning is the development of problem-solving skills, which occurs when students first gain an understanding of a particular problem and then actively engage in learning to devise a solution to the problem.[6] These problems include basic elements of learning, such as learning music fundamentals, and extend to developing social skills and improving attitudes toward learning. Developing decision-making skills contributes to elevating student ownership in the music class and ensemble. When students engage in meaningful learning, you can also guide them through the process of engaging in critical thinking, where they question and reflect on what they are learning, thus developing a heightened understanding of subject material.[7] As a result, students can learn new knowledge from their peers more comprehensively when relating it to their prior knowledge.[8] An important characteristic of meaningful learning is you can learn from your students,[9] too, and develop new understanding about who your students are, including what they know and what they do not know.[10]

When students have opportunities to engage in meaningful learning under your guidance during peer mentoring, learning in the music classroom becomes decentralized.[11] Decentralized learning involves you *and* the students sharing leadership in the learning process when constructing new knowledge in the music class and ensemble, similar to Mrs. Jackson and her students. Under your supervision, you and your students comprise a multitude of learning resources that help develop student learning and heightened critical thinking skills.[12] A synergy between you and students is then created, where everyone learns new knowledge.[13] For meaningful learning to occur, you must first play an important role in creating a positive learning environment. This includes modeling how to learn and continued guidance and support for students through the process of learning.[14]

Quick tip: Decentralized learning

I find that when I have a bunch of kids who are section leaders, helpers, and co-directors, it makes rehearsals more efficient and saves a lot of time. Plus, the confidence they get out of mentoring is tremendous. It's an incredible way to empower students.

—*David Cosby, Music Director,*
Holderness School, Holderness, NH

Before students lead learning by sharing their knowledge with each other, you need to be aware of what knowledge they possess when pairing them together in peer mentoring.[15] For example, when you introduce new knowledge, it needs to be relevant and relate to the students' prior knowledge for context.[16] Thus, you play an important role in making the relationships between prior knowledge and new knowledge clear to the students.[17] You also play an important role in scaffolding learning opportunities.[18] In scaffolding, you decide what content will be learned, when it will occur, and how students will engage with each other to optimize sharing their knowledge to learn new knowledge.[19] Scaffolding in this context enables students to engage in musical independence.[20]

Leadership with authority of knowledge is shared by you and students, who all engage in sharing their knowledge and experiences. At its core, then, meaningful learning is collaborative in nature.

Characteristics of peer mentoring

Peer mentoring refers to peers' mentoring and learning from each other[21] and the actions that occur when they lead each other in the process of sharing prior knowledge and experiences and constructing new knowledge with each other.[22] During peer mentoring, both mentors and mentees learn. Through the socializing that occurs, students develop leadership skills,[23] provide support for each other,[24] and form friendships.[25] Peer mentoring can be formal in structure, with the teacher designating who will serve as mentor and mentee, when peer mentoring will take place, and to what extent. Formal mentoring can occur in dyads, such as when one student helps a peer learn their parts, or in groups, such as a section leader rehearsing their peers in a sectional. Another example of a group structure might have all students engaged in peer mentoring at the same time. Peer mentoring can also be informal, with students mentoring each other on their own, often without the supervision of their teacher.[26] Peer mentoring can occur for both musical and nonmusical reasons and can include verbal and nonverbal interactions between students.

> **Quick tip: Peer mentoring for nonmusical reasons**
>
> Students can help new students in the music program to facilitate logistics that go beyond music, such as mentoring them in things in the rest of the school. These include figuring out where to get a locker and who do they go speak to when they have questions about X, Y, or Z. These social mentorships are really valuable and help new students acclimate not only to the music program but to life in school.
> —Troy Davis, former Band and Jazz Band Director at Aragon High School, San Mateo, CA; current Director of Instrumental Music and Jazz Studies at West Valley College, Saratoga, CA

There are many approaches to peer mentoring. Peer mentoring is considered *hierarchical* when a knowledgeable and experienced individual (the mentor) guides someone considered to possess less knowledge (the mentee).[27] A common type of hierarchical peer mentoring is cross-age mentoring. For example, an older, high school-aged student mentors a younger, elementary-aged student, under the guidance of a teacher,[28] such as when a first-year high school student mentors a fourth-grade student on the fundamentals of playing the recorder. Cross-age mentoring typically occurs in school outside of class during lunch or before or after school, and mentors can provide "guidance, social support, and when appropriate, academic assistance."[29] It can occur in a variety of settings and with diverse student populations, including students with disabilities. It can also increase social skills and self-confidence for both the mentor and the mentee in addition to increasing their knowledge.[30] We saw this in Snapshot 1 when Beth, a university student, helped the trombone section of the high school jazz ensemble. Although a student mentor can often be older than the mentee, this is not always the case, for student mentors possess more knowledge than the mentee, regardless of age.

Peer mentoring can also involve *nonhierarchical* structures, such as when peers serve concurrently as mentor and mentee.[31] Co-mentoring is an approach to peer mentoring that is *nonhierarchical*. In this approach, a reciprocal relationship exists between the mentor and the mentee, as both people learn simultaneously.[32] Neither the mentor nor the mentee necessarily has more knowledge or experience than the other person. For example, beginning band students can concurrently share their knowledge when learning key signatures.[33]

You can use hierarchical and nonhierarchical structures for peer mentoring depending upon the specific learning needs at any given time in any class or ensemble. A mentoring system that works well for one class may not work as well for the other. You do not have to choose only one structure; you may use a combination of these two systems, even during the same music class or ensemble rehearsal.[34] Regardless of whether peer mentoring is hierarchical or nonhierarchical, learning is multi-faceted: Not only does the mentee learn, but student mentors learn as well.[35] For example, when student mentors explain musical concepts, such as fundamentals of breathing to produce a good tone on an instrument,[36] the experience reinforces their existing knowledge.[37]

Mentoring—in terms of knowledge transfer—shares some characteristics with teaching, but the two terms do not necessarily mean the same thing. One important distinction is that a teacher does not always serve as a mentor to their students. Teaching typically involves a person, who is considered the specialist, guiding students through learning by way of a pedagogical process. A teacher knows a variety of ways to explain concepts and deliver information to students. In addition, teachers are in charge of administrative duties—tasks outside of knowledge transfer and sharing.

According to Dewey, the teacher plays an important role in guiding the sharing of knowledge and experiences between students.[38] The success of students in sharing and constructing knowledge with each other depends in large measure on your ability to guide them through the process of understanding what it is they are learning in the classroom. Mentoring involves significant work in addition to your normal responsibilities, including an initial investment of time to help students become independent learners instead of learning solely from the you, the music teacher. However, achieving that goal will ultimately establish a degree of autonomy with the implementation of peer mentoring, which will decenter learning in the music program so you are not always the sole dispenser of knowledge. The students and you can then contribute all your voices—including their knowledge and experiences—for meaningful learning in the music program. As a departure point for our exploration into the various ways you can use peer mentoring in the classes and ensembles you teach, the next section highlights the disparate characteristics of the various types of student-centered learning and separates them from the topic of peer mentoring.

Foundations of peer mentoring summary

- Meaningful learning involves students engaged in active learning, where they share prior knowledge and construct new knowledge when interacting with their peers during peer mentoring.
- Meaningful learning embodies problem-solving skills and critical-thinking skills.
- An important part of meaningful learning is scaffolding, where you decide what content will be learned, when it will occur, and how students will engage with each other to optimize their learning.
- When you and your students share authority in leading learning, learning becomes decentralized, and both you and your students can learn new knowledge.
- Peer mentoring includes hierarchical and nonhierarchical structures and can be formal or informal in nature. How you structure peer mentoring depends upon the specific learning needs at any given time in any class or ensemble.
- A major benefit of peer mentoring is that both mentors and mentees learn.

Other types of student-centered learning

The term *peer mentoring* is often used interchangeably with other types of student-centered learning, including cooperative learning, collaborative learning, peer tutoring, and peer-assisted learning. Because these terms convey or suggest a similar meaning, they are often confused even though each term specifies a unique type of student-centered learning.

Cooperative learning

Cooperative learning is a student-centered learning practice set up by the teacher[39] that originated in the common school movement in the early 19th century.[40] It gained momentum in the 20th century with efforts to integrate students from diverse backgrounds, ethnicities, and abilities in classrooms[41] following the US Supreme Court's decision in *Brown v. Board of Education of Topeka*. Cooperative learning can help "break social barriers, meet the needs of marginalized groups, and build social bridges among and between members of a diverse student body"[42] that lead toward opportunities to develop positive relationships among all students.[43] It can also help improve student self-esteem, improve attitudes toward learning, and decrease social segregation and isolation. Cooperative learning does not embody a single teaching technique or method but rather comprises learning strategies that include groups of students organized by the teacher based on academic and social goals.[44] The teacher-assigned task is designed to help the students learn the subject matter while also achieving social goals as they work together in a group toward a specific goal or end product.[45] Cooperative learning involves a division of labor, with the teacher assigning each student a separate task to complete. Each member of the group participates in the learning process and is accountable for both their own learning and that of their classmates during the activity.

In order for a music teacher to implement successful cooperative learning experiences for their students, five elements must be considered: Positive interdependence (students working together), individual accountability (students are held accountable by the teacher and each other for their individual contributions to the group), face-to-face promotive interaction (students praise each other to encourage achievement as a group), social skills (teachers need to teach students how to be leaders and help them develop their communication skills for meaningful interactions), and group processing (students describing what actions are helpful and not beneficial to learning).[46]

This instructional technique shares some similarities with peer mentoring, including the role of the teacher with organizing learning activities that involve student interactions and development of students' social skills. But cooperative learning involves assigning specific roles within the learning group. In peer mentoring, students can switch between roles of mentor and mentee and provide input for learning goals, and music teachers can use it for objectives beyond learning subject matter, such as classroom management. It is the flexibility of peer mentoring structures—hierarchical or nonhierarchical, dyads or groups—that can provide music teachers with more opportunities for engaging students in meaningful learning in the music classroom.

Collaborative learning

Similar to cooperative learning, collaborative learning engages students in working together toward a common goal.[47] Collaborative learning is considered one of the oldest forms of learning and became prominent in the 20th century through the work of Russian psychologist Lev Vygotsky. Vygotsky posited that learning occurs between students who acquire their cultural values, beliefs, and problem-solving strategies from interacting with more-knowledgeable peers. In collaborative learning, peers who are considered to have a better understanding of subject matter and skills are referred to as the *more-knowledgeable other* (MKO). Learning occurs in the *zone of proximal development*, where the MKO collaborates with the less-knowledgeable student until the student becomes competent with learning a specific task.[48]

At the core of collaborative learning are the social interactions between students, which involve two processes: Intersubjectivity and interdependence. *Intersubjectivity* refers to the social relationships that are developed between peers as they collaborate with each other,[49] while *interdependence* refers to the way in which students guide each other through the learning process. Unlike in cooperative learning, which is highly structured with specific tasks set up by the teacher and students assuming ownership of their learning in addition to helping each other learn,[50] in collaborative learning responsibility for learning is in the hands of the students. Similar to peer mentoring, when students engage in collaborative learning the teacher may learn from their students.[51] In peer mentoring, however, both the music teacher and students share in the responsibility of engaging in meaningful learning opportunities,[52] and students of equal knowledge and abilities can mentor each other.

Peer tutoring

Peer tutoring and peer mentoring are perhaps the most often confused types of student-centered learning. This confusion is most likely due to different authors in different countries publishing in different sources.[53] Although they do share some characteristics, peer tutoring refers to a more advanced student, either in age or knowledge, working with a less advanced student in assigned coursework.[54] The roots of peer tutoring go back to ancient Rome, but the version we know of today originated in the late 18th century with Andrew Bell, who found that students who tutored each other had increased motivation and improved attitudes toward learning.[55]

Peer tutoring is usually highly structured, set up by a teacher or an adult, with one student helping another. Although peer tutoring generally occurs with just one student helping another, it can also work in groups of two or more students.[56] The teacher's role with structuring peer tutoring includes matching a tutor with a tutee, scheduling tutoring sessions, guiding students through the process of learning how to tutor, making sure the tutors understand the subject matter, supervising tutoring, and making evaluations. The teacher's role in peer tutoring is similar to the one played in creating and maintaining peer mentoring. The sole goal of peer tutoring is improvement in some aspect of learning subject matter, unlike in peer mentoring, where the music teacher can set myriad musical and nonmusical goals for learning. Peer mentoring, then, can include students working toward nonmusical goals, such as learning the expectations of the music classroom, continuing traditions from year to year, and learning how to interact with their peers via socializing.[57]

Peer-assisted learning

Unlike peer mentoring, which can include more-knowledgeable students mentoring less-knowledgeable students, peer-assisted learning entails students of similar knowledge and abilities developing knowledge during the process of teaching and learning.[58] The roots of this style of learning go back to ancient Greece; more recently, its main proponents are Keith Topping and Stewart Ehly. It can include aspects of peer tutoring, peer modeling, peer monitoring, and peer assessment.[59] Because at its core the focus is on students of similar knowledge and abilities, peer-assisted learning is an effective way of learning for students regardless of age, gender, race, and ethnicity.[60] In peer-assisted learning, students actively help each other with learning, and through their interactions they learn themselves.[61] Not only does it help students with learning new information, concepts, and skills, but it can also help improve behavior in the classroom.[62] Thus, peer-assisted learning goes beyond simply learning subject matter in the classroom. Because peer tutoring is a component of peer-assisted learning, the teacher's role is similar to their role with peer tutoring: Pairing students for successful learning experiences, maintaining a schedule for when students can engage in peer-assisted learning, and preparing students to tutor.

The characteristic common to all these student-centered learning approaches is that students share or construct some type of knowledge with each other. To develop an understanding of the connection between peer mentoring and knowledge, it is beneficial to recognize the different types of knowledge.

The nature of knowledge

As mentioned earlier in the chapter, John Dewey's work on the sharing of knowledge and experiences[63] provides the foundation for learning during peer mentoring. Students possess prior knowledge that they learn from their music teachers, other teachers in the school, their private teachers, family members, and each other.[64] When students share their knowledge and experiences with each other,[65] you serve a vital role with facilitating this process.[66] Knowledge transfer occurs through the processes of socializing (sharing what one knows) and internalization (learning by doing).[67] When students learn new knowledge from a more experienced and knowledgeable peer, they engage in social interactions as they learn new information about music performance, expectations of the ensemble or classroom, and traditions embodied within the ensemble and classroom.[68] Knowledge can be described as foundational or non-foundational and as tacit or explicit. Having a basic understanding of the different types of knowledge provides a basis for considering how you can use peer mentoring with your students.

> **Quick tip: Where students get their knowledge**
>
> When students mentor each other, I do sometimes hear what I've said in class mimicked. I remember doing that in high school, too, with trying to imitate my orchestra teacher and the things that he said. The students also gain knowledge when taking private lessons, and they share that information with their peers. Ultimately, they take initiative and share knowledge with what they think is a good idea that could help their peers.
> —Helene Grotans, Band, Orchestra, and Choir Director, Borel Middle School, San Mateo, CA

Foundational knowledge

Foundational knowledge is that which is basic to a particular subject. In music, examples include the understanding of note lengths, the ability to count rhythms, and the use of the correct fingerings. Through instruction in music, students accrue knowledge that all musicians understand. As students engage in peer mentoring, they learn how to both share and construct foundational knowledge. An example of foundational knowledge is found in Snapshot 1, when Pam mentored her peers in the trumpet section about playing the *forte* dynamic softer.

Non-foundational knowledge

Sharing foundational knowledge provides the basis for students to continue learning new knowledge through their interactions, a process called non-foundational knowledge "whereby further inquiry may be directed."[69] With this type of knowledge, not everyone necessarily agrees with how to convey a concept. For example, in ensemble rehearsals, non-foundational knowledge might include how to play with a good sound. In a traditional learning environment, students place their trust in the authority in the room—the music teacher—to guide them through these types of musical decisions. In successful peer mentoring, students begin to place their trust in each other to help make musical decisions. In Snapshot 1, Beth shared non-foundational knowledge when she mentored the trombone section in the efficient use of air to support their sound.

Tacit knowledge

Tacit knowledge is information learned from experience, usually through verbal interactions. Students do not always know how or when they learned this information, and they are not always able to clearly articulate what that knowledge entails. Using the knowledge does not require much conscious thought.[70] For example, an experienced musician can play with accurate dynamics without much thought about technique but may not recall how they learned to do so. Furthermore, a student may not be able to conceptualize how to play dynamics or be able to clearly articulate to a peer the process of how to play dynamics. This could explain why in Snapshot 1 Pam was able to help the trumpet players with how to play the correct dynamics in their parts, but she did not mentor them other than telling them they were playing too loud. Peer mentoring enables students to reflect upon what they have learned so that in turn they can share and construct knowledge with others.

Explicit knowledge

Explicit knowledge is "readily communicated and shared through print, electronic methods, and other formal means."[71] Although this type of knowledge is relatively easy to acquire, students need prior knowledge to understand it. The Duke Ellington song "In a Mellow Tone" served as explicit knowledge in Mrs. Jackson's jazz band rehearsal. The students had already learned how to read music, so they had a basic understanding of how to play the song, which helped them when they mentored each other on various musical elements, such as beginning and releasing notes together. As students engage in peer mentoring, the knowledge they share and construct can become prior knowledge for new learning opportunities in the music ensemble and classroom.

> **Quick tip: Sources of knowledge**
>
> Students pick up knowledge from myself, from other clinicians that come in, from honor bands that they've been to, and from coaches that come into rehearse them. The knowledge is not all coming from me. Oftentimes, they're giving tips that they've learned on YouTube that's helped them individually as players, and then they'll pass that on to their peers. And it's cool, because it's not always coming from me, and it doesn't always have to come from me, the music teacher.
> —*Esteban Adame, Band Director,*
> *Artesia High School, Lakewood, CA*

Knowledge summary

- Music teachers play an important role in guiding students through the process of sharing and constructing their knowledge. Peer mentoring provides abundant opportunities for them to do so.

- Students have prior knowledge from a variety of sources that include music teachers in the school, other teachers in the school, their private teachers, each other, and family members.
- Sometimes, students understand what they know—their foundational knowledge. Other times, they do not understand what they know—their tacit knowledge.
- When students share and construct knowledge by way of peer mentoring, their levels of comprehension go up, and they have more meaningful learning experiences.

Questions for discussion

1. What are the major attributes of meaningful learning?
2. How might you create a positive learning environment for meaningful learning?
3. How can you use hierarchical structures to help your students with elevating their learning in the music class or ensemble? How might nonhierarchical structures help elevate your students' learning in the music class or ensemble?
4. How might you use the four types of knowledge presented in this chapter (foundational, non-foundational, tacit, and explicit) with peer mentoring and your students?
5. What characteristics of peer mentoring, co-mentoring, and cross-age mentoring resonate with your current use of peer mentoring with your students?
6. In this chapter, we identified cross-age mentoring as being between an older student and a younger student. How might you use this type of peer mentoring to recruit students into your music program?

Reflection

In this chapter, you have taken the first steps toward learning more about peer mentoring by understanding meaningful learning and decentralized learning and defining peer mentoring. Creating an environment for meaningful learning is an important step in using peer mentoring with your students. As you reflect on the qualities of meaningful learning, it is important to determine your comfort level with sharing your authority of knowledge with your students. With these fundamental components of meaningful learning in place, you can begin to think about how to guide your students through the process of sharing and constructing knowledge. You also explored the different types of peer mentoring, segregating different types of student-centered learning, and clarifying the different types of knowledge used in peer mentoring. As you reflect on what you have read, think about the knowledge that your students have, try to determine where you think they learned it, and create a way you can help them share their knowledge with each other.

Recall Snapshot 1 documenting Mrs. Jackson's jazz ensemble rehearsal, and consider whether any of the peer mentoring seems familiar to you, as well as ways in which it was different than how you use peer mentoring or how you anticipate using it. Think about how—or if—Mrs. Jackson's way of using peer mentoring could be applicable in your own teaching settings. Either way, you may want to write some notes to help focus your ideas about what your goals are with peer mentoring. The next chapter focuses on how you can begin to set up—and then maintain—peer mentoring in music classes and ensembles.

Notes

1. This snapshot is inspired from my personal experiences teaching jazz ensembles, from observing master teachers work with their high school students, and from the following studies I conducted: Andrew Goodrich, "Utilizing Elements of the Historic Jazz Culture in a High School Setting," *Bulletin of the Council for Research in Music Education*, no. 175 (2008): 11–30, www.jstor.org/stable/40319410; Andrew Goodrich, "Peer Mentoring in a High School Jazz Ensemble," *Journal of Research in Music Education 55*, no. 2 (2007): 94–114, https://doi.org/10.1177/002242940705500202.
2. Barry Bozeman and Mary Kay Feeney, "Toward a Useful Theory of Mentoring: A Conceptual Analysis and Critique," *Administration and Society* 39, no. 6 (2007): 719–739, https://doi.org/10.1177/0095399707304119.
3. John Dewey, *Experience and Education* (New York: Collier, 1938).
4. Peter R. Webster, "Construction of Musical Learning," in MENC *Handbook of Research on Music Learning*, ed. Richard Colwell and Peter Webster, vol. 2, *Strategies* (New York: Oxford University Press, 2011); Jackie H. Wiggins, *Teaching for Musical Understanding* (Rochester, MI: Center for Applied Research in Musical Understanding, 2009).
5. Richard Mayer, "Rote Versus Meaningful Learning," *Theory into Practice* 41, no. 4 (2002): 226–232, https://doi.org/10.1207/s15430421tip4104_4; Yael Sharan, "Meaningful Learning in the Cooperative Classroom," *International Journal of Primary, Elementary, and Early Years of Education* 43, no. 1 (2015): 83–94, https://doi.org/10.1080/03004279.2015.961723; Antoni B. Valori, "Meaningful Learning in Practice," *Journal of Education and Human Development* 3, no. 4 (2014): 199–209, https://doi.org/10.15640/jehd.v3n4a18.
6. Mayer, "Rote Versus Meaningful Learning."
7. Sharan, "Cooperative Classroom."
8. Valori, "Meaningful Learning in Practice."
9. Frank Abrahams, "The Application of Critical Pedagogy to Music Teaching and Learning: A Literature Review," *Update: Applications of Research in Music Education* 23, no. 2 (2005): 12–22, https://doi.org/10.1177/87551233050230020103.
10. Sharan, "Cooperative Classroom."
11. Valori, "Meaningful Learning in Practice."
12. Brian N. Weidner, "Developing Musical Independence in a High School Band," *Bulletin of the Council for Research in Music Education*, no. 205 (2015): 71–86, https://doi.org/10.5406/bulcouresmusedu.205.0071; Brian N. Weidner, "A Grounded Theory of Musical Independence in the Concert Band," *Journal of Research in Music Education* 68, no. 1 (2020): 53–77,

https://doi.org/10.1177/0022429419897616; Valori, "Meaningful Learning in Practice."
13. David Jonassen and Johannes Strobel, "Modeling for Meaningful Learning," in *Engaged Learning with Emerging Technologies*, ed. David Hung and Myint Swe Khine (Dordrecht: Springer, 2006), 1–27.
14. Weidner, "Developing Musical Independence."
15. Valori, "Meaningful Learning in Practice."
16. Joseph D. Novak, "Meaningful Learning: The Essential Factor for Conceptual Change in Limited or Inappropriate Propositional Hierarchies Leading to Empowerment of Learners," *Science Education* 86, no. 4 (2002): 548–571, https://doi.org/10.1002/sce.10032.
17. Novak, "Conceptual Change."
18. Jackie Wiggins, "Constructivism, Policy, and Arts Education: Synthesis and Discussion," *Arts Education Policy Review* 116, no. 3 (2015): 155–159, https://doi.org/10.1080/10632913.2015.1038674.
19. Wiggins, "Constructivism."
20. Weidner, "Developing Musical Independence"; Wiggins, "Constructivism."
21. Andrew Goodrich, Elizabeth Bucura, and Sandra Stauffer, "Peer Mentoring in a University Music Methods Class," *Journal of Music Teacher Education* 27, no. 2 (2018): 1–16, https://doi.org/10.1177/1057083717731057.
22. Richard S. Webb, "An Exploration of Three Peer Tutoring Cases in the School Orchestra Program," *Bulletin of the Council for Research in Music Education*, no. 203 (2015): 63–80, https://doi.org/10.5406/bulcouresmusedu.203.0063; Jacqueline H. Wiggins, "The Nature of Shared Musical Understanding and Its Role in Empowering Independent Musical Thinking," *Bulletin of the Council for Research in Music Education*, no. 143 (1999–2000): 30, www.jstor.org/stable/40319013.
23. Andrew Goodrich, "Peer Mentoring and Peer Tutoring Among K-12 Students: A Literature Review," *Update: Applications of Research in Music Education* 36, no. 2 (2018): 13–21, https://doi.org/10.1177/8755123317708765; Bernadette Butler Scruggs, "Learning Outcomes in Two Divergent Middle School String Orchestra Classroom Environments: A Comparison of a Learner-Centered and a Teacher-Centered Approach" (PhD dissertation, Georgia State University, 2008), ProQuest (AAT 3371516).
24. Janet W. Colvin and Marinda Ashman, "Roles, Risks, and Benefits of Peer Mentoring Relationships in Higher Education," *Mentoring & Tutoring: Partnership in Learning* 18, no. 2 (2010): 121–134, https://doi.org/10.1080/13611261003678879.
25. Goodrich, "High School Jazz Ensemble."
26. Andrew Goodrich, "Peer Mentoring in a University Jazz Ensemble," *Visions of Research in Music Education* 28 (2016), www-usr.rider.edu/~vrme/v28n1/visions/Goodrich_Mentoring_in_Jazz_Ensemble.pdf
27. Bozeman and Feeney, "Useful Theory of Mentoring."
28. Clifford K. Madsen, "Music Teacher Education Students as Cross-Age Reading Tutors in an After-School Setting," *Journal of Music Teacher Education* 20, no. 2 (2011): 40–54, https://doi.org/10.1177/1057083710371441.
29. Michael J. Karcher, "The Cross-Age Mentoring Program: A Developmental Intervention for Promoting Students' Connectedness across Grade Levels," *Professional School Counseling* 2 (2008): 137, https://doi.org/10.1177/2156759X0801200208.
30. Madsen, "After-School Setting."
31. Erik Johnson, "Peer Teaching in the Secondary Music Ensemble," *Journal of Education Training Studies* 3, no. 5 (2015): 35–42, https://doi.org/10.11114/jets.v3i5.906.

32. Andrew Goodrich et al., "Comentoring in a University Jazz Ensemble," *Visions of Research in Music Education* 25 (2014), https://opencommons.uconn.edu/vrme/vol25/iss1/6; Carol A. Mullen, *Mentorship Primer* (New York: Peter Lang, 2005).
33. Lucille Alexander and Laura G. Dorow, "Peer Tutoring Effects on the Music Performance of Tutors and Tutees in Beginning Band Classes," *Journal of Research in Music Education* 31, no. 1 (1983): 33–47, https://doi.org/10.2307/3345108.
34. Goodrich, "Extracurricular Music Class."
35. Goodrich, "Peer Mentoring and Peer Tutoring"; Christine Howe, *Peer Groups and Children's Development* (Hoboken, NJ: John Wiley & Sons, 2009).
36. Andrew Goodrich, "Peer Mentoring in an Extracurricular Music Class," *International Journal of Music Education* 39, no. 4 (2021): 410–423, http://doi.org/10.1177/0255761420988922.
37. Goodrich, "Extracurricular Music Class"; Howe, "Peer Groups."
38. Dewey, *Experience and Education*.
39. David Johnson and Roger T. Johnson, "Making Cooperative Learning Work," *Theory into Practice* 38, no. 2 (1999): 67–73, https://doi.org/10.1080/00405849909543834.
40. James E. Schul, "Revisiting an Old Friend: The Practice and Promise of Cooperative Learning for the Twenty-First Century," *The Social Studies* 102, no. 2 (2011): 88–93, https://doi.org/10.1080/00377996.2010.509370.
41. Judith Jellison, *Including Everyone: Creating Music Classrooms Where All Children Learn* (New York: Oxford University Press, 2015).
42. Schul, "Revisiting," 92.
43. David Johnson and Roger T. Johnson, "Essential Components of Peace Education," *Theory into Practice* 44, no. 4 (2005): 280–292, https://doi.org/10.1207/s15430421tip4404_2.
44. Phyllis R. Kaplan and Sandra Stauffer, *Cooperative Learning in Music* (Reston, VA: MENC, The National Association for Music Education, 1994).
45. Kaplan and Stauffer, *Cooperative Learning in Music*.
46. Johnson and Johnson, "Making Cooperative Learning Work."
47. Lev Vygotsky, *Mind in Society: The Development of Higher Psychological Processes* (Cambridge, MA: Harvard University Press, 1978).
48. Vygotsky, *Mind in Society*.
49. Vygotsky, *Mind in Society*.
50. Kaplan and Stauffer, *Cooperative Learning in Music*.
51. Kenneth Bruffee, "Sharing Our Toys: Cooperative Learning Versus Collaborative Learning," *Change: The Magazine of Higher Learning* 27, no. 1 (1995): 12–18.
52. Goodrich, "Peer Mentoring and Peer Tutoring."
53. Keith J. Topping and Stewart Ehly, "Peer Assisted Learning: A Framework for Consultation," *Journal of Educational and Psychological Consultation* 12, no. 2 (2001): 113–132, https://doi.org/10.1207/S1532768XJEPC1202_03.
54. Colvin and Ashman, "Roles, Risks, and Benefits."
55. Keith J. Topping, *The Peer Tutoring Handbook: Promoting Co-operative Learning* (Cambridge, MA: Brookline Books, 1988).
56. Andrea Fernández-Barros, David Duran, and Laia Viladot, "Peer Tutoring in Music Education: A Literature Review," *International Journal of Music Education* (2022): 1–12, https://doi.org/10.1177/02557614221087761.
57. Goodrich, "Peer Mentoring and Peer Tutoring."
58. Topping and Ehly, "Peer Assisted Learning," 140.
59. Topping and Ehly, "Peer Assisted Learning."

60. Topping and Ehly, "Peer Assisted Learning."
61. Topping and Ehly, "Peer Assisted Learning."
62. Keith J. Topping and Stewart Ehly, "Introduction to Peer Assisted Learning," in *Peer-Assisted Learning*, ed. Keith Topping and Stewart Ehly (New York: Routledge, 1998).
63. Dewey, *Experience and Education*.
64. Webb, "Exploration."
65. Webb, "Exploration."
66. Goodrich, "High School Jazz Ensemble."
67. Walter Swap et al., "Using Mentoring and Storytelling to Transfer Knowledge in the Workplace," *Journal of Management Information Systems* 18, no. 1 (2001): 95–114, https://doi.org/10.1080/07421222.2001.11045668.
68. Vygotsky, *Mind in Society*.
69. Dewey, *Experience and Education*, 10.
70. Jay Liebowitz and Thomas Beckman, *Knowledge Organizations: What Every Manager Should Know* (Boca Raton, FL: St. Lucie Press, 1998).
71. Elizabeth Smith, "The Role of Tacit and Explicit Knowledge in the Workplace," *Journal of Knowledge Management* 5, no. 4 (2001): 315, https://doi.org/10.1108/13673270110411733.

2 The role of the music teacher

When you decide to use peer mentoring, one of the challenges confronting you is figuring out how to accommodate student involvement and still preserve control as classroom instructor. You may wonder, "What if the students share misinformation with each other? What if they overlook information required for learning in their enthusiasm for what they have to share?" If you find yourself pondering these questions, you can take comfort in the reality that well-prepared student mentors can participate in peer mentoring and even assume leadership without forgetting who is ultimately in charge of the classroom. In fact, peer mentoring actually supports your role as the music teacher in the classroom, as learning becomes more meaningful for both the mentor and mentee when the students help in providing class content.

As you learned in Chapter 1, situated within Dewey's concepts of learning is the idea that students share their knowledge and experiences with their peers. You play a vital role in structuring peer mentoring for your students.[1] Creating and maintaining peer mentoring are a fluid and dynamic process. It is your responsibility as the music teacher to implement and maintain learning conditions that promote opportunities for peer mentoring.[2]

This chapter focuses on your role in guiding students through the peer mentoring process. To help contextualize your role as the music teacher with peer mentoring, it is important to understand the importance of addressing diversity, equity, inclusion, and access when structuring peer mentoring, and how peer mentoring can help all students to engage in active learning, including students who are often marginalized (including, but not limited to, students with disabilities, students who identify as LGBTQ+, and minoritized students). Embedded within this discussion is becoming aware of power structures inherent in peer mentoring and how this instructional technique can other marginalized students.

After gaining insights on this information, you will then learn how to set up and maintain a peer mentoring program: How to select student mentors and mentees, how to design peer mentoring so that all students mentor concurrently, how to tap into the knowledge and experience students have to share, and how to help mentors and mentees successfully give as well as

DOI: 10.4324/9781003243618-4

receive information. In addition, this chapter provides a review of the different types of learning and levels of engagement used in peer mentoring. The opening snapshot of Ms. San Pedro at work in her choral practice room portrays a first step in the peer mentoring process—getting her students excited about her plans for introducing peer mentoring the next school year.

Snapshot 2: Ms. San Pedro's summer choir meeting

Shelby High School is a private high school located in an urban area in Southern California. The choral program includes an audition-only jazz show choir, an audition-only choir, and a choral ensemble open to all students.

It is early August, and the only sound inside the music wing of the high school is the whirr of the floor buffer driven by Mr. Watkins as he prepares the building for the opening of school next month. Near the end of the hallway, student murals of musical notes and instruments and of people singing brighten the walls. At the end of the hall is the entrance to the choir room, where a couple of students in shorts and t-shirts disappear through a doorway.

The students are now in the choir room, and there are unmistakable signs that it is still summer: The whiteboards are spotless, the folio cabinets are empty, and tall stacks of chairs frame the empty riser in the back of the room. The only sign that something is about to happen is a semicircle of seven chairs set up at the front of the room. Ms. San Pedro, the choir director, greets the students as they enter the choir room. She asks them how their summers have been going, and soon a din of conversation about summer vacation fills the emptiness.

"Hey, Ms. San Pedro, how's your summer?" hollers José, a rising sophomore.

"It's been fine!" she answers. "I've managed to take some time off and get to some of the books on my reading list."

"Awesome!" Sandra says.

"Should we sit in the chairs?" asks D'nissa, a senior and choir council president.

Ms. San Pedro nods. "Yes! Let's have a seat." She joins the students in the semicircle and begins the meeting. "Thank you for coming in. I've missed you, and I want to give you a heads-up on what we are going to do this year. I want to talk with you about peer mentoring."

Lisa leans forward expectantly and asks, "Ms. San Pedro, is this like last year when we helped each other in sectionals?"

"Yes, just like that, but this year we are actually going to do more of it in the choral ensemble, and I wanted to meet with you choir council members today so we can begin learning how to do it. I spoke with the principal and guidance counselors, and they all think it is a great idea. They said they look forward to hearing more about it."

Ms. San Pedro begins to share her enthusiasm for peer mentoring and explains how it can help improve the sound of the choir. She also explains how it can also help with making sure all students are learning their parts and paying attention in rehearsals. She pauses for a moment and then announces, "I brought you here because you are going to be our first mentors."

"Oh, cool!" says D'nissa. "But how do we do that?"

"And what does first mentors mean?" asks José.

"First mentors means we will eventually have everyone in the choral ensemble engaged in peer mentoring, where they serve as a mentor, a mentee, or both. But I need your help with getting this process started." José nods his head and quietly remarks, "Got it."

"In terms of how we go about this, I'm going to show you," promises Ms. San Pedro. "I'll walk you through how to share what you know with your peers as the peer mentor, and I'm also going to work with you to learn how to take information from each other as the mentee." She pauses for a brief moment and then continues. "We will have you mentor a peer individually during choral rehearsal, so one-on-one, while I'm on the podium conducting. I'm also going to ask you to work with your own sections while I'm rehearsing the choral ensemble." Ms. San Pedro waits for a minute for this to sink in before continuing. "This fall, we're going to keep it simple. I want you to help the other students with basic things, like posture, not holding the music in front of their faces, little things like that that are actually big things to help us improve."

"For sure," José laughs and adds, "the choir needs that kind of help." Everyone giggles.

"But," Ms. San Pedro continues, "you will also mentor the other students in music fundamentals, such as how to use their air for more relaxed singing. You will also help lead sectionals and work on correcting pitches that are out of tune."

Suddenly, Raul has an inspiration. "Mr. Niles has been doing breathing exercises with us in band to help our sound. I can totally share what I learned with everyone!"

"Perfect!" Ms. San Pedro says.

"Hey," Sandra breaks in, "this sounds like what Mr. Jefferson has us doing in tennis practice, where we are assigned in pairs to help each other with our tennis strokes."

"Yes, that is very much like what you will be doing this year. Not only will I pair you up with a student who could use the help, but I'll also have you mentoring in groups. Once we get this up and running, we will add more mentors."

"But how do we know if we're mentoring correctly?" D'Nissa wonders.

"I'll keep working with you throughout the year. I don't just disappear. I'll set goals before each rehearsal when we do peer mentoring. Then, hopefully, after each rehearsal we'll have a quick moment to debrief."

"That may be tough sometimes," Raul reasons. "I have chemistry right after choir, and Mrs. Swanson doesn't like for us to be late to her class."

"Maybe we could email you, Ms. San Pedro, with how we think peer mentoring went," suggests Sandra.

"Great idea! I was actually thinking we could use Google Docs as a type of journal to stay in touch with how peer mentoring is going," Ms. San Pedro adds. She stops for a minute before shifting to her next point. "So, our first step," she continues, "is to decide what you think our musical goals for peer mentoring should be and what our classroom management goals should be as well. Let's write some ideas on the board and come up with a list of goals for the semester. In fact, why don't you work together to come up with the goals, and if you get stuck, I'll help." The students get out of their seats and begin writing ideas on the board. Ms. San Pedro smiles, breathes deeply, and whispers to herself, "This is going to be a wonderful year . . ."

Getting started: Creating a supportive learning environment

You can help shape students' learning experiences by implementing peer mentoring that can lead to musical growth and development of leadership.[3] To do so, you need to empower your students to be active in their learning.[4] Creating a supportive learning environment provides a foundation for sociocultural learning that creates optimal conditions for students to successfully share what they know with each other.[5] These conditions, which include students' attitudes, beliefs, behaviors, and customs, influence students' behaviors in the music classroom[6] and can bring about changes in student attitudes toward learning that can also influence behaviors outside of the classroom.

Quick tip: Creating a supportive learning environment

I am involved in Orff Schulwerk and Project-Based Learning. There are facets within these two that have helped me to incorporate elements of constructive feedback that builds students up and ultimately the community of students too. For example, in Orff Schulwerk, we do a lot of group music making, where students will often create a rhythmic ostinato in separate groups and then perform them for each other. After a group performs, I ask them, "What did you like about this particular group's performance?" "What was your favorite part?" These compliments help build a safe classroom culture that instills in students the idea that we appreciate each other and to appreciate the risks that we take when performing music.

—*Tiffany Unarce Barry, former Music Teacher at Steindorf K-8 STEAM School, San Jose, CA; current Professor of Music Education at San Jose State University, San Jose, CA*

Peer mentoring can serve a variety of objectives, and you can use it in a variety of ways to promote active learning and elevated performance levels among your students.[7] There are important differences between the formal hierarchical structures and informal egalitarian models discussed in Chapter 1 that will affect your planning. The composition of peer mentoring varies from program to program and, within programs, from ensemble to ensemble and class to class.[8] Your first step, then, is to formulate a clear idea of why you want to use this instructional technique with your students. This requires you to think about and define what your goals for peer mentoring are. For example, Chapter 1 pointed out that peer mentoring can occur for both musical and nonmusical reasons, so think about how peer mentoring can help students elevate their musical skills in the classroom, as well as nonmusical goals, such as improved classroom management and greater student motivation. Even if you currently use peer mentoring and have a clear idea of why you are using it, it can still help to revisit your objectives on a semester or yearly basis to make sure it is meeting the needs of your students. Coming up with an overarching goal provides the platform on which you will build your program. Short-changing this step will make others more difficult.

The next consideration is whether you want peer mentoring to occur in dyads, groups, or possibly a combination of the two. These structures are considered in greater detail in Chapter 3. You should also decide when you want peer mentoring to take place: Should it be scheduled before, during, or after rehearsals? Perhaps each time has advantages for your program. Write these ideas down and develop a specific plan that will work for your students.

In considering peer mentoring and the issue of shared responsibility for curriculum content with your students, you will be faced with the nagging question of where students learn their knowledge in the first place.[9] This concern is one of the biggest issues you may face when using peer mentoring. Students already possess various levels of knowledge gained from a variety of sources: You, previous and current music teachers of other classes and ensembles, private teachers, other teachers in the school, and teachers and conductors of ensembles outside of school.[10] That being said, a major concern with peer mentoring is the potential for students to share misinformation with each other.[11] Although students are already in possession of knowledge, one of your most vital tasks is making sure that knowledge is accurate. As the music teacher, you play an important role in monitoring what knowledge students share with each other and helping potential student mentors figure out how to give information to—and receive information from—their peers.

Creating a supportive learning environment is an important dimension to implementing and maintaining a peer mentoring program. Snapshot 2 illustrates the need to clearly articulate the objectives of the program and the roles of mentors and mentees, and providing a structure to keep the peer mentoring system healthy once it is up and running. Ms. San Pedro spent some of her own time off during the summer to meet with students and get them excited about peer mentoring in the choir program. Her objective for this meeting was to get peer mentoring started with a few student leaders, who will in turn help to build excitement for peer mentoring among the entire ensemble. Getting students on board is important because many students may be hesitant or lack the desire to actively contribute to the learning process.[12] Furthermore, many students may be accustomed to their teachers not sharing authority in the classroom and dictating how and when learning will occur.[13] Creating a supportive learning environment conducive to peer mentoring is a crucial first step. If you are excited about peer mentoring, your students will be too.

Diversity, equity, inclusion, and access

Most music classrooms contain a diverse array of students.[14] Music teachers are aware of the importance of diversity in the content that is taught in music classes and ensembles (e.g., programming music written by people of color), and making sure that learning is equitable and accessible for all students. But many music teachers struggle at times to figure out how to effectively reach and teach all students in their music program. If this dilemma resonates with you, you can co-create a supportive learning environment with your students so everyone, regardless of race, cultural background, ethnicity, gender identity, sexual orientation, or abilities, can engage in meaningful learning in the music class and ensemble.[15] Peer mentoring, then, can aid with diversity, equity, inclusion, and access.

To help you consider how peer mentoring contributes to diversity, equity, inclusion, and access, this section focuses primarily on how you can co-create meaningful learning experiences with your students. Although marginalized populations encompass a broad array of students, examples will be drawn upon research in music education and education that involve students with disabilities,[16] students who identify as LGBTQ+,[17] and students from underrepresented minorities.[18] To contextualize marginalized populations for this discussion, a student with a disability is someone who has undergone a formal assessment by a professional, acting with parental support, to determine if a disability exists.[19] The term *disabilities* is wide ranging and may include behavioral, emotional, cognitive, or physical impairments.[20] Students who do not meet diagnostic criteria for any disabilities are referred to as typically developing students.[21] The *LGBTQ+* designation refers to students who identify as lesbian, gay, bisexual, transgender, queer, or other related identities.[22] The term *minoritized students* refers to students devalued in terms of race (e.g., Black, Native American, Hispanic, and Asian).[23] That is, it does not refer to students in terms of their relative numbers within the population but how they are considered lower status in society.[24]

Co-creating brave spaces for learning

When creating learning opportunities, you can construct supportive learning environments where all students feel welcome and safe and can contribute their voices to the learning process. The term *safe spaces* is often used to denote a classroom where the music teacher creates a learning environment where students feel safe. Yet, when the music teacher is the sole individual who creates a safe space for learning, it may not meet the needs of all students, especially marginalized students, who may not feel safe in the music classroom.[25] Recently, scholars and teachers have begun to use the term *brave spaces* to indicate spaces for learning that are co-created by the music teacher and students. Co-creating brave spaces for learning values contributions from all students.[26] In this setting, you can facilitate the inclusion of issues surrounding diversity, equity, inclusion, and access into the learning process in tandem with students, who provide their input into what makes the learning environment a brave space for their learning.[27]

When co-creating brave spaces for learning, it is important to consider where and how peer mentoring occurs, including location, and whether you will use dyads or groups or both. It is important to establish guidelines for how peer mentoring will occur among students[28] combined with setting realistic expectations for what students can learn.[29] With the initial guidelines and expectations communicated to the students, you can ask students for their input to aid with ownership in the learning process. Including input from students in these formative stages not only helps to build trust and strengthen relationships between students but also between you and your students. You and your students will need to establish clear goals and objectives for what you wish to accomplish via peer mentoring.[30] Students can help you create objectives for learning in addition to planning for performances. For example, student interactions can form the basis for *inclusion*—including students with disabilities in music classes and ensemble rehearsals so that they become full participants in the learning process.[31] When students with disabilities participate in peer mentoring activities, many benefits arise that enhance the overall musical experience,[32] including developing friendships, sharing humor, and connecting with peers.[33] Further, co-creating brave spaces for learning with typically developing students and students with disabilities helps to develop positive attitudes[34] among all students and heightened ownership in the music program for meaningful learning. On the contrary, not including students with disabilities into music classes and ensembles creates an environment conducive to negative stereotyping.[35]

To promote inclusive learning, it is important for you to co-create a positive SEL environment where students engage in positive interactions with each other during peer mentoring.[36] The first step in this process involves reflecting on your own attitudes and potential stereotypes you may have regarding students with disabilities.[37] Understanding these stereotypes is an important first step that will help you to understand how to more effectively co-create an inclusive learning environment with your students, including learning how to accommodate differently abled students in the music class and ensembles. As the music teacher, you can work with typically developing student mentors to become advocates for those with disabilities and structure the peer mentoring process so that students with disabilities feel welcome and included in rehearsal and performance activities.

> **Quick tip: Preparing peer mentoring for students with disabilities and typically developing students**
>
> When creating opportunities for typically developing students and students with disabilities, you can't just drop them in a room and expect them to do something without some type of scaffolding or training. It is important to structure peer mentoring so everybody takes turns as mentor and mentee, so everyone is included. I find that this helps all students to take a leadership role, particularly for students with disabilities who thrive in music. Because of peer mentoring, the students with disabilities succeed very well in music compared to their other courses outside of music.
>
> —*Troy Davis, former Band and Jazz Band Director at Aragon High School, San Mateo, CA; current Director of Instrumental Music and Jazz Studies at West Valley College, Saratoga, CA*

There are many complexities embedded within co-creating a learning environment that includes both students with disabilities and typically developing students. Because of the uniqueness of each music class and ensemble, and because each student experiences a disability differently,[38] it is important to understand how to guide typically developing students toward engagement with students with disabilities for meaningful learning experiences for all students. Judith Jellison, one of the leading researchers in peer learning and inclusion, recommended several steps toward creating an inclusive learning environment. To begin, it is important to create opportunities for interactions between typically developing students and students with disabilities early in the school year.[39] Doing so helps to emphasize the importance of student interactions toward meaningful learning. It is also helpful to consult with fellow teachers, guidance counselors, administration, paraprofessionals, and staff at your school who can provide additional assistance.[40] Administration in particular can play an important role in establishing those connections.[41] Parents will also have additional insights into the learning styles of their children and are usually willing to share this information to help you create meaningful learning opportunities.[42]

Brave spaces for learning can also provide a supportive learning environment for students who identify as LGBTQ+, where they feel safe contributing to the learning process. Even though establishing brave spaces for learning is vitally important, not every student who identifies as LGBTQ+ will want to reveal their sexual or gender identity to peers or music teacher. Therefore, you will want to set up peer mentoring to aid LGBTQ+ students without asking them to reveal their identity.

> **Quick tip: Peer mentoring and non-binary students**
>
> When I see a student at school with potential to be a role model for another student of the same sexual identity, or gender identity, I try to pair the students together if at all possible. As an example, I have had non-binary students who have wanted to pair up with another non-binary student. I place them together for peer mentoring because I think that it's really important to feel comfortable and safe when learning.
> —Helene Grotans, Band, Orchestra, and Choir Director, Borel Middle School, San Mateo, CA

Co-creating brave spaces for learning can aid LGBTQ+ students with resilience. Before co-creating peer mentoring opportunities to aid with resilience, it is important to be aware of and understand issues that affect LGBTQ+ students.[43] These issues include understanding the complexities of what each sexual or gender identity entails within the LGBTQ+ designation. It also helps to understand how homophobia and heterosexism play a role in school bullying and harassment. LGBTQ+ students can experience myriad issues in and out of school, including peer harassment,[44] nonacceptance from family,[45] health risks at a higher rate than their peers who do not identify as LGBTQ+,[46] and violence.[47] To develop this understanding, it may be helpful to develop a support network with your colleagues, including administration, counselors, staff, and school psychologists. This network can also help you to develop support structures for LGBTQ+ students, including promoting brave spaces for learning, which are necessary for using peer mentoring to aid with resilience. To help students deal with these issues, you can co-create a learning environment that aids LGBTQ+ students with feeling comfortable in the music classroom and ensemble. You can accomplish this by co-creating brave spaces for learning that aid with resilience, which can help students learn coping mechanisms to deal with adversity.[48] Furthermore, through peer mentoring, students who do not identify as LGBTQ+ can gain a deeper understanding of the experiences of LGBTQ+ students,[49] thus improving their attitudes toward LGBTQ+ individuals and, ultimately, reducing prejudice.[50] It is important to prepare heteronormative students for peer mentoring so they understand issues surrounding LGBTQ+ students, and through this process they become more empathetic.[51]

Co-creating brave spaces for learning can also provide a foundation for understanding the backgrounds and experiences of all students, including those who are minoritized, in the music classroom and ensemble. Through peer mentoring, you and your students can dialogue about racism and promote anti-racism.[52] Not only do students gain a heightened understanding of each other's experiences, but you can also gain a heightened understanding about the individual experiences of minoritized students in your music class or ensemble, especially with racism.[53] The knowledge and experiences shared by the students continue to inform how you guide all students through these conversations during peer mentoring.[54] Thus, by integrating conversations about race and racism into the objectives for peer mentoring, learning outcomes can extend beyond comprehension of subject matter and the elevation of performing skills. Student interactions during peer mentoring, then, can lead to in-depth conversations about racism and learning to value the voices of all students.[55] When minoritized students contribute their voices to learning, they become leaders in the classroom. Further, students of color often benefit from being mentored by peers of the same race.[56] Over time, then, leadership can become a cyclical process, where mentees eventually become the leaders in learning, a process referred to as *lateral mentoring*.[57] In addition, the connections between students established and nurtured through peer mentoring contribute to heightened meaningful learning when students challenge their assumptions and long-held beliefs about their prejudices, privilege, and racism.[58]

Meaningful learning occurs when marginalized students contribute their voices to learning via peer mentoring in the music class or ensemble.[59] Peer mentoring, then, can supersede a model of teaching and learning solely for mastering subject matter or elevating musical performance levels[60] by providing a conduit for you to aid students with understanding and valuing all perspectives regardless of race, cultural background, ethnicity, gender identity, sexual orientation, or abilities.[61] When co-creating an atmosphere conducive for meaningful learning for all students, however, it is highly important to consider power structures inherent in peer mentoring and the potential for othering students.

Power relationships

When students share their knowledge and experiences, they play a role in controlling what knowledge and experiences are being shared. Power relationships exist in peer mentoring and can be found in both hierarchical and nonhierarchical structures. In peer mentoring, micro- and macro-relationships typically comprise two types of power structures.[62] Microstructures entail the relationships that develop during interactions between mentor and mentee, and macrostructures involve the power relationships in the music program. These power relationships are influenced by each other and may affect the ways in which students interact with one another. Thus, it is important for you to structure peer mentoring to intentionally encourage students to contribute their voices to learning.

Despite the numerous benefits of using peer mentoring for meaningful learning, it is important for you to be aware of power structures and to continually monitor student interactions, for some students from dominant populations may not be willing to give up power[63] or be willing to invest their time.[64] Therefore, it is a crucial role for you as the music teacher to continually emphasize to the students that knowledge and experiences are a shared endeavor between everyone, regardless of background.[65] Modeling peer mentoring for students provides opportunities for students to ask questions about the goals for mentoring and how to go about mentoring, and having them reflect on what they are learning helps them build a higher level of self-confidence that in turn leads to a higher level of motivation to contribute to meaningful learning. Modeling is discussed in greater depth later in this chapter. Through peer mentoring, learning becomes a transformational process when marginalized students share their voices to guide learning in the music classroom, particularly when students from dominant populations and marginalized populations are placed together.[66] The end result is that marginalized students will feel more comfortable contributing their voices to meaningful learning in the music class and ensemble.

Another facet to power structures is that as the music teacher, you typically serve as the focal point for students learning how to mentor and be mentored. You play a powerful role with deciding how peer mentoring is structured and how it will be used to create meaningful learning experiences for students. For example, you need to be aware of whether you are simply giving permission to marginalized students to engage in peer mentoring, and thus reaffirming a dominant power structure. Instead, if you are flexible when structuring peer mentoring so that you facilitate peer mentoring experiences instead of being the sole authority in the classroom, you and your students can engage in dialogic interactions to help counter prejudice, homophobia, bias, and racism. As a result, marginalized students can share their knowledge and experiences, and contribute their voices toward meaningful learning in the music class and ensemble. As the music teacher, you play an important role not only in monitoring the knowledge and experiences shared by students but also by encouraging students to be open to each other's perspectives so that they all have a voice in the learning process.[67]

Othering students

Embedded within power relationships is the potential for marginalized students to be *othered* during peer mentoring.[68] *Othering* occurs when an excluded group of students, such as those who are marginalized due to skin color, are viewed as being different in some manner because they are not part of the dominant group.[69] Thus, othering is the dominant group considering the marginalized group as deficient in some way.[70] Othering can serve as a foundation for prejudice among students due to differences, including race, class, gender, sexual identity, and ability,[71] and it can perpetuate hierarchies that continue to perpetuate racist oppression.[72] As a result of othering, marginalized students can experience alienation, internalized oppression, and repression.[73] Because hierarchies are inherent in many peer mentoring scenarios and because othering is based upon a perceived deficit of some type, peer mentoring has a danger of reaffirming power structures of dominant populations as being superior in the music classroom and ensemble.[74] Thus, it is imperative to set up opportunities for marginalized students to contribute their voices to learning.[75]

Diversity, equity, inclusion, and access summary

- It is important to co-create learning opportunities so that students who are marginalized due to race, cultural background, ethnicity, sexual identity, and abilities can contribute to meaningful learning in the music class and ensemble.
- Brave spaces for learning are co-created by you and the students. Co-creating brave spaces for learning values contributions from all students and helps facilitate the inclusion of issues surrounding diversity, equity, inclusion, and access into the learning process.
- Micro- and macro-power relationships exist in peer mentoring. Microstructures involve mentor and mentee, and macrostructures involve the power relationships in the music program. You play an important role in monitoring power structures so that all students can participate in peer mentoring.
- As the music teacher, you need to be aware of othering. Othering occurs when an excluded group of students, such as those who are marginalized due to skin color, is viewed as being different in some manner because the students are not part of the dominant group.

Constructing the peer mentoring system

With an awareness of how to co-create a supportive learning environment with your students for meaningful learning, the next section explores the various ways you can construct peer mentoring for your students. As you learned in Chapter 1, designing and implementing peer mentoring can be challenging time-wise with your busy schedule.[76] In a day crowded with duties and packed with responsibilities, finding time to lead a peer mentoring program presents unique challenges. Tasks, like planning performances, performing administrative chores, dealing with classroom management issues, finishing up school duties, and attending meetings, consume in-school hours, and that is before the teaching even begins! Despite those distractions, investing time in planning for peer mentoring is necessary for it to be successful.[77] As you read in Snapshot 2, Ms. San Pedro had the support of her administration. She understood the importance of full transparency and informed her administration and staff that she planned to use peer mentoring in her music program. Having the support of faculty, administration, and personnel when implementing peer mentoring is critical to its success.[78]

Selection of mentors and mentees

Although research and common sense suggest that teachers should design peer mentoring for all students,[79] it helps for the teacher to have a clear idea of who will serve as a good mentor, especially when introducing peer mentoring for the first time. How mentors and mentees are selected is one of the main predictors of success in a peer mentoring program.[80] Selecting a small group of students at first can help ensure the system is manageable and set up for optimum success. As time progresses and word of your successful program spreads, additional mentors and mentees can be recruited until *all* students participate in peer mentoring. This can include hierarchical structures with a mentor/mentee relationship, or nonhierarchical structures, where students concurrently serve in roles as mentor and mentee.[81]

When creating a peer mentoring program, you probably already have a pretty good idea of which students would make effective mentors. These are students that you know will take the responsibility seriously and who have the potential to become leaders (if they are not already) in the music program. Tap into existing groups as Ms. San Pedro did with her choir council members in Snapshot 2. Another option is to meet with section leaders, who likely possess more knowledge and have accumulated more experiences from their time as a member in the music ensemble. In addition to maturity and experience, mentors should have positive attitudes,[82] a strong academic record, a high level of performance skills, an ability to be empathetic, and a personality conducive to working with people.[83]

Quick tip: Selecting mentors

I am incredibly careful about who I pick to be my mentors. Mentoring is a huge responsibility, because during peer mentoring students are not always under my direct supervision but working with their peers. I find that it's got to be someone that I absolutely trust and also someone who has the sensibilities as an individual to be patient, to not make fun of the other students, and to just really be there to help and mentor their peers. Because I'm careful about who I pick, when students mentor each other, I have no reservations about their abilities, for I think they are capable of doing the job.

—David Cosby, Music Director,
Holderness School, Holderness, NH

Once you have a squad of mentors, the next task is to pair mentors with mentees. Mentees can include students who would benefit the most from receiving additional help with learning. Although helping struggling students may be your primary goal, you might also consider students who are at risk of quitting the music program. It is important that the mentors and mentees will work well together.[84] Although this outcome is not always easy to predict, try to match up students you know will get along well and who will respect each other. For peer mentoring experiences that involve nonhierarchical structures, you can designate which students will serve in the role of mentor and mentee, and make it clear to them that they will swap these roles. These considerations underline the importance of setting up specific goals and objectives prior to implementing peer mentoring so that no possibility is overlooked.

> **Quick tip: Keeping track of mentors and mentees**
>
> To organize peer mentoring for our after school peer mentoring program, I use a Google spreadsheet to keep track of who's a mentor and who's a mentee. We now have a running sidebar of kids that are waiting for a mentor or waiting to be a mentor. This system works great because I work with the other band teacher so if one of us is ever sick, the other person can keep it running. And if a student says they can't make it that day, I can look at the Google Docs and see who they are paired with for peer mentoring. It's a great reference document and really helps the peer mentoring program run itself.
> —Helene Grotans, Band, Orchestra, and Choir Director,
> Borel Middle School, San Mateo, CA

Meeting with mentors and mentees

Meeting with the students you have selected to be mentors and mentees is the next step in the process of implementing peer mentoring. Although scheduling conflicts are the norm,[85] it is essential to meet with the students prior to their beginning peer mentoring.[86] In Snapshot 2, Ms. San Pedro avoided scheduling conflicts by meeting with the students for the first time during the summer. During that meeting, she clearly articulated why she wanted to have them engage in peer mentoring.[87]

Establish simple goals for the students at first, nothing too complex. Initial goals might include musical topics, such as learning words to a song, intonation, instrument fundamentals like fingerings,[88] or understanding key signatures.[89] Writing them down on a whiteboard, SMART Board, Google Docs, or anything that works in your situation can help clarify those goals for the students and allow for questions when necessary. When you and your students think about goal setting, be sure to communicate that you also want them to help with nonmusical goals, such as classroom management, or have them mentor students considered at risk for quitting music.[90] Keep the list short and manageable. You might also consider having the students help you create the goals, as Ms. San Pedro did.[91] This adds another layer of student buy-in and ownership of the peer mentoring process. When you ask students to help you to establish these goals, be sure to appreciate their efforts—their responses may surprise you! Their resulting excitement about the program will help other students accept it as well. By seeking your students' help in creating these goals, you have provided them opportunities to take a leadership role in the peer mentoring process.

Another consideration is to make sure mentors and mentees understand the expectations for learning,[92] for it is important that students clearly understand why they are engaged in peer mentoring. This includes careful planning on who is paired with whom during peer mentoring. For example, you may want to use different combinations of students that include pairing by race[93] and by matching students from the dominant population with one from a marginalized population. When making these decisions, the objectives for learning can help guide you, such as peer mentoring for musical reasons (e.g., students teaching each other a song by ear) or nonmusical reasons (e.g., reflecting on and understanding one's privilege). This is a multi-faceted endeavor, and rotating different pairings and groupings for different reasons can help all students to not only elevate their knowledge about music, but they also gain a deeper understanding of each other's racial, ethnic, and cultural backgrounds.[94]

> **Quick tip: Monitoring peer mentoring**
>
> As a facilitator of peer mentoring, you're not sitting back and kicking your feet up and just hoping things work out well. You're constantly observing the students to make sure that what they are conveying to each other is accurate.
> —*Warren Gramm, former Music Teacher in Jersey City Public Schools, NJ; current Assistant Professor of Music Education at Lebanon Valley College, Annville, PA*

Not to be overlooked is the importance of having clear guidelines for peer mentoring behavior.[95] For example, students need to understand that they must be mindful of what they are saying to their peers and that they avoid peer pressure and sarcasm. It is important that you and your students work together to actively create brave spaces for learning. By working on this challenge with your group of mentors and mentees, you will help them feel comfortable when participating in mentoring, which will in turn contribute to meaningful learning experiences.

> **Quick tip: Modeling feedback**
>
> When I model peer mentoring for students, I start with providing a positive remark, then share what I noticed was a musical issue, ask if they corroborate with it, and then provide a solution. During this process, we talk about respect and knowing your audience, imagining ourselves being in that person's shoes, and the importance of thinking about the things you're going to say before you say them. This helps them understand ways to give and receive feedback in a way that feels safe to build people up instead of tearing them down. Guiding students through the process of giving feedback helps them to understand how it makes you feel to receive feedback, including learning how to receive criticism. I then pair them together and have them practice peer mentoring.
> —*Tiffany Unarce Barry, former Music Teacher at Steindorf K–8 STEAM School, San Jose, CA; current Professor of Music Education at San Jose State University, San Jose, CA*

Once mentoring begins, continue to communicate regularly with your mentors. Emphasize why they need to mentor, recap the specific objectives or goals for their mentoring, and provide guidance about how they share their knowledge and experiences.[96] This is a great opportunity to continue modeling proper peer mentoring behavior to help remind the students of how they should interact with each other when sharing their knowledge and experiences. Give the students opportunities to ask questions. These meetings help ensure long-term mentoring effectiveness.[97]

Make sure you take time to debrief with students after each mentoring experience. This reflection should involve mentors as well as mentees. This can be tricky, as students may have to hurry to their next class, but even a quick one-minute check-in can pay big dividends. If even a one-minute exchange is impossible, create additional ways to solicit feedback on how peer mentoring is going. Journaling is an effective way for students to reflect upon the mentoring process[98] and can be accomplished by way of an online platform, such as Google Docs. Today's mentees have the potential to become tomorrow's mentors, and having mentors and mentees engage in reflection together adds another layer of understanding to their experience.[99] Chapter 3 goes into reflection and journaling in greater detail.

Whether you meet with students during the summer, before or after school, or before or after rehearsals, continued conversations are extremely important. They provide opportunities to work with students to review goals, to remind them how to mentor and be mentored, and to continue monitoring their work. Talking with students also gives you time to provide feedback and to follow up on any questions they come up with during mentoring.

Mentor modeling

An important aspect of guiding students through the mentoring process is showing them how to mentor and be mentored, which you can do by modeling for your students.[100] Demonstrating peer mentoring by acting in the role of a student mentor and student mentee helps guide students through every step of the process.[101] As part of the demonstration, you can model improper behaviors, such as using sarcasm, so students can understand what not to say. Modeling the roles of mentor and mentee for the students is an important part of setting up peer mentoring in your music class and ensemble.[102]

> ### Quick tip: Modeling peer mentoring
>
> Before I begin modeling peer mentoring for my students, I pull a student off to the side and instruct them to provide feedback that is kind of brash and blunt after my modeling. I then use my trumpet for band, or violin for orchestra, and play for the students and have them critique my playing. I purposefully play things incorrectly during these demonstrations. The students have the music that I am playing so they can provide specific feedback. I also project three sentence frames for affirmation and three sentence frames for constructive criticism/feedback on the board to help encourage students to be detailed and specific. For example, "At measure _____, I like how you _____." "At measure _____, you need to _____ by doing _____." I explain how to use these sentences during peer mentoring, and I find it really helps them. I also post these sentences online, where I post their homework so they can look at them later. Through this process, they begin to understand how to listen, how to give affirming and constructive feedback, and what it is like to receive harsh feedback. I then ask all the students, "How do we talk to people? What's appropriate? And how do we give constructive feedback without being a jerk about it?" Giving the students this kind of structure really helps them to mentor each other because they're sixth, seventh, and eighth graders.
> —*Lieven Smart, Music Teacher Grades 6–8,*
> *Junction Avenue K–8 School, Livermore, CA*

You can model for students how to concurrently engage in roles of mentor and mentee, and you can actively guide them through the mentoring process, such as mentoring each other for musical reasons. For example, students can mentor each other to elevate their comprehension of key signatures.[103] The process would begin with you leading students through the steps to understanding a particular key signature, starting with determining which notes comprise the key signature and then figuring out the correct fingerings or how to properly produce sound depending upon the vocal range in the scale. Next, the students would mentor each other with learning key signatures, with the mentors guiding mentees through the process of how to successfully play or sing a scale in the key signature. Then, under your directive, the students would swap roles with the former mentees serving in the role of mentor. Serving in the role of mentor provides students with the opportunity to engage in leadership, and serving in the role of mentee helps them to critically reflect on the learning process.[104] Having students serve in both roles helps them to more thoroughly comprehend subject matter by having to explain it to their peers.[105] Thus, having students engage in both roles of mentor and mentee in the same lesson provides a more holistic learning experience for all students.

Students can also model peer mentoring for each other. By explaining how to mentor and be mentored in their own words, they gain a deeper understanding of the peer mentoring process.[106] For example, two students might form a dyad and role-play a mentoring experience, with one taking the role of the mentor and the other in the role of the mentee. Or, several students could role-play a group mentoring experience. Finding the time to model remains a difficult part of the equation, but many possibilities exist. You might find time to set up modeling workshops before school, or you could have a group of students demonstrate mentoring in front of the entire ensemble during a rehearsal, allowing class time for students to ask the mentor/mentee models any questions they have. Relinquishing even five minutes of packed class or rehearsal time for modeling demonstrations will promote peer mentoring among your students.

Of course, you should clear even the briefest modeling sessions with your students before scheduling them. You want them to feel comfortable with sharing their method of mentoring and being mentored in front of their peers. As the system develops, you can begin to have experienced students guide new students in the program more frequently with how to mentor and be mentored. Having students guide their peers through the process of learning how to mentor and be mentored adds an additional layer of leadership to peer mentoring, further supporting your students' commitment to remain actively involved with growing peer mentoring in your music program.

Constructing the peer mentoring system summary

- Co-creating goals and objectives with students helps to increase their ownership in the music class and ensemble. Meet with students

before peer mentoring sessions so that everyone understands the goals and objectives for the day.
- Meet with students after peer mentoring assignments to debrief with both mentors and mentees.
- You can select who will serve as mentors and who will serve as mentees. You can also design peer mentoring so that all students engage in the roles of mentor and mentee.
- Monitor students who are doing well as mentors and as mentees, and adjust if necessary.
- You can demonstrate peer mentoring by acting in the role of a student mentor and student mentee, guiding them through every step of the process. You can model improper behaviors, such as using sarcasm, so students can understand what not to say.
- When students model peer mentoring and explain how to mentor and be mentored to each other, they gain a deeper understanding of the peer mentoring process.

Instruction options for peer mentoring

How peer mentoring helps develop student leadership depends on the instructional format, and it is important to understand the different types of instruction that can form the basis for peer mentoring experiences. Although many different types of instructional formats exist, two that allow for student leadership—individualized instruction and differentiated instruction—are pertinent to peer mentoring.

Individualized instruction

Individualized instruction is that which is designed to accommodate the learning style of an individual student. Peer mentoring can help provide opportunities for individualized instruction in the music classroom. When the classroom consists of many students, the task of designing different learning activities for each student is daunting. Using peer mentors can be beneficial because they can help individual students with a particular learning style while you lead the class. For example, you could ask a peer mentor to work one-on-one with a student or to help individual students within their section while you are busy rehearsing the rest of the group, similar to what Ms. San Pedro envisioned as part of the peer mentoring program she was creating with her choir. Because students progress at different paces when learning their music, it can be helpful to have peer mentors, who are more advanced musically, facilitate learning. In music classrooms, then, the concept of individualized instruction can extend to helping individual students with their learning.[107]

Individualized instruction has four components, each of which you need to consider: Learning each student's interests, creating learning opportunities for each student based upon these interests, scaffolding learning through peer interactions, and monitoring student progress.[108] These components provide a basis for student interactions when making decisions in peer mentoring. As a music teacher, you play an important role in the process of determining the needs of each student: You are responsible for understanding what your students already understand, what they are capable of learning, and how this influences your expectations about their learning.[109]

Differentiated instruction

In differentiated instruction, teachers identify the needs of groups of students within the larger class and address those needs by presenting learning activities that create meaningful learning experiences for all students. Your role in this format of instruction is consequential, for when you can identify the various interests of students,[110] you can establish expectations for groups of learners within the classroom.[111] For example, when you plan rehearsals, you can then provide opportunities for all learners to achieve success with a particular task.[112] Using a variety of instructional approaches, you can help all students achieve success in rehearsals.[113]

> Quick tip: Differentiated instruction
>
> Peer mentoring is a great opportunity to differentiate instruction. If a student is struggling with playing their music, I can pair them up with a peer whom they're able to work with and learn from them. For example, I can ask the students, "Why don't you go outside, and can you help them get the major scale fingering correct? And then, make sure you can play it in quarter notes and half notes." And that gets that student out of the classroom where they're feeling overwhelmed and into a situation where they feel like they're learning. I feel like I can move forward with teaching the class without leaving the struggling student behind.
>
> —David Cosby, Music Director,
> Holderness School, Holderness, NH

Peer mentoring provides a conduit for differentiated instruction in music classrooms and ensembles. In Snapshot 2, Ms. San Pedro explained to the students that they would mentor their entire section. For example, as you rehearse one section or sections in an ensemble, a peer mentor could take on a leadership role by providing rehearsal directives in their own section.

You may wish to designate a section leader to be a mentor; however, the mentor could be an older student, a student with a leadership position (e.g., orchestra council), or a student with prior mentoring experience (e.g., former

TK student who is now in kindergarten). Another option is to rotate who serves as a student mentor to provide opportunities for as many students as possible to serve in this role. Decide ahead of time whether you are comfortable having students engage in verbal mentoring while you are conducting a rehearsal. The upside is that having more than one leader in the classroom allows you and your students to achieve several musical goals for a rehearsal all at one time.[114] If you have space, you can send mentors and students having difficulty learning their music in a group to an adjacent room while you rehearse the rest of the students. Conversely, peer mentors could also run through sections of music or entire compositions with advanced students while you rehearse with other students. These options can work in any setting, from large ensembles, such as a marching band or choir, to smaller chamber ensembles, such as a string quartet, to general music classrooms.

> **Quick tip: Comfort level with verbal mentoring**
>
> When we're playing in rehearsal, and I ask the student leaders to take five minutes and address musical issues amongst their sections, the leaders will address that issue. It gets noisy, but that's the way we gotta do it. You gotta have a high tolerance for the noise, though.
> —*Esteban Adame, Band Director, Artesia High School, Lakewood, CA*

Teacher authority and peer mentoring

Including peer mentoring in your program does not mean that you are sacrificing any of your authority as the teacher in the music classroom. As discussed earlier in this chapter, your role as the teacher is vitally important. Setting up and maintaining peer mentoring in the program require that you take an active role in guiding all students through the steps of how to mentor and be mentored, continuously communicate goals and objectives with the students, and checking in with them to find out how the mentoring process is going. These responsibilities come with many layers of authority. Ultimately, you retain authority even when students share in the delivery of information in class, because you have the final say on the musical decisions and you are responsible for classroom management. Also, keep in mind that peer mentoring does not occur every moment of every rehearsal;[115] it is up to you to determine how often, when, and where it will occur. Even being in charge of the logistics of peer mentoring adds to your authority as students engage in peer mentoring.

> **Quick tip: Balancing your authority and peer mentoring**
> - Authority is best when shared with the students.
> - Authority is earned by students and then handled with care.

- Even though the teacher is a "specialist," the rehearsal room is full of intelligent people.
- Chances are that someone else in the room has a better answer than you, the teacher!
- When students invest in the process (e.g., musical decision-making), they are apt to "buy in" to a much greater extent.
- By involving all students in everything, the creative process is enlightened and wonderful surprises can happen!
- Art is nurtured with collaboration.
- The ensemble as a whole is the blending together of individual inputs.

—Gary Gillett, retired Band Director at Sentinel High School, Missoula, MT

Questions for discussion

1. How might you use peer mentoring to create learning opportunities so that students can reflect on their prejudices and attitudes and promote anti-racism?
2. In what ways can you set up peer mentoring so marginalized students can contribute their voices to learning?
3. In what ways can you design and monitor peer mentoring to avoid othering students?
4. What might your primary musical and nonmusical goals be for using peer mentoring in the music program?
5. How can you use hierarchical peer mentoring structures to create meaningful learning opportunities?
6. How can you use nonhierarchical peer mentoring structures to create meaningful learning opportunities?
7. How might you use individualized instruction with peer mentoring?
8. How might you use differentiated instruction with peer mentoring?
9. How can you retain your authority as the music teacher while sharing authority with students during learning?

Reflection

In this chapter, you learned about the teacher's role in peer mentoring. Peer mentoring holds potential for misuse of power structures and othering of students. As a music teacher, you play an important role in co-creating brave spaces for learning with your students and careful monitoring of student interactions. Through these processes, all students can engage in meaningful learning, regardless of race, class, gender, sexuality, and ability. As you already know, setting up peer mentoring can take a lot of time and energy, but the investment can pay huge dividends by creating more meaningful learning experiences for all the students in your music program.

If you have not used peer mentoring before, reflect on how Ms. San Pedro began the process of setting up peer mentoring in Snapshot 2, and think about how you can talk to your school's administration and key personnel to generate interest and support. This is also a good time to think about the goals and objectives you have for peer mentoring—or to revisit them—and how you can involve your students in co-creating these goals and objectives.

Selecting students is a pivotal part of setting up peer mentoring. Think about which students have the potential to become mentors. Begin with section leaders, older students, and students in leadership positions. Next, think about which students will be open to being mentees. Consider which students you think could use extra help from mentors. You can also structure peer mentoring so that all students are mentors and mentees and then swap roles. The ultimate goal is to provide opportunities for all students in the music class and ensemble to engage in peer mentoring as both mentors and mentees. Because every music program is different and every class and ensemble within that program has different learning needs, consider how peer mentoring can adapt to both individualized and differentiated instruction, and how different levels of engagement might work with your students.

Now that you have a good understanding of why and how to use peer mentoring, or have reexamined why and how you use it, the next step is understanding the student's role in the process. That is the topic of the next chapter.

Notes

1. Alice-Ann Darrow, Pamela Gibbs, and Sarah Wedel, "Use of Classwide Peer Tutoring in the General Music Classroom," *Update: Applications of Research in Music Education* 24, no. 1 (2005): 15–26, https://doi.org/10.1177/87551233050240010103; Erik A. Johnson, "Peer Teaching in the Secondary Music Ensemble," *Journal of Education Training Studies* 3, no. 5 (2015): 35–42, https://doi.org/10.11114/jets.v3i5.906.
2. Carol A. Mullen, *Mentorship Primer* (New York: Peter Lang, 2005), 2.
3. Mullen, *Mentorship Primer*, 2–3.
4. John Dewey, *Experience and Education* (New York: Collier, 1938); Candace Spigelman, "Reconstructing Authority: Negotiating Power in Democratic Learning Sites," *Composition Studies* 29, no. 1 (2001): 27–49, www.jstor.org/stable/43501474.
5. Mullen, *Mentorship Primer*, 2.
6. Dewey, *Experience and Education*; Lev Vygotsky, *Mind in Society: The Development of Higher Psychological Processes* (Cambridge, MA: Harvard University Press, 1978).
7. Lucille Alexander and Laura G. Dorow, "Peer Tutoring Effects on the Music Performance of Tutors and Tutees in Beginning Band Classes," *Journal of Research in Music Education* 31, no. 1 (1983): 33–47, https://doi.org/10.2307/3345108; Mullen, *Mentorship Primer*.

8. Susan Dennison, "A Win-Win Peer Mentoring and Tutoring Program: A Collaborative Model," *The Journal of Primary Prevention* 20, no. 3 (2000): 161–174, https://doi.org/10.1023/A:1021385817106.
9. Erik A. Johnson, "The Effect of Peer-Based Instruction on Rhythm Reading Achievement," *Contributions to Music Education* 38, no. 2 (2011): 43–60, www.jstor.org/stable/24127190.
10. Richard S. Webb, "An Exploration of Three Peer Tutoring Cases in the School Orchestra Program," *Bulletin of the Council for Research in Music Education*, no. 203 (2015): 63–80, https://doi.org/10.5406/bulcouresmusedu.203.0063.
11. Dewey, *Experience and Education*; Johnson, "Secondary Music Ensemble."
12. Russel K. Durst, *Collision Course: Conflict, Negotiation, and Learning in College Composition* (Urbana, IL: National Council of Teachers of English, 1999).
13. Spigelman, "Reconstructing Authority."
14. Judith Jellison, Laura Brown, and Ellary Draper, "Peer-Assisted Learning and Interactions in Inclusive Music Classrooms: Benefits, Research, and Applications," *General Music Today* 28, no. 3 (2015): 18–22, https://doi.org/10.1177/1048371314565456; Yael Sharan, "Meaningful Learning in the Cooperative Classroom," *International Journal of Primary, Elementary, and Early Years of Education* 43, no. 1 (2015): 83–94, https://doi.org/10.1080/03004279.2015.961723.
15. Brent C. Talbot, "Introduction," in *Marginalized Voices in Music Education*, ed. Brent Talbot (New York: Routledge, 2018), 1–12.
16. Jellison, Brown, and Draper, "Inclusive Music Classrooms."
17. John Cawley et al., "Effect of HealthCorps, a High School Peer Mentoring Program, on Youth Diet and Physical Activity," *Childhood Obesity* 7, no. 5 (2011): 364–371, https://doi.org/10.1089/chi.2011.0022; Andrew Goodrich, "Counterpoint in the Music Classroom: Creating an Environment of Resilience with Peer Mentoring and LGBTQIA+ Students," *International Journal of Music Education* 38, no. 4 (2020): 582–592, https://doi.org/10.1177/0255761420949373; Jeananne Nichols, "Rie's Story, Ryan's Journey: Music in the Life of a Transgender Student," *Journal of Research in Music Education* 61, no. 3 (2013): 262–279, https://doi.org/10.1177/0022429413498259; Joshua Palkki, "'My Voice Speaks for Itself:' The Experiences of Three Transgender Students in Secondary School Choral Programs" (PhD dissertation, Michigan State University, 2016), ProQuest (AAT 10141543).
18. Tabbye Chavous et al., "Gender Matters, Too: The Influences of School Racial Discrimination and Racial Identity on Academic Engagement Outcomes among African American Adolescents," *Developmental Psychology* 44, no. 3 (2008): 637–654, https://doi.org/10.1037/0012-1649.44.3.637; Karin Hendricks and Dorothy, "Negotiating Communities of Practice in Music Education: Dorothy's Narrative," in *Marginalized Voices in Music Education*, ed. Brent Talbot (New York: Routledge, 2018), 65–79.
19. Judith Jellison, *Including Everyone: Creating Music Classrooms Where All Children Learn* (New York: Oxford University Press, 2015).
20. Jellison, *Including Everyone*.
21. Jellison, *Including Everyone*.
22. Christopher Cayari, "Demystifying Trans*+ Voice Education: The Transgender Singing Voice Conference," *International Journal of Music Education* 37, no. 1 (2019): 118–131, https://doi.org/10.1177/0255761418814577; Karin S. Hendricks and June Boyce-Tillman, *Queering Freedom: Music, Identity, and Spirituality* (Bern: Peter Lang, 2018).
23. Talbot, "Introduction to *Marginalized Voices*."

24. Özlem Sensoy and Robin DiAngelo, *Is Everyone Really Equal? An Introduction to Key Concepts in Social Justice Education* (New York: Teachers College Press, 2017).
25. Brian Arao and Kristi Clemens, "From Safe Spaces to Brave Spaces: A New Way to Frame Dialogue around Diversity and Social Justice," in *The Art of Effective Facilitation: Reflections from Social Justice Educators*, ed. Lisa M. Landreman (Sterling: Stylus Publishing, 2013); Karin S. Hendricks and Gary E. McPherson, "Reconsidering Musical Ability Development Through the Lens of Diversity and Bias," in *The Oxford Handbook of Compassion and Care in Music Education*, ed. Karin S. Hendricks (New York: Oxford University Press, 2023).
26. Johnson, "Secondary Music Ensemble"; Michael Karcher et al., "Pygmalion in the Program: The Role of Teenage Peer Mentors' Attitudes in Shaping Their Mentees' Outcomes," *Applied Developmental Science* 14, no. 4 (2010): 212–227, https://doi.org/10.1080/10888691.2010.516188.
27. Arao and Clemens, "From Safe Spaces."
28. Jellison, Brown, and Draper, "Inclusive Music Classrooms."
29. Jellison, *Including Everyone*.
30. Michael Karcher et al., "Mentoring Programs: A Framework to Inform Program Development, Research, and Evaluation," *Journal of Community Psychology* 34, no. 6 (2006): 709–725, https://doi.org/10.1002/jcop.20125.
31. Judith A. Jellison and Donald. M. Taylor, "Attitudes Toward Inclusion and Students with Disability: A Review of Three Decades of Music Research," *Bulletin of the Council for Research in Music Education*, no. 172 (2007): 9–23, www.jstor.org/stable/40319362.
32. Jellison, Brown, and Draper, "Inclusive Music Classrooms."
33. Zachary S. Rossetti, "'That's How We Do It': Friendship Work between High School Students with and without Autism or Developmental Delay," *Research & Practice for Persons with Severe Disabilities* 36, no. 1–2 (2011): 23–33, https://doi.org/10.2511/rpsd.36.1-2.23.
34. Jellison and Taylor, "Attitudes Toward Inclusion."
35. Jellison, *Including Everyone*.
36. Jellison, *Including Everyone*.
37. Hendricks and McPherson, "Reconsidering Musical Ability"; Jellison, *Including Everyone*.
38. Rossetti, "That's How We Do It."
39. Jellison, *Including Everyone*.
40. Jellison, *Including Everyone*.
41. Erik W. Carter et al., "Peer Network Strategies to Foster Social Connections among Adolescents with and without Severe Disabilities," *Exceptional Children* 46, no. 2 (2013): 51–59, https://doi.org/10.1177/004005991304600206
42. Jellison, Brown, and Draper, "Peer-Assisted Learning."
43. Heather Murphy, "Improving the Lives of Students, Gay and Straight Alike: Gay-Straight Alliances and the Role of School Psychologists," *Psychology in the Schools* 49, no. 9 (2012): 883–891, https://doi.org/10.1002/pits.21643; Richard A. Stevens, "Understanding Gay Identity Development within the College Environment," *Journal of College Student Development* 45, no. 2 (2004): 185–206, https://doi.org/10.1353/csd.2004.0028.
44. Benjamin J. Corbitt, "A Qualitative Exploration of Schools with Gay-Straight Alliances as Learning Environments for LGBTQ Students" (PhD dissertation, California State University, Long Beach, 2016), ProQuest (AAT 10076450).
45. Caitlin Ryan et al., "Family Rejection as a Predictor of Negative Health Outcomes in White and Latino Lesbian, Gay, and Bisexual Young Adults," *Pediatrics* 123, no. 1 (2009): 346–352, https://doi.org/10.1542/peds.2007-3524.

46. Michael P. Marshal et al., "Suicidality and Depression Disparities between Sexual Minority and Heterosexual Youth: A Meta-Analytic Review," *Journal of Adolescent Health* 49, no. 2 (2011): 115–123, https://doi.org/10.1016/j.jadohealth.2011.02.005.
47. Catherine Taylor and Tracey Peter, *Every Class in Every School: Final Report on the First National Climate Survey on Homophobia, Biphobia, and Transphobia in Canadian Schools* (Toronto, ON: Egale Canada Human Rights Trust, 2011).
48. Michael Ungar, "The Social Ecology of Resilience: Addressing Contextual and Cultural Ambiguity of a Nascent Construct," *American Journal of Orthopsychiatry* 81, no. 1 (2011): 1–17, https://doi.org/10.1111/j.1939-0025.2010.01067.x.
49. Goodrich, "Counterpoint."
50. Darrel Higa et al., "Negative and Positive Factors Associated with the Well-Being of Lesbian, Gay, Bisexual, Transgender, Queer, and Questioning (LGBTQ) Youth," *Youth & Society* 46, no. 5 (2014): 663–687, https://doi.org/10.1177/0044118X12449630.
51. Goodrich, "Counterpoint."
52. Deborah Bradley, "The Sounds of Silence: Talking Race in Music Education," *Action, Criticism, and Theory for Music Education* 6, no. 4 (2007): 132–162, http://act.maydaygroup.org/articles/Bradley6_4.pdf; Deborah Bradley, "Hidden in Plain Sight: Race and Racism in Music Education," in *The Oxford Handbook of Social Justice and Music Education*, ed. Cathy Benedict, Patrick Schmidt, Gary Spruce, and Paul Woodford (New York: Oxford University Press, 2015), 190–203; Ibrim X. Kendi, *How to Be an Anti-Racist* (New York: Penguin Random House, 2019).
53. Ruth Gustafson, *Race and Curriculum: Music in Childhood Education* (New York: Macmillan, 2009).
54. Andrew Goodrich, "Valuing Racialized Student Voices: Transforming Learning Through Peer Mentoring," *Action, Criticism, and Theory for Music Education* 21, no. 1 (2021): 142–171, https://doi:10.22176/act21.2.142.
55. bell hooks, *Teaching to Transgress* (New York: Routledge, 2014).
56. Connie Tingson-Gatuz, "Mentoring the Leader: The Role of Peer Mentoring in the Leadership Development of Students-of-Color in Higher Education" (PhD dissertation, Michigan State University, 2009), ProQuest (AAT 3381412).
57. Tingson-Gatuz, "Mentoring the Leader."
58. Goodrich, "Valuing Racialized Student Voices."
59. Andrew Goodrich, "Peer Mentoring in an Extracurricular Music Class," *International Journal of Music Education* 39, no. 4 (2021): 410–423, https://doi.org/10.1177/0255761420988922; Goodrich, "Valuing Racialized Student Voices."
60. Goodrich, "Valuing Racialized Student Voices."
61. Goodrich, "Extracurricular Music Class"; Goodrich, "Valuing Racialized Student Voices."
62. Catherine Hansman, "Diversity and Power in Mentoring Relationships," in *Critical Perspectives on Mentoring: Trends and Issues*, ed. Catherine Hansman (Columbus, OH: ERIC Clearinghouse on Adult, Career, and Vocational Education, Center of Education and Training for Employment, College of Education, the Ohio State University, 2002), 39–48.
63. Jennifer Lindwall, "Will I Be Able to Understand My Mentee? Examining the Potential Risk of the Dominant Culture Mentoring Minority Youth," *Journal of Youth Development* 12, no. 1 (2017): 1–20, https://doi.org/10.5195/jyd.2017.485.

64. Semiyu Aderibigbe, Djonde Frega Antiado, and Annaliza Sta Anna, "Issues in Peer Mentoring for Undergraduate Students in a Private University in the United Arab Emirates," *International Journal of Evidence Based Coaching and Mentoring* 13, no. 2 (2015): 65–80, https://radar.brookes.ac.uk/radar/items/1641d9e8-3d45-424b-8f50-6b0096075df0/1/.
65. Hansman, "Diversity and Power."
66. Goodrich, "Valuing Racialized Student Voices."
67. Goodrich, "Valuing Racialized Student Voices."
68. Goodrich, "Valuing Racialized Student Voices."
69. Noah Borrero et al., "School as a Context for 'Othering' Youth and Promoting Cultural Assets," *Teachers College Record* 114, no. 2 (2012): 1–37, https://doi.org/10.1177/016146811211400207.
70. Gill Crozier, Penny Jane Burke, and Louise Archer, "Peer Relations in Higher Education: Raced, Classed and Gendered Constructions and Othering," *Whiteness and Education* 1, no. 1 (2016): 39–53, https://doi.org/10.1080/23793406.2016.1164746.
71. Crozier, Burke, and Archer, "Peer Relations."
72. Hess, *Music Education for Social Change*.
73. Mary Canales, "Othering: Toward an Understanding of Difference," *Advances in Nursing Science* 22, no. 4 (2000): 16–31, https://journals.lww.com/advancesinnursingscience/Fulltext/2000/06000/Othering_Toward_an_Understanding_of_Difference.3.aspx.
74. Crozier, Burke, and Archer, "Peer Relations"; Goodrich, "Valuing Racialized Student Voices."
75. Hess, *Music Education for Social Change*.
76. Darrow, Gibbs, and Wedel, "Classwide Peer Tutoring"; Andrew Goodrich, "Peer Mentoring in a High School Jazz Ensemble," *Journal of Research in Music Education* 55, no. 2 (2007): 94–114, https://doi.org/10.1177/002242940705500202; Johnson, "Rhythm Reading Achievement"; Jeff Taylor, "Peer Mentoring within the Middle and High School Music Department of the International School of Kuala Lumpur: A Case Study" (DMA dissertation, Boston University, 2016), ProQuest (AAT 10135020).
77. Goodrich, "High School Jazz Ensemble."
78. Richard D. Sawyer, "Mentoring but Not Being Mentored: Improving Student—Student Mentoring Programs to Attract Urban Youth to Teaching," *Education* 36, no. 1 (2001): 39–59, https://doi.org/10.1177/0042085901361004.
79. David L. Stader, "Lifeworld and System: Promoting Respect and Responsibility in High School," *Journal of School Improvement* 2, no. 2 (2001): 11–15, https://eric.ed.gov/?id=EJ637703.
80. Andrew J. Hobson, "Fostering Face-to-Face Mentoring and Coaching," in *The Sage Handbook of Mentoring and Coaching in Education*, ed. Sarah Fletcher and Carol Mullen (Thousand Oaks, CA: SAGE, 2012), 59–73.
81. Johnson, "Secondary Music Ensemble."
82. Goodrich, "High School Jazz Ensemble."
83. Hobson, "Fostering."
84. Hobson, "Fostering."
85. Taylor, "Kuala Lumpur."
86. Hobson, "Fostering."
87. Johnson, "Rhythm Reading Achievement."
88. Goodrich, "High School Jazz Ensemble."
89. Alexander and Dorow, "Peer Tutoring Effects."
90. Goodrich, "High School Jazz Ensemble."
91. Johnson, "Peer Teaching."

92. Heather Shotton, Star Oosahwe, and Rosa Cintrón, "Stories of Success: Experiences of American Indian Students in a Peer-Mentoring Retention Program," *Review of Higher Education* 31, no. 1 (2007): 81–107, https://doi.org/10.1353/rhe.2007.0060.
93. Hansmann, "Diversity and Power."
94. Hansmann, "Diversity and Power."
95. Hobson, "Fostering," 59–73.
96. Darrow, Gibbs, and Wedel, "Classwide Peer Tutoring."; Hobson, "Fostering."
97. Hobson, "Fostering."
98. Johnson, "Peer Teaching."
99. Hobson, "Fostering."
100. Darrow, Gibbs, and Wedel, "Classwide Peer Tutoring"; Goodrich, "Extracurricular Music Class"; Johnson, "Peer Teaching."
101. Goodrich, "Extracurricular Music Class"; Johnson, "Peer Teaching."
102. Pierre Jean Ensergueix and Lucille Lafont, "Reciprocal Peer Tutoring in a Physical Education Setting: Influence of Peer Tutor Training and Gender on Motor Performance and Self-Efficacy Outcomes," *European Journal of Psychology of Education* 25, no. 2 (2010): 222–42, https://doi.org/10.1007/s10212-009-0010-0.
103. Alexander and Dorow, "Peer Tutoring Effects."
104. Johnson, "Peer Teaching."
105. Goodrich, "Extracurricular Music Class"; Christine Howe, *Peer Groups and Children's Development* (Hoboken, NJ: John Wiley & Sons, 2009).
106. Albert Bandura, "Social Cognitive Theory," in *Annals of Child Development*, ed. Ross Vasta (Greenwich, CT: JAI Press, 1989), 1–60; Kathryn Byrne, "The Give and Take of Peer Review: Utilizing Modeling and Imitation" (PhD dissertation, Kent State University, 2015); Darrow, Gibbs, and Wedel, "Classwide Peer Tutoring."
107. Alexander and Dorow, "Peer Tutoring Effects"; Goodrich, "High School Jazz Ensemble."
108. Kristi Pretti-Frontczak and Dianne Bricker, *An Activity-Based Approach to Early Intervention* (Baltimore, MD: Brookes Publishing, 2004).
109. Mary B. Boat, Laurie A. Dinnebeil, and Youlmi Bae, "Individualizing Instruction in Preschool Classrooms," *Dimensions of Early Childhood* 38, no. 1 (2010): 3–11, www.jcsicsa.ir/article_85708_66c5d66c5a0798df29d8296d54c273e9.pdf.
110. Carol Ann Tomlinson and Layne Kalbfleisch, "Teach Me, Teach My Brain: A Call for Differentiated Classrooms," *Educational Leadership* 56, no. 3 (1998): 52–55, https://eric.ed.gov/?id=EJ575232.
111. Diana Lawrence-Brown, "Differentiated Instruction: Inclusive Strategies for Standards-Based Learning That Benefit the Whole Class," *American Secondary Education* 32, no. 3 (2004): 34–62, www.jstor.org/stable/41064522.
112. Lawrence-Brown, "Differentiated Instruction."
113. Lawrence-Brown, "Differentiated Instruction."
114. Goodrich, "High School Jazz Ensemble."
115. Andrew Goodrich, Elizabeth Bucura, and Sandra Stauffer, "Peer Mentoring in a University Music Methods Class," *Journal of Music Teacher Education* 27, no. 2 (2018): 1–16, https://doi.org/10.1177/1057083717731057.

3 The role of the student

Any relationship takes time and effort to be successful, and the relationship between the participants in peer mentoring is no different. Having explored the teacher's role in the peer mentoring partnership, it is now time to look at the student's responsibility in the process. Your role as the teacher is certainly significant, but students are central to peer mentoring. Assigning students to the role of mentor or mentee provides a structure for sharing knowledge and experiences with each other. You will learn about these roles in detail, including how they function in both hierarchical and nonhierarchical mentoring structures. Next, you will gain insights into your role and the students' roles for peer mentoring that occur outside of the music classroom and ensemble rehearsal space. These types of peer mentoring include online peer mentoring in remote learning environments and peer mentoring that occurs outside of the school setting and not under your direct supervision. Finally, the processes of how students can engage in the reflection process both during and after peer mentoring sessions portray how you can use these approaches to provide meaningful learning experiences for your students. To help contextualize peer mentoring from a music student's perspective, Snapshot 3 presents peer mentoring between Takisha and DeeJay, two trumpet players in Mr. Gardner's youth orchestra, who are working on their parts for Beethoven's Symphony no. 5.

Snapshot 3: Mr. Gardner's youth orchestra rehearsal

The Youth Orchestra is an audition-only ensemble comprising students from public and private high schools in a large metropolitan area in the Upper Midwest. The orchestra rehearses on Monday evenings from seven to nine o'clock throughout the school year.

Mr. Gardner and the Youth Orchestra are rehearsing for their upcoming spring concert. The concert program is an aggressive one: It includes Symphony no. 5 by Beethoven, *St. Paul's Suite* by Holst, and *Rhosymedre* by Vaughan Williams. The time is 7:20 p.m., and rehearsal has been underway for 20 minutes. As Mr. Gardner conducts the second movement of Symphony no. 5, he stops frequently to work on intonation.

"Okay, so the intonation is *much* improved since last week's rehearsal, but I still hear a few issues," remarks Mr. Gardner. "Remember that we talked about the importance of playing with proper balance, especially with our dynamics, and if we play too loud it can really effect the pitch."

Mr. Gardner continues rehearsing for several measures, stops conducting, and proclaims, "That's more like it! Trumpets, I like how you played a bit softer this time. It's getting much better!"

Takisha, principal trumpet and a senior, and DeeJay, second trumpet and a sophomore, have huge smiles on their faces and give each other a thumbs-up. Mr. Gardner adds, "The trombones are back in the room from working with each other in the hallway, so trumpets, it's your turn to go out and work with each other on the Beethoven. I suggest you continue to work on balance with your parts to help further improve intonation. Takisha, go ahead and take ten minutes for you and DeeJay to work on your intonation."

"Will do, Mr. Gardner!" responds Takisha. She quietly says to DeeJay, "Grab your music stand and your tuner, and let's go."

"You got it," responds DeeJay.

Takisha and DeeJay grab their instruments and music and head out to the hallway outside of the rehearsal room. Takisha pulls the two music stands into a slight arc, and she and DeeJay stand next to each other. "Let's run the passage," begins Takisha, pointing to the music.

"Which one?" asks DeeJay.

"The section in movement two, Andante con moto."

"Oh, yeah. Got it."

Takisha counts them off, and they play the excerpt. "I think the problem is your D-naturals, DeeJay. Are you pushing your third valve slide out?"

DeeJay shrugs and says, "Nah. I didn't think it was that necessary."

"Doing that helps to lower the pitch on that note," Takisha explains.

"Oh, yeah," concedes DeeJay.

Takisha continues, "Play your low D with the third valve slide out, and I'll play the same note." They play the note. "Much better!" Takisha points out. "So, do you remember Janice, principal trumpet player who graduated last year?"

"Oh, yeah. I know who she was," says DeeJay. "She could play the trumpet!"

Takisha adds, "When I was in orchestra last year, she showed me a couple of ways to play in tune that she learned from her band director. I checked these out with Mr. Gardner, who said they were solid ideas, and so I should share them with you tonight, so let's try them."

"All right," agrees DeeJay.

"First, let's tune with the tuner." Takisha sets the tuner on the stand, and they play their D-naturals. "Okay, we are actually both a bit sharp on that note, so we should both pull out our tuning slides a little bit, and don't forget to push out your third valve slide as well."

"All right," says DeeJay. They play the note again, and Takisha gives an enthusiastic thumbs-up.

"We got it!" she notes. "Now, I'm gonna play the D-natural an octave higher like it's written in my part." They play the D-naturals. "Now that sounds pretty good to me. Okay, so Janice also showed me another way to practice playing in tune. "If you drone a concert C on the tuner . . .

DeeJay interrupts, "Concert C? What's that?"

Takisha responds, "So, because we are trumpets in B-flat, we read our notes one note higher than the piano, which is in concert key. At least, that's how I think of it."

DeeJay nods his head knowingly. "Oh, okay. That's why Mr. Gardner always says let's tune to a concert A, and we play a B."

"Exactly!" Takisha continues, "So, if you set it to play a concert C, [she turns on the tuner] "you can play your note with the tuner." She demonstrates and remarks, "And see? I'm still out of tune with the tuner, so I need to adjust." They play their D-naturals while the tuner sounds a concert C. They both pull out their tuning slides a little bit and play again. "Now, that's pretty much in tune. Janice said she did this every day in her warm-up. I now do it too and find it really helps."

DeeJay gets it and volunteers, "That's really cool. I'm gonna try that when I practice."

They gave each other a high five and then play through the excerpt a couple of times. Finally, Takisha says, "I think that's a lot better. We better get back to rehearsal." They pick up their music and walk back to the ensemble room. After they sit down, Mr. Gardner asks them, "Well, how did it go?"

"It went really well," responds Takisha. DeeJay chimes in, "Yeah, I learned how to play my D-naturals in tune!"

Mr. Gardner responds, "Wonderful! Now, if both of you could remember to fill out a quick reflection in the Google Docs that would be great. I'd like to hear more about how it went."

"You got it!" remarks Takisha with DeeJay adding, "I'll do it right after rehearsal!" Mr. Gardner nods his head in approval and continues with the rehearsal.

Prior knowledge in the peer knowledge exchange

Research indicates students possess prior knowledge and have experiences they can share with their peers. As you learned in Chapter 1, students accumulate that knowledge from you, other teachers in the school—those of both music and other classes—private instructors, and each other.[1] This stockpile of knowledge includes four levels presented in Chapter 1: Foundational knowledge, non-foundational knowledge, tacit knowledge, and explicit knowledge.

Peer mentoring allows students to play an important role in their own learning; they learn a great deal from each other.[2] In fact, they retain subject matter learned from their peers more easily than that which is learned from their teachers,[3] such as Takisha explaining to DeeJay in Snapshot 3 about how to play the note D-natural in tune. When students share their knowledge with each other, they are more likely to remember what they learned.[4]

> **Quick tip: Peers learning from their peers**
>
> I love when students help each other learn. Sometimes, I let my kids teach my class while I'm in there, and what I find is occasionally I'll explain something and I'll get nothing but blank stares. Then, I'll have one of my students teach the class. Even though they say the exact same thing that I did, everyone's like, "Oh, yeah, I get it now." Students relate to each other so well, and sometimes my role is simply being an interpreter during learning.
> —David Cosby, Music Director,
> Holderness School, Holderness, NH

The exchange of knowledge and experiences during peer mentoring is both comprehensive and mutual.[5] Comprehensiveness embodies the relationship between the mentor and the mentee. Beyond simply sharing musical information, students can exchange personal experiences and develop friendships. For peer mentoring to provide a platform for sharing knowledge and experiences, students need to have a mutual understanding of both the reasons for participating in mentoring and the importance of valuing the mentoring process. Comprehensiveness and mutuality help to set peer mentoring apart from other relationships between students.[6]

In peer mentoring, the exchange of knowledge is informal, interactive, and enduring.[7] These qualities enable students to gain a mutual understanding of what they are learning, which then provides the basis for increased musical and verbal interactions. Furthermore, they create an atmosphere, in which students feel comfortable sharing and receiving knowledge and experiences, which in turn contributes to a more meaningful learning experience. Students create these relationships themselves, and thus assume a greater role in the peer mentoring process.[8]

Student roles in peer mentoring

Music teachers play a pivotal role in setting up and maintaining a peer mentoring program, but they depend on those they select to be mentors and mentees to make the process run smoothly. Students generally engage in two different types of peer mentoring: Fixed role and reciprocal role. Whether in a fixed or reciprocal role, students carry out goals for learning, elevate their musical knowledge, develop their musical skills, and provide clarity with instruction for each other.[9]

Fixed role

Hierarchical structures, such as fixed-role peer mentoring, situate the more-knowledgeable students as mentors and those considered to have less knowledge as the mentees. This is the structure portrayed in Snapshot 3 between Takisha and DeeJay. Although the goal of fixed-role mentoring is to strengthen the learning for the mentee, mentors experience musical growth as well.[10] Fixed-role mentoring shares similarities with cross-age mentoring, discussed in Chapter 1, and also with differentiated instruction, which you learned about in Chapter 2. Students in fixed roles take on additional responsibilities beyond instruction, which could include setting up the room for class, distributing sheet music, writing information on the whiteboard, and helping organize materials for instruction.[11] Having these kinds of responsibilities engages students and helps them to learn to stay on task when learning their music,[12] which will increase their comprehension of their parts.[13] Mentors in fixed roles can help students in their own sections, or they can mentor across sections.[14] In fixed-role mentoring, students sometimes take on leadership roles, such as running sectionals; this can contribute to elevated performance levels in school music programs.

In fixed-role mentoring, student mentors have their own unique styles of sharing their knowledge and experiences with mentees. For example, some students prefer to mentor in dyads, similar to how Takisha worked one-on-one with DeeJay in Snapshot 3. Other students, however, will be more comfortable in leading larger groups, such as an entire section or even working with multiple sections through cross-section mentoring. Mentors in a fixed role often model musical sounds using their voice or instrument instead of—or as a supplement to—verbal instruction.

Reciprocal role

When peer mentoring takes on a nonhierarchical structure, there is a two-way sharing of knowledge. In reciprocal-role peer mentoring, students concurrently serve in the roles of mentor and mentee, and they learn regardless of whether they are the mentor or the mentee.[15] When students engage in these less-hierarchical approaches, they often have a more comprehensive learning experience than would be expected based on the original goal of the mentoring session.[16] In addition, they often demonstrate higher achievement than when they learn from their instructors.[17]

One type of reciprocal-role mentoring is co-mentoring, such as when a high school senior mentors a freshman about playing a particular style of music, and the freshman in turn contributes knowledge about playing in tune that the senior was unaware of. The reciprocal-role approach can also happen sequentially; for example, students who are mentors or mentees on Monday might switch their roles on Tuesday, with the mentor assuming the mentee role and vice versa.[18] Students can also swap roles as mentors and mentees during class or rehearsal and help each other with learning musical concepts, such as key signatures,[19] sight-reading, music theory,[20] and with music fundamentals, such as intonation.[21] For example, a third-grade student could mentor their peer by singing the correct pitches to a song. The student could then swap roles so that the mentee is now the mentor who makes sure their peer, formerly the mentor, is singing the correct words. Even though reciprocal-role peer mentoring is less hierarchical in structure and at times informal in concept, you still play an important role in guiding students through the tasks of identifying their roles in this process, including how to share and receive knowledge, when to engage in peer mentoring, and when to swap roles as mentor and mentee.

Student roles summary

- In hierarchical structures, more-knowledgeable students mentor less-knowledgeable students (fixed roles).
- In nonhierarchical structures, students equal in ability and knowledge mentor each other (reciprocal roles).
- Students and the teacher can explore opportunities and preferences for mentoring in dyads, groups, or both.

Levels of engagement in peer mentoring

When students engage in meaningful learning during peer mentoring, instruction can be grouped into three main categories: Low-, mid-, and high-level engagements.[22] These levels of engagements pertain to both fixed-role and reciprocal-role peer mentoring.

Low-level engagement refers to situations, where you can encourage students to ask and answer simple questions, such as how to finger a particular note or which bar to play on a xylophone. These interactions provide opportunities for mentors to answer questions that are easy for them and at the same time can make learning in the classroom flow more smoothly because the class does not get bogged down with minor details.

Mid-level engagement gives student leaders a chance to mentor their peers during rehearsals in a way that goes beyond answering simple questions. For example, mentors might reinforce the correct words to a song and how to play or sing rhythms; indicate where to breathe with phrasing; explain articulations, proper diction, and style; or point out musical issues that need to be addressed.

Using high-level engagement, peer mentors might mentor throughout the music class and ensemble and not necessarily just in their own sections. For example, a trumpet player who is a senior might mentor a freshman clarinetist in aligning intonation between their parts. Mentoring for nonmusical issues, such as classroom management, is another example of high-level engagement.

Online peer mentoring

Students today are constantly plugged in by way of their smartphones or other devices, where they can engage with each other online on social media platforms. As technology progresses, the use of peer mentoring in remote learning environments is becoming more widespread. The term *online peer mentoring* entails students engaging in peer mentoring in a remote learning environment that includes many similarities with in-person peer mentoring, such as learning subject matter, and involves social interactions.[23] Online peer mentoring, which is sometimes referred to as e-mentoring or digital mentoring, creates new spaces for students to engage in meaningful learning.[24] For example, students can share recordings to help each other learn their music,[25] share their knowledge with each other,[26] lead group discussions, and even mentor each other with how to use technology.[27] Online peer mentoring in remote learning environments is multi-faceted, just as it is in music programs at school. Social connectedness among students in these environments is an important component of online peer mentoring.[28] With student access to digital devices, "mentoring travels with you in your pocket."[29]

Asynchronous and synchronous structures

There is considerable diversity in online peer mentoring structures. As with face-to-face peer mentoring, online peer mentoring includes hierarchical and nonhierarchical structures. Similarly, both dyadic mentoring and group mentoring structures can exist in online environments.[30] For example, online peer mentoring can be instrumental, with students providing advice and support for learning subject matter, or psychosocial, with participants discussing their problems and modeling proper behavior for each other.[31]

A beneficial aspect of online peer mentoring is that students can interact with each other at times convenient for them. When guiding students through the process of online peer mentoring, you can create asynchronous opportunities, such as mentors posing questions for mentees via email or discussion boards. In addition, you could facilitate synchronous peer mentoring opportunities for students at times mutually convenient for them, where they can engage in private lessons, web chats, or live interactions via Zoom or Skype, where they can share their knowledge with each other.[32]

Engaging with peers at other institutions

Another benefit of online peer mentoring is the potential for students to interact with peers from other institutions[33] and music teachers and specialists outside of school.[34] These interactions can occur through virtual mentoring communities and social media platforms, such as Facebook.[35] With asynchronous learning, students can share knowledge with peers at other institutions within their own time frame.[36] Furthermore, they can interact with multiple peers from multiple institutions, providing an abundance of opportunities to access a vast array of knowledge.[37] Although there are many benefits to students' interacting with peers from other schools, synchronous online peer mentoring can be difficult when the students live in different time zones.[38]

Providing resources beyond the music classroom

Online peer mentoring serves a similar function to face-to-face peer mentoring in that students can provide learning resources beyond those offered by the music teacher.[39] Immediate access to information provides numerous opportunities for students to quickly expand their knowledge. Under your guidance, students can create databases and organize links to helpful resources so they have access to this information to use when mentoring each other. You can also encourage students to create podcasts, where they focus on some aspect of sharing their experiences with developing their musicianship. In turn, this can help student mentors, who reinforce what they know when explaining musical concepts to their peers, and can aid mentees, who learn new information. You can help facilitate student access to this information by using existing online platforms, such as your school or music program website.[40]

Online peer mentoring and learning

Online peer mentoring provides numerous experiences for students to learn from each other. Mentoring can also occur in the form of private lessons between students, sectionals, or online group discussions. Online peer mentoring, then, helps to develop individual musicianship of mentors and mentees and can ultimately help to elevate the knowledge level of students in the music class and ensemble.[41] One of the first steps toward setting up online peer mentoring is to post goals and objectives for peer mentoring.[42] Once the online peer mentoring system is up-and-running, students can play an important role in creating their own goals for learning. Initial goals may include students mentoring each other for music fundamentals or helping each other to learn their music.

Although the access to a vast multitude of sources provides many benefits for online peer mentoring, you need to carefully monitor what information the students share with each other due to the great potential for students to share misinformation. This task is further compounded if students are interacting with peers at other institutions.[43] Conducting periodic check-ins on students' online peer mentoring experiences can help you to keep track of what information students are sharing with each other in the music program, and also with students at other institutions when they engage in digital peer mentoring.[44] You can do this in a variety of ways, such as online journaling (e.g., Google Docs) or online meetings (e.g., Zoom), where students write down or talk about what knowledge they are sharing during peer mentoring and what they are learning.

You will also want to carefully monitor your mentors and mentees to determine if they are actually interacting with each other. Although monitoring can be time-consuming, it is important to ensure that students are mentoring each other and if they are staying on task. To aid with this issue, you could designate specific time frames for when peer mentoring will occur and then check in with the students to see how peer mentoring is going, when they met, and how the learning process is working for them.[45]

Online peer mentoring provides additional ways for students to interact with each other to create meaningful learning opportunities. Although this presents some challenges, such as the need to set aside time to monitor student learning, online peer mentoring provides a platform for music teachers to create continuity with learning as schools continue to develop hybrid and remote learning environments for students.

Quick tip: Supplementing classroom instruction

Our online mentorship program is deeply integrated into the learning that happens in the classroom. Everyone's a mentor and everyone's a mentee. We use discussion boards, where students post a video of their playing on Wednesday, and then respond to two different peer's videos on Thursday. We're using a method book, so everybody's doing the same exercise. The students use their different experiences to provide all kinds of feedback, and it's not just limited to a peer who plays the same instrument.

—*Lieven Smart, Music Teacher Grades 6–8,*
Junction Avenue, Livermore, CA

Issues with online access

Some students cannot take advantage of the numerous benefits of online peer mentoring because they do not have access to a computer.[46] Others may not be literate about how to use a computer, or the music classroom only has one computer.[47] The lack of access to technology further exacerbates the divide between students from high-income households, who likely own their own computers and have internet access, and students from low-income households.[48]

Peer mentoring outside of school

Not to be overlooked are the situations where peer mentoring takes places beyond school walls and teacher observation and control. Students commonly help each other outside of an academic setting through activities that include learning popular music tunes,[49] transcribing jazz solos,[50] learning songs by ear from recordings, and composing and arranging songs, often engaging in informal music learning.[51] This type of student-centered learning, such as two or more students helping each other learn a song by ear, typically occurs without teacher-imposed structures or goals. Teachers should encourage their students to get together outside of rehearsals to mentor each other[52] so that they can play an active role in their own learning.[53]

> **Quick tip: Peer mentoring outside of school**
>
> Once peer mentoring was up and running in the jazz band, it evolved to where the students started practicing together outside of class. They would get together and jam on the weekends, they formed their own bands, and they were taking gigs. In all this, they were teaching each other the ways that they learned jazz improvisation, and it eventually got to the point where I could introduce concepts in rehearsals but then didn't have to teach improvisation because they were teaching each other.
> —*Troy Davis, former Band and Jazz Band Director at Aragon High School, San Mateo, CA; current Director of Instrumental Music and Jazz Studies at West Valley College, Saratoga, CA*

Certain characteristics exist whether mentoring exists inside or outside of school. In informal peer mentoring, students still reinforce existing knowledge and learn new knowledge. But, with no teacher present, peer mentoring outside of school puts greater responsibility on the student. However, you can still monitor mentoring and check in with students to give them the opportunity to share with you what they are learning or have learned. You can also get a sense of how peer mentoring is helping the students by how they sound in music class or ensemble rehearsal.

Student reflection

One of the most important commitments for students and teachers engaging in peer mentoring is reflecting on what occurred during the mentoring session.[54] While teachers probably have experience with reflection as part of their professional practice, students need to be guided through the process, which goes hand in hand with sharing their knowledge and experiences. Reflection feeds metacognition, the process of actively thinking about what knowledge they are learning and how their experiences contribute to enhancing their growth in learning.[55] When students reflect on their own experiences, they determine what they know and why they know it. Explaining their experiences to someone else helps them reaffirm what they already know.[56] As students reflect on their roles as mentors and mentees, they begin to figure out what knowledge they have, what they do not know, what went well and did not go so well, and how their experiences shape future peer mentoring assignments.

Quick tip: Checking in with students

We don't have any formal written reflections, but I do a check-in with students after class. I ask them, "How did things go? What did you work on? Did you have any challenges?" The students are very good at thinking about, "Okay, what did we do? Was this successful? Is there something else that I noticed that this particular student needs to work on?" The students are very perceptive, and the reflection helps me to make sure that things are going okay and if there are any questions or concerns.
—*Terri Knight, Transitional Kindergarten through
fifth-grade General Music, Band, and Orchestra,
Greenbrook Elementary and Twin Creeks Elementary,
San Ramon Valley Unified School District, Danville, CA*

Types of reflection

Two primary types of reflection are helpful in learning: Reflection-in-action and reflection-on-action. When taking part in reflection-in-action, students think critically about their learning while engaged in that learning.[57] It is an informal process that helps students figure out how they share their knowledge and experiences and make adjustments in the moment. Reflection-on-action is a process that takes place after a peer mentoring session; this type of reflection allows students to make future adjustments to their process if they feel it necessary.[58]

Ways to reflect

Reflection can occur in a variety of ways. Students and the teacher can verbally discuss how peer mentoring went and what was learned, or students can reflect on the process with each other. For example, in reflection-in-action, music teachers can structure reflection so that students can reflect on their learning either during or immediately after a peer mentoring activity. When Takisha and DeeJay returned to orchestra rehearsal and Mr. Gardner asked them how peer mentoring went in Snapshot 3, they engaged in a basic form of reflection-in-action. Reflection-in-action can be more structured, too, and can occur in the form of reflection amplifiers, which are designed to elicit "a deliberate object of attention and reflection . . . that offer learners structured opportunities to examine and evaluate their own learning."[59] For example, you can guide students through the process of learning how to engage in reflection-in-action by providing a single prompt that mentors and mentees could use, such as, "What did I just learn in this activity?" Ideally, you would be present for the peer mentoring activity and reflection to understand how students are engaged in reflection and what they are learning. Recently, researchers have explored how teachers and students can use mobile technologies, such as smartphones, to access reflection prompts and enter reflections.[60] Although these tools have been found to be effective, if you are considering adopting them for classroom use you need to consider school policies for use of mobile technologies in the school, and also be aware that not all students will have access to them.

However, it can be difficult in some peer mentoring scenarios for you to always be present for reflation-in-action, so you should explore options to supplement students' verbal reflections.

A primary approach for student reflection is reflection-on-action, which occurs later, after the peer mentoring activity. Journaling is an effective way for students to record how they went about mentoring and also reflect on outcomes of the process.[61] For example, students could enter their reflection into an online application, such as a Google Docs, for you to review later, similar to Mr. Gardner's request for Takisha and DeeJay to do so in Snapshot 3. It is helpful if you can structure the reflection process for students. Questions, such as *what did I do, why did I do that*, and *what came of it*[62] are helpful prompts for journal entries. When engaging in reflection-on-action, students can focus on three areas: They can return to the experience, mentally reliving what happened; they can concentrate on their feelings, writing about their emotional response to the learning that occurred; and they can reevaluate the experience, reflecting on what worked or did not work when mentoring.[63] Reflection is an ongoing endeavor and provides another avenue for students to increase ownership in their own learning.

> ### Quick tip: Reflecting on learning
>
> To help students reflect on their learning after peer mentoring in sectionals, I use a Google Form so they don't have to say in front of the whole group how it went. I have every single student complete the form, which takes under three minutes. I ask them to rate their learning experience in terms of productivity. I use a scale of one through five, five being the best, one being the worst. I also ask them how it went, and without even being in the room I can tell you if it was chaos or if it was awesome just by their responses. I can also tell how

invested students are in learning if they barely make any effort to fill out that form, or if someone writes a few sentences per answer about major details that happened. It's good information for me to check in on, and it's a way for students to not have to share in front of the entire group and call somebody out in front of their peers.

—Allison Lacasse, Band Director,
Belmont High School, Belmont, MA

Reflection summary

- Reflection is an important part of the peer mentoring process.
- Guided reflections help the students identify and understand what they know and do not know.
- Reflection-in-action occurs during peer mentoring and helps students enhance the mentoring process.
- Reflection-on-action occurs after peer mentoring. In addition to a student–teacher verbal review of peer mentoring, journaling is an effective way for students to engage in this type of reflection.

Questions for discussion

1. How can students engage in comprehensiveness and mutuality when using knowledge learned from other sources?
2. Consider both fixed-role and reciprocal-role mentoring. How might you use these structures with your students?
3. How could you incorporate dyad and group mentoring structures in the music class and ensemble?
4. What types of online peer mentoring activities might you use with students enrolled in your music classes or ensembles?
5. How can you design reflection-in-action and reflection-on-action with your students?

Reflection

Peer mentoring is, of course, ultimately about the students. The role in which the students are placed—mentor, mentee, or both—helps determine how they share what they know and their willingness to receive help from their peers. Research indicates that students bring prior knowledge to the music class and ensemble and that they can share this knowledge to help create meaningful learning experiences. Sharing knowledge involves comprehensiveness in that learning can go beyond learning solely for subject matter and can include students learning from each other's personal experiences. It is also important for students to have a mutual understanding of why they are participating in mentoring and why it is important.

76 *Foundations of peer mentoring and student leadership*

In this chapter, you learned about two primary peer mentoring structures: Fixed role and reciprocal role. As you think about how you use these structures with students in your music program, remember that your options are broad. You may use each type at different times, depending on what you and your students want to learn. For example, think about how the hierarchical structure of fixed-role peer mentoring could help those students that need additional help in mastering their music. Remember Takisha and DeeJay and their interactions. Takisha, designated as the mentor by Mr. Gardner, helped DeeJay to not only play the excerpt in the second movement of Beethoven's Symphony no. 5 with improved intonation but also to elevate his understanding of different ways of improving his intonation in the future.

Peer mentoring can occur in remote learning environments, and even though you may be absent from their conversations, you should be aware of how the students are mentoring each other. Peer mentoring can also occur outside of the school setting. When you check in with your students to see how the in-school mentoring is going, ask if they get together outside of the school to hang out and make music. From their responses, you can get a sense of what knowledge and experiences they are sharing with each other. You can also get an understanding of how peer mentoring is working by simply hearing how they are performing in music class or ensemble rehearsal.

Reflection is a major component of the learning that occurs during peer mentoring. Provide opportunities for your students to reflect during peer mentoring (reflection-in-action) and after peer mentoring (reflection-on-action). Teach them how to reflect on what they are learning.

In the next chapter, you will learn more about socializing, one of the essential aspects of developing leadership with peer mentoring. You will learn how to develop leadership through peer mentoring, how students interact with each other verbally and nonverbally, and how peer mentoring and student leadership can help accomplish musical and nonmusical objectives for the music program.

Notes

1. Richard S. Webb, "An Exploration of Three Peer Tutoring Cases in the School Orchestra Program," *Bulletin of the Council for Research in Music Education*, no. 203 (2015): 63–80, https://doi.org/10.5406/bulcouresmusedu.203.0063.
2. Lucille Alexander and Laura G. Dorow, "Peer Tutoring Effects on the Music Performance of Tutors and Tutees in Beginning Band Classes," *Journal of Research in Music Education* 31, no. 1 (1983): 33–47, https://doi.org/10.2307/3345108; Lucy Green, *How Popular Musicians Learn: A Way Ahead for Music Education* (Burlington, VT: Ashgate, 2002); Lucy Green, *Music, Informal Learning, and the School: A New Classroom Pedagogy* (Burlington, VT: Ashgate, 2008); David Hebert, "Music Competition, Cooperation, and Community: An Ethnography of a Japanese School Band" (PhD dissertation, University of Washington, 2005), ProQuest (AAT 3163382); Bernadette

Butler Scruggs, "Learning Outcomes in Two Divergent Middle School String Orchestra Classroom Environments: A Comparison of a Learner-Centered and a Teacher-Centered Approach" (PhD dissertation, Georgia State University, 2009), ProQuest (AAT 3371516).
3. Alice-Ann Darrow, Pamela Gibbs, and Sarah Wedel, "Use of Classwide Peer Tutoring in the General Music Classroom," *Update: Applications of Research in Music Education* 24, no. 1 (2005): 15–26, https://doi.org/10.1177/87551233050240010103; Andrew Goodrich, "Peer Mentoring in a High School Jazz Ensemble," *Journal of Research in Music Education* 55, no. 2 (2007): 94–114, https://doi.org/10.1177/002242940705500202; Scruggs, "Learning Outcomes."
4. Webb, "Exploration."
5. Beverly Hardcastle, "Spiritual Connections: Protégés' Reactions on Significant Mentorships," *Theory into Practice* 27, no. 3 (1988): 201–208, https://doi.org/10.1080/00405848809543352.
6. Hardcastle, "Spiritual Connections."
7. Hardcastle, "Spiritual Connections."
8. Katharina F. Lucas, "The Social Construction of Mentoring Roles," *Mentoring & Tutoring: Partnership in Learning* 9, no. 1 (2001): 23–47, https://doi.org/10.1080/13611260120046665.
9. Lucas, "Social Construction"; Scruggs, "Learning Outcomes."
10. Shirley Hill, Brian Gay, and Keith Topping, "Peer-Assisted Learning beyond School," in *Peer Assisted Learning*, ed. Keith Topping and Stewart Ehly (New York: Routledge, 1998).
11. Darrow, Gibbs, and Wedel, "Classwide Peer Tutoring"; Hebert, "Music Competition."
12. Alexander and Dorow, "Peer Tutoring Effects"; Scruggs, "Learning Outcomes."
13. Alexander and Dorow, "Peer Tutoring Effects"; Goodrich, "High School Jazz Ensemble"; Jeff Taylor, "Peer Mentoring within the Middle and High School Music Department of the International School of Kuala Lumpur: A Case Study" (DMA dissertation, Boston University, 2016), ProQuest (AAT 10135020).
14. Kaitlyn A. Fay, "In Search of Effective Jazz Education: An Analysis and Comparison of Pedagogical Methods Employed by Directors of Successful High School Jazz Ensembles" (PhD dissertation, William Patterson University, 2013), ProQuest (AAT 1538595).
15. Michael Harvey et al., "Mentoring Global Female Managers in the Global Marketplace: Traditional, Reverse, and Reciprocal Mentoring," *International Journal of Human Resource Management* 20, no. 6 (2009): 1344–1361, https://doi:10.1080/09585190902909863.
16. Erik Johnson, "Peer Teaching in the Secondary Music Ensemble," *Journal of Education Training Studies* 3, no. 5 (2015): 35–42, https://doi.org/10.11114/jets.v3i5.906.
17. Erik A. Johnson, "The Effect of Peer-Based Instruction on Rhythm Reading Achievement," *Contributions to Music Education* 38, no. 2 (2011): 43–60, www.jstor.org/stable/24127190.
18. Darrow, Gibbs, and Wedel, "Classwide Peer Tutoring."
19. Darrow, Gibbs, and Wedel, "Classwide Peer Tutoring."
20. Johnson, "Secondary Music Ensemble."
21. Andrew Goodrich et al., "Comentoring in a University Jazz Ensemble," *Visions of Research in Music Education* 25 (2014), https://opencommons.uconn.edu/vrme/vol25/iss1/6.
22. Goodrich, "High School Jazz Ensemble."

23. Laura Bierema and Sharan B. Merriam, "E-Mentoring: Using Computer Mediated Communication to Enhance the Mentoring Process," *Innovative Higher Education* 26, no. 3 (2002): 214, https://link.springer.com/content/pdf/10.1023/A:1017921023103.pdf.
24. Irja Leppisaari, "Exploring Emerging Mentoring Practices in New Ecosystems of Learning in Finland," *International Association for Development of the Information Society* (2019): 97–108, https://files.eric.ed.gov/fulltext/ED601177.pdf.
25. Sarah Evans et al., "More Than Peer Production: Fanfiction Communities as Sites of Distributed Mentoring," in Proceedings of the 2017 ACM Conference on Computer Supported Cooperative Work and Social Computing, 259–272, https://doi.org/10.1145/2998181.2998342.
26. Janice Kinghorn, "The New Digital Divide: Peer Collaboration as a Bridge," *Association for University Regional Campuses of Ohio Journal* 20, no. 6 (2014): 109–116, https://aurco.org/Journals/AURCO_Journal_2014/Digital_Divide_Rye-Kinghorn_AURCO_Vol20_2014.pdf.
27. Kurt Kraiger, "Transforming Our Models of Learning and Development: Web-Based Instruction as Enabler of Third-Generation Instruction," *Industrial and Organizational Psychology* 1, no. 4 (2008): 454–467, https://doi.org/10.1111/j.1754-9434.2008.00086.x.
28. Charles Kivunja, "Innovative Methodologies for 21st Century Learning, Teaching and Assessment: A Convenience Sampling Investigation into the Use of Social Media Technologies in Higher Education," *International Journal of Higher Education* 4, no. 2 (2015): 1–26, https://doi.org/10.5430/ijhe.v4n2p1
29. Irja Leppisaari, "Emerging Mentoring Practices," 107.
30. Kraiger, "Transforming."
31. Josh McCarthy, "International Design Collaboration and Mentoring for Tertiary Students Through Facebook," *Australasian Journal of Educational Technology* 28, no. 5 (2018): 755–75, https://doi.org/10.14742/ajet.1383.
32. Francesco Cavallaro and Kenneth Tan, "Computer-Mediated Peer-to-Peer Mentoring." *Association for the Advancement of Computing in Education Journal* 14, no. 2 (2006): 129–38, www.learntechlib.org/primary/p/6219/.
33. Kraiger, "Transforming"; Hugh Miller and Mark Griffiths, "E-Mentoring," in *The Handbook of Youth Mentoring*, ed. David Dubois and Michael J. Karcher (Thousand Oaks, CA: SAGE, 2005), 300–313.
34. Heidrun Stoeger, Manuel Hopp, and Albert Ziegler, "Online Mentoring as an Extracurricular Measure to Encourage Talented Girls in STEM (Science, Technology, Engineering, and Mathematics): An Empirical Study of One-on-One Versus Group Mentoring," *Gifted Child Quarterly* 61, no. 3 (2017): 239–249, https://doi.org/10.1177/0016986217702215.
35. McCarthy, "International Design Collaboration."
36. Evans et al., "Distributed Mentoring."
37. Evans et al., "Distributed Mentoring"; Andrew Goodrich, "Online Peer Mentoring and Remote Learning," *Music Education Research* 23, no. 2 (2021): 256–269, https://doi.org/10.1080/14613808.2021.1898575.
38. Bierema and Merriam, "E-Mentoring."
39. Kivunja, "Innovative Methodologies."
40. Carmit-Noa Shpigelman, Patrice Weiss, and Shunit Reiter, "E-Mentoring for All," *Computers in Human Behavior* 25 (2009): 919–928, https://doi.org/10.1016/j.chb.2009.03.007.
41. Phillip M. Hash, "Remote Learning in School Bands During the COVID-19 Shutdown," *Journal of Research in Music Education* 68, no. 4 (2021): 381–397, https://doi.org/10.1177/0022429420967008.

42. Miikka Salavuo, "Social Media as an Opportunity for Pedagogical Change in Music Education," *Journal of Music Education and Technology* 1, no. 2–3 (2008): 121–136, https://doi:10.1386/jmte.1.2; John Robert Stoszkowski, Liam McCarthy, and Joana Fonseca, "Online Peer Mentoring and Collaborative Reflection: A Cross-Institutional Project in Sports Coaching," *Journal of Perspectives in Applied Academic Practice* 5, no. 3 (2017): 118–121, https://clok.uclan.ac.uk/19860/.
43. Yves Punie and Kirsti Ala-Mutka, "Future Learning Spaces: New Ways of Learning and New Digital Skills to Learn," *Nordic Journal of Digital Literacy* 2, no. 4 (2008): 210–225, https://doi.org/10.18261/ISSN1891-943X-2007-04-02.
44. Goodrich, "Online Peer Mentoring."
45. Darrow, Gibbs, and Wedel, "Classwide Peer Tutoring"; Andrew Goodrich, "Peer Mentoring in an Extracurricular Music Class," *International Journal of Music Education* 39, no. 4 (2021): 410–423, https://doi.org/10.1177/0255761420988922.
46. McCarthy, "International Design Collaboration"; Peg Boyle Single and Richard M. Single, "E-Mentoring for Social Equity: Review of Research to Inform Program Development," *Mentoring and Tutoring: Partnership in Learning* 13, no. 2 (2005): 301–320, https://doi.org/10.1080/13611260500107481.
47. Cavallaro and Tan, "Computer-Mediated."
48. Punie and Ala-Mutka, "Future Learning Spaces."
49. Green, *New Classroom Pedagogy*.
50. Goodrich, "High School Jazz Ensemble."
51. Goodrich, "High School Jazz Ensemble"; Green, *How Popular Musicians Learn*; Green, *New Classroom Pedagogy*; Robert H. Woody, "Popular Music in School: Remixing the Issues," *Music Educators Journal* 93, no. 4 (2007): 32–37, https://doi.org/10.1177/002743210709300415.
52. Goodrich, "High School Jazz Ensemble"; Woody, "Popular Music in School."
53. Green, "New Classroom Pedagogy."
54. Jenepher L. Terrion and Ruth Philion, "The Electronic Journal as Reflection-on-Action: A Qualitative Analysis of Communication and Learning in a Peer Mentoring Program," *Studies on Higher Education* 33, no. 5 (2008): 583–597, https://doi.org/10.1080/03075070802373073.
55. Terrion and Philion, "The Electronic Journal as Reflection-on-Action."
56. Vicki Coppock, "Children as Peer Researchers: Reflections on a Journey of Mutual Discovery," *Children & Society* 25, no. 6 (2001): 435–446, https://doi.org/10.1111/j.1099-0860.2010.00296.x.
57. Donald A. Schön, *Educating the Reflective Practitioner: Toward a New Design for Teaching and Learning in the Professions* (San Francisco, CA: Jossey Bass, 1987).
58. Schön, *Educating the Reflective Practitioner*.
59. Bernardo Tabuenca et al., "Fostering Reflective Practice with Mobile Technologies," in Proceedings of the 2nd Workshop on Awareness and Reflection in Technology Enhanced Learning (Technical University of Aachen, 2012), 88, http://hdl.handle.net/2268/151980.
60. Tabuenca et al., "Reflective Practice."
61. David Boud, "Using Journal Writing to Enhance Reflective Practice," *New Directions for Adult and Continuing Education*, no. 90 (2001): 9–17, https://doi.org/10.1002/ace.16.
62. Terrion and Philion, "Electronic Journal."
63. Boud, "Journal Writing."

4 Socializing and leadership

In the first three chapters, you learned about the foundations of peer mentoring, your role as the music teacher with implementing and sustaining peer mentoring, and the role of the students in these processes. Peer mentoring involves socializing, which provides the platform for student interactions and subsequent learning. Leadership is a salient component of socializing. Student leadership not only contributes to elevated learning of subject matter and performance skills in the music class and ensemble, but it also helps to improve attitudes toward learning, heightens ownership, and aids in co-creating brave spaces for learning. This chapter explores the various ways socializing contributes to meaningful learning in the music class and ensemble. Gaining insights into socializing will help you consider the benefits and issues that can occur during student interactions. You will examine the important role student leaders play in helping you make musical and non-musical decisions, and you will learn how to facilitate leadership opportunities for groups of students and all students simultaneously. To begin, Mr. Ramirez facilitates peer mentoring among fourth- and fifth-grade students as they learn how to play the recorder in a general music class.

Snapshot 4: Mr. Ramirez's fourth-grade general music class

Morris Elementary School, which enrolls students in kindergarten through fifth grade, is located in a medium-sized town approximately 45 miles from a large metropolitan area in the Pacific Northwest. The music program at the school includes K–5 general music, fifth grade band, and fifth-grade choir.

As the fourth-grade students walk into the music classroom, they notice several unfamiliar students. "Welcome 5th Graders!" is written on the markerboard in Mr. Ramirez's handwriting, a clue as to who they might be. The class recently started playing recorders. At the end of the prior class, Mr. Ramirez introduced "Hot Cross Buns" and informed the students that they would be responsible for helping each other with the fingerings for G, A, and B.

Socializing and leadership

Mr. Ramirez begins, saying, "I'm happy to announce that we have several guests today. Let's welcome Mary, Wendell, Emily, Lily, and Marcello to the class."

"Yeah!" says one of the fourth graders.

Mr. Ramirez continues, "They're here today to help us learn some additional notes on the recorder that we'll use when playing 'Hot Cross Buns.'" A fourth-grade student raises her hand. "Yes, Alicia?"

"How'd they get out of class?"

"It's their lunch hour, and they are kindly giving up some free time to help us out. Okay, before they help us, let's check to see if we remember our mentoring groups. All students in Group A raise your hands." Half of the students raise their hands. "Good," says Mr. Ramirez. "Then group B . . ."

Having confirmed that the students know which group they are in, Mr. Ramirez says, "Group A, let's begin with showing all of us how to hold the recorder." The Group A students hold the recorder in front of them and model how to hold it. "Good. Group B, let's see you hold the recorder," he says, and the Group B students do the same. "Excellent. Now, Group B, show us how to finger B." As the students hold their recorders in front of them and demonstrate, Mr. Ramirez walks around the room to double-check that they are fingering the note correctly.

Emily, a fifth-grade student, raises her hand and Mr. Ramirez responds, "Yes, Emily."

"Remember to keep your fingers slightly curved, like you're holding an orange. Like this." She demonstrates holding an orange and then fingers B.

"Thanks, Emily," says Mr. Ramirez. "That's great advice. Thanks Group B, looking good. Group A, let's see the fingering for B." After seeing how Group A models the fingering, he says, "Very good. Now, let's play. Remember, I'll count you off 1-2-3-4 and then we play the note B. Watch me for the cutoff." Mr. Ramirez counts them off and the students play B. "Not too bad, but you all need to watch me for the note release. Let's try it again." They play again. "Much better! Now, Group A, we learned another note last week. Can someone raise their hand and tell me what note it was?" A student in Group A raises his hand. "Yes, Walter."

"It was A."

"Correct! Now, Group A students, talk among yourselves using indoor voices and remind each other about how to finger the A. While you do that, I'll work with Group B to remind them how to use their air. Mary, Wendell, Emily, Lily, and Marcello, please help Group A as needed. Once you know they can play A, show them how to play G."

The students in Group A begin to talk about how to finger A as Mr. Ramirez works with the students in Group B with their air. Marcello is the first to speak, asking, "Who can show me the fingering for A?" Most students in Group A hold their recorders in front of them and demonstrate the fingering."

Lily chimes in, "Most of you have it, but some of you are using the wrong fingering. Let me show you."

While Lily demonstrates the correct fingering, Emily says, "Lily has it. She's showing you the correct fingering. Notice that it's fingers one and two on your left hand, not all three."

"You're such a rock star, Lily," chimes Wendell. "But she's right," he says to the class. "This is how you finger it. Marcello and I will walk in front of you to double-check again."

Mary asks, "Mr. Ramirez, shall we have Group A play the note?"

"Not yet," he responds. "Are they fingering it correctly?"

"Yes," replies Mary.

"Great." Mr. Ramirez moves to the front of the students. "Group A, show us the fingering for A." The Group A students model the fingering for the Group B students. "Good. Now, let's have Group A play A for four beats so we can hear how it sounds. Group B, I want you to watch and listen to Group A while they play. Here we go, get ready, 1-2-3-4." Group A plays the note. "Not too bad," remarks Mr. Ramirez. "Group B, join in and play with Group A this time. Here we go, 1-2-3-4." The entire class plays A. "Sounds good. Way to go! Now, Mary, Wendell, Emily, Lily, and Marcello will show us how to play G."

Mary, Wendell, Emily, Lily, and Marcello proceed to the front of the class while Mr. Ramirez stands among the students. Marcello holds up his recorder and models the fingering for G. Lily adds, "Notice how Marcello is covering all three of the top holes with his left-hand fingers."

Mary chimes in, "And see how his fingers are slightly curved."

Wendell says, "Before we all play this note, the five of us will demonstrate it. Who's going to count us in?"

Mary and Emily laugh, and Mary says, "I don't know. Lily, can you count us in?"

"Sure thing!" Lily responds enthusiastically. She counts "1-2-3-4," and the fifth-grade students play G. "Now," adds Lily, "let's all play it together, including you Mr. Ramirez!" Some of the students chuckle at Lily's remark.

Marcello adds, "When you play G, you'll need to use more air . . ."

"But just a little bit more," says Wendell, "otherwise it will be WAY too loud."

Lily counts them off again. After the entire class plays the note, she says, "Now, we'll play the note again, and then you can all repeat it after we play. I'll conduct for you." Lily counts off the fifth-grade students and they play the G. She then does the same with the fourth graders. "Not too bad," she remarks.

Wendell adds, "It's pretty loud, though. Listen to how loud we play it and then try to match our sound level." Lily counts the fifth graders off again followed by the fourth-grade class. "Much better," responds Wendell.

Mr. Ramirez walks to the front of the class again. "Now, let's play these three notes one at a time. Mary, Wendell, Emily, Lily, and Marcello will play the note first, then we will all respond. After we do that a couple of times, they'll teach us how to play "Hot Cross Buns."

Socializing as springboard for student interaction in peer mentoring

In Snapshot 4, the students in Mr. Ramirez's music class interacted with each other as they engaged in peer mentoring to learn "Hot Cross Buns" on their recorders. The interactions included sharing knowledge and experiences in a friendly and supportive manner as they encouraged each other to learn "Hot Cross Buns." Mr. Ramirez alternated between the roles of teacher and facilitator with leading the class, guiding mentoring between the Group A and Group B students, and allowing the fifth-grade students to mentor the fourth-grade students. When socializing, students develop relationships that aid with building friendships and acceptance by their peers[1] in the music classroom. Researchers have found that these friendships are an important component of the learning process and are closely related to social and academic growth.[2] The relationships that develop can also help students develop stronger bonds with each other that in turn help with increased motivation and elevated learning in the music classroom.[3] The friendships that develop during peer mentoring also help provide the foundation for students to be able to give and accept critique from their peers.[4]

Socializing

When students interact with each other,[5] their sharing of their knowledge and experiences becomes a catalyst for socializing.[6] Socializing is critical in a community of learners,[7] such as Mr. Ramirez's general music class, where learning is a shared endeavor between students when they share their knowledge and experiences. Socializing during peer mentoring can include dyads and groups of students. Interactions between students comprise the core of socializing, and additional components of learning include using *concrete objects* (e.g., a metronome); *procedures* (e.g., a warm-up routine); and, most importantly, *language*.[8] These three components aid in establishing an environment for learning, where students play an active role in sharing knowledge and experiences via peer mentoring.[9]

The individual characteristics of each music classroom or ensemble create a shared social and cultural context that provides opportunities for students to effectively share their knowledge and experiences with each other.[10] Socializing aids with effective communication between students and works best in learning environments that focus on cooperation and less on competition between students.[11] Socializing, then, provides a foundation for students to share what they know with their peers,[12] and it aids with developing connections between what knowledge they already possess and what new knowledge they are learning.[13] Thus, it is one of the most important parts of the peer mentoring process,[14] where it begins at the onset of student interactions and helps to establish a positive learning environment.[15] It is interesting to note that the use of humor has been found to help create a positive learning environment during socializing that helps to create a welcoming and relaxing atmosphere for students.[16]

Benefits of socializing

There are numerous benefits to socializing during peer mentoring, including elevated performance skills and comprehension of subject matter.[17] Nonmusical benefits include leadership[18] and students encouraging each other to help them "[feel] supported and uplifted."[19] For example, in Snapshot 4, the fifth-grade students encouraged the fourth-grade students throughout the entire class as they learned "Hot Cross Buns." The impact of this encouragement can be more beneficial than approval from the music teacher and plays a major role in the success of peer mentoring.[20] Socializing can help students who often feel like they are excluded from activities to feel like they are included.[21] It also helps to develop an overall cohesiveness among students[22] in that when they bond through their interactions, they can develop heightened ownership in the music program.[23] Socializing, then, helps students to develop individuality and a sense of community with a music program.[24]

> **Quick tip: Building community**
>
> Peer mentoring is really about building community, and this looks different from section to section and student to student. For the most part, I give my older students a little bit more of a free reign when it comes to building community and bonding and friendships, but my message to them is always about, "You know, remember when you were a freshman and a sophomore, and you didn't know the school, and you didn't know the systems that were in place. What would you have liked to know and what can you do with a freshman or sophomore who's really shy and not super social?" It's the relationship bonding moments that mean the most.
> —*Allison Lacasse, Band Director,*
> *Belmont High School, Belmont, MA*

When students socialize during peer mentoring and share their knowledge, they are leading the learning in the music class, and researchers have found that engaging in leadership aids with heightened learning.[25] Socializing leads to learning social skills and development of self-esteem[26] that contributes to building positive relationships between students.[27] Students also develop responsibility as they work together to establish group goals for learning.[28]

Socializing occurs in a variety of ways in the music program and can occur before class,[29] during class,[30] and after class.[31] For example, students might discuss musical issues, such as performing at the correct tempo.[32] Students can work together as they engage in conversations with each other about learning. These conversations help students to gain a better understanding of each other, both personally and their musical abilities, as they set musical goals for the class. Students can also share their musical interests with each other, such as which performers they enjoy listening to.[33]

> **Quick tip: Students connecting with each other**
>
> Socializing builds relationships, and kids need to build those very strong, lasting relationships. In the 20+ years of my teaching, peer mentorship has helped student mentors connect with student mentees in ways that I could not because of that peer connection. Kids are always more open with their peers.
> —*Terri Knight, transitional kindergarten through fifth-grade General Music, Band, and Orchestra, Greenbrook Elementary and Twin Creeks Elementary, San Ramon Valley Unified School District, Danville, CA*

Interruptions, peer pressure, sarcasm, and disparate abilities

Despite the many benefits of socializing during peer mentoring, problems can arise, particularly with verbal interactions. In particular, there is an increased possibility that students will interrupt you.[34] Furthermore, sarcasm and negative humor can hinder students' learning.[35] Peer pressure is a concern as well.[36] As the music teacher, you can decide when and to what extent you are comfortable with students verbally sharing their knowledge.

Another concern is the potential for hierarchies and power structures involving students of different performing abilities to hinder learning during peer mentoring.[37] For example, a student with higher musical performance ability might reject mentoring from a less-proficient peer, or a student of lower musical ability may not feel they have something to share. A student who identifies as part of the popular crowd might not want to participate in mentoring with a student who is seen as less popular. As discussed in Chapter 2, you play an important role in guiding students through the processes of understanding how to engage with each other when socializing.

Role of the music teacher with socializing

You play an important role in helping student mentors demonstrate empathy and showing them how to praise mentees.[38] It is also important for you to help student mentors develop listening skills that emphasize empathy among all students, which will help bolster confidence and develop positive relationships during socializing.[39] In turn, mentees will feel more comfortable and develop a sense of belonging in the music program.[40] Throughout this process, students can also develop a healthy self-image.[41]

In Snapshot 4, Mr. Ramirez played an active role with facilitating peer mentoring that included creating two mentoring groups, inviting the fifth-grade students to class, and constantly guiding and monitoring students during socializing. In your role as a facilitator, you play an important role with creating socializing opportunities during peer mentoring that can help build trust between students.[42] As students develop trust, they form stronger bonds between each other, and the comfort level between students is elevated.[43] Trust is also heightened between the music teacher and students as they co-create learning opportunities, such as Mr. Ramirez and his students, and students develop trust among each other as well, who can then experience the friendships and sense of community that grow out of that trust.[44]

The many dimensions of socializing

As a part of peer mentoring, socializing is a holistic process that is multidimensional for you and students. It can include "formal peer mentors [who] may be particularly beneficial in facilitating socialization of protégés,"[45] but it is also a process that benefits all students, regardless of whether at any given moment it is hierarchical or nonhierarchical, or whether students are in fixed roles or reciprocal roles. Successful socializing does not depend upon a certain number of students,[46] nor does it necessarily involve a student mentor to mentee relationship, for it can also include mentees sharing knowledge with mentors.[47] As the teacher, you can decide whether to designate formal relationships between students and/or use informal learning structures. Thus, all students can engage in proactive socialization, where they seek information, feedback, and initiate relationships with their peers.[48]

When you create socializing opportunities during peer mentoring, you *can* include individual student needs, but you *must* include group needs.[49] Group needs may involve learning goals created by the music teacher and students. Knowledge shared during socializing helps to develop and reinforce class and ensemble norms, rituals, and traditions.[50]

Socializing also helps students entering a music program (e.g., a new student to a second-grade music class; first-year students in high school) feel welcome.[51] As with socializing to aid in meaningful learning, it is not necessarily a "top-down process," where current students dictate what knowledge and experiences new students need to know.[52] It can also be a "bottom-up process," where new students initiate relationships with their peers through socializing and ask questions and seek new knowledge they deem necessary for acclimating to the music program.[53]

Socializing can be identified and organized with six dimensional traits:[54] (1) performance proficiency, which is the level of musical performance attained by a student during socializing; (2) people, which refers to the development of successful peer relationships that are shaped by the learning that happens during peer mentoring; (3) politics, or students' understanding of power structures and relationships in terms of how they work together in the music classroom; (4) language, referring to students' abilities to convey knowledge and experiences to their peers in a manner that they can understand; (5) organizational goals and values, which describe how students create, learn, and value the music program's goals and values and also understand the rules; and (6) history, which is understanding the music program's history, traditions, and rituals, as well as understanding the backgrounds of peers.[55]

Socializing summary

- Socializing provides the basis for students to share their knowledge and experiences.
- Socializing occurs in hierarchical and nonhierarchical peer mentoring structures.
- Benefits of socializing include increased responsibility, stronger bonds between students, increased motivation and self-esteem, comprehension of subject matter, elevated performance levels, and heightened ownership in the music class and ensemble.
- You play an important role in developing socializing that helps to build trust between students.
- Socializing helps students engage in meaningful learning and feel like they are part of the group.

Verbal and nonverbal interactions

In peer mentoring, the verbal and nonverbal interactions between students when they share their knowledge and experiences during peer mentoring are at the core of socializing.[56] Within these interactions, modeling and imitating peers serve as the foundations of socializing.[57]

Verbal interactions

An important part of socializing during peer mentoring are the verbal interactions between students.[58] Students share their knowledge verbally to explain a multitude of concepts, such as music fundamentals, including articulations, style, and dynamics.[59] These interactions provide opportunities for both student mentors and mentees to not only reinforce prior knowledge but also learn new knowledge as they engage in meaningful learning.[60] For example, when sharing their knowledge about the composing process with mentees, student mentors can develop a heightened understanding of the composition process.[61] Verbal interactions can also include sharing experiences, such as providing advice on how to audition for music ensembles.[62] Student mentors can be proactive and verbally explain concepts to mentees, help supplement knowledge concurrently with the music teacher,[63] and give additional feedback to the mentee.[64] Mentees can ask the mentor questions for clarification.[65]

Nonverbal interactions

Nonverbal interactions are also part of the socializing that occurs during learning and can occur at any time.[66] For example, before rehearsal, students might play or sing during warm-ups to inspire and motivate their peers.[67] During rehearsals, mentors and mentees can cue each other.[68] Embedded within nonverbal interactions are two important components of learning during peer mentoring: Modeling[69] and imitation.[70] These concepts are often grouped together as similar, especially because Vygotsky viewed them as opportunities for mentors and mentees to elevate their knowledge and skills.[71] However, there is a distinction: Modeling implies demonstrating something, such as musical phrases, whereas imitation can denote attempting to implement what is heard via modeling.

Modeling

Modeling during socializing refers to students engaged in "demonstrating or instructing"[72] knowledge, including musical sounds or behaviors,[73] and can help students with learning new subject matter.[74] For example, Lily modeled a correct fingering on the recorder in Snapshot 4. Modeling is a vital aspect of peer mentoring, for it helps mentors and mentees to elevate their performance skills by not only learning new knowledge but can also help them to refine their current knowledge about performing.[75] An interesting aspect of modeling is that students sometimes do not realize they are modeling, but a peer may be observing them perform[76] or may be engaged in another musical task (parallel activity) and not specifically focusing on the performance.[77]

Ultimately, behaviors exhibited by students during modeling play an important role in influencing how their peers learn, and they can "serve as social prompts that actuate and channel behavior in social transactions."[78] During these social transactions, desirable behavior is reinforced,[79] such as talking only when it is appropriate.

Imitation

Imitation refers to copying, emulating, and learning by doing and typically refers to a peer "doing the imitation or observing another [peer] with the intent of imitating."[80] Imitation is an important part of peer mentoring because it helps increase student comprehension of subject matter.[81] Whereas modeling is typically a one-way instructional approach with a student modeling for a peer, imitation involves a two-way approach to learning, where a peer imitates what is being modeled to them. Thus, modeling occurs first, then students engage in imitation.[82] Imitation surpasses strict repetition, however, for imitation requires context and motivation.[83] That is, the imitator needs to be able to comprehend what is being modeled and possess the desire to imitate toward improving some aspect of their knowledge and skills.[84] Music teachers, then, need to carefully construct opportunities for students to engage in imitation, where mentors are at the level of the mentees at least initially, but they should also take into consideration the potential for the mentee to develop their skills as the result of interacting with more advanced mentors and fellow peers.[85]

Verbal and nonverbal interactions summary
- Verbal interactions during peer mentoring provide students with opportunities to learn new knowledge, reinforce prior knowledge, and share experiences.
- Examples of nonverbal interactions include performing and cuing and are based in modeling and imitation.
- Modeling plays an important role in influencing how students learn and is a one-way exchange of instruction that includes demonstrating musical sounds and classroom behavior.
- Imitation is a response to modeling and refers to copying, emulating, and learning by doing.
- It is important for the music teacher to structure learning opportunities so that modeling and imitation are at the knowledge levels of students but also provide opportunities for musical growth and development.

Socializing: The building blocks of leadership

When students share their knowledge and experiences during peer mentoring, they develop their leadership skills.[86] Researchers have discovered that peer mentoring and leadership form a symbiotic relationship in that the two practices complement each other as part of meaningful learning:[87] "The learning and development of leadership capacities are inextricably intertwined" and "leadership educators can purposefully foster learning environments that help students integrate knowledge, skills, and experiences in meaningful ways."[88] Leadership is closely linked to learning[89] and academic achievement;[90] active learning is an important part of developing leadership skills.[91] Leadership in peer mentoring is an important and effective way to give students opportunities to have a voice in their learning.[92]

> **Quick tip: Socializing and leadership**
>
> Peer mentoring brings about a higher level of accountability within my ensembles because peers interact both socially and musically when mentoring each other and are careful when disseminating opinions and information to one another. This creates a greater sense of ownership in the ensemble and the development of leadership skills for the students.
>
> —Warren Gramm, former Music Teacher in
> Jersey City Public Schools, NJ; current Assistant Professor
> of Music Education at Lebanon Valley College, Annville, PA

Through leadership, students can assist each other with learning music fundamentals[93] or concepts such as improvisation and composition,[94] share their knowledge about technique,[95] or simply discuss their musical interests.[96] The fifth-grade students in Snapshot 4 demonstrated leadership when teaching the fourth-grade students how to play "Hot Cross Buns." During peer mentoring, then, students exhibit leadership when they share their knowledge and experiences via verbal and nonverbal interactions. For example, student leaders can share pedagogical knowledge when they contribute to making musical decisions during peer mentoring.[97] When student leaders contribute to learning, they can help improve the quality of learning that occurs, which can help to elevate musical performance levels and problem-solving skills, and have increased participation with making musical decisions.[98]

Because of the intertwined nature of these two practices, peer mentoring becomes a way for students to develop their leadership skills[99] "by making room for demonstrating learning, and building collaborative leadership."[100] In addition, peer mentoring helps students "to become collaborative leaders, shifting into a collaborative mindset, guiding [their peers] through process, and embracing coactive power."[101] Through these student collaborations, students gain confidence and increase their self-esteem.[102] Thus, when students engage in peer mentoring, they are also engaging in leadership, for they contribute to heightened musical learning.

Leadership for musical reasons

During peer mentoring, students take on important leadership roles when sharing their knowledge to help their peers improve in some aspect of musical performance.[103] For example, student leaders can help their peers to be prepared for classes and rehearsals. Preparing for rehearsal could involve demonstrating proper musical procedures, such as warming up correctly before rehearsal,[104] or modeling how to play notes correctly, as the fifth graders did in Snapshot 4. Class and rehearsal preparation can also include working with peers on fundamentals of music, such as articulations, dynamics, and note lengths, and can extend to even more advanced concepts, such as sound production, balance, and intonation. Student leaders can also help reinforce the importance of performing at a high level, both during classes, rehearsals, and performances.[105] During peer mentoring, they can help their peers with problem-solving when encountering musical performance issues.

Leadership for nonmusical reasons

Student leadership extends beyond helping peers be prepared for classes, rehearsals, and performances. Student leaders can help increase participation from both mentors and mentees, such as helping you with classroom management by maintaining order in the music classroom[106] or by modeling proper music classroom behavior. Student leaders can also help you with developing team building in the music class and ensemble.[107] This type of leadership can help reinforce high-level performance expectations and help sustain these traditions from year to year.[108]

Effective traits of student leadership

You can use peer mentoring to help students become decision-makers to prepare them for leadership roles in the music program.[109] When creating leadership opportunities, you can strive to integrate student leadership into music classroom activities.[110] Student leadership has several important components, including modeling effective leadership, engaging in a shared vision of what needs to be accomplished, being open to new ideas and ways to improve learning, building trust and developing relationships, and recognizing individual and group accomplishments. Through these processes, student leaders can develop their peers' confidence during peer mentoring.[111]

Student leadership gives students in the music program opportunities to practice developing their leadership skills when engaged in peer mentoring.[112] An effective student leader is "a person who is able to communicate well, engage in critical thinking, lead groups in problem solving and planning, and able to structure goals and objectives for the group."[113] You play an important role along with the students in creating a welcoming and supportive atmosphere that helps student leaders to be successful but also allows them to make errors and learn from them.[114]

Effective student leadership embodies a wide array of different leadership roles. For example, student leaders can help prepare the next generation of leaders in roles as lead mentor and advanced mentor[115] through a process known as *lateral mentoring*.[116] *Lead mentors* are students with at least two or more years of mentoring experience who can help with administrative duties in the music program (e.g., taking attendance) but primarily help guide other mentors toward music program goals. They are responsible for mentoring several protégés at once and checking in with other mentors and mentees about how mentoring is going.[117] *Advanced mentors* have at least one year of mentoring experience and will typically mentor one mentee and one protégé, who they are preparing to become a future mentor. Unlike the lead mentor, advanced mentors focus solely on mentoring the protégés;[118] however, student leaders can also engage in *shared responsibility*, where they rotate leadership roles so all students engage in leadership, such as the two mentoring groups set up by Mr. Ramirez in Snapshot 4, so all students could engage in leadership when mentoring their peers.[119] The rotation of leadership can lead to heightened ownership in learning and facilitates switching between roles of mentor and mentee during peer mentoring. As the music teacher, you play an important role in facilitating these leadership experiences and determining when you will want to use lateral mentoring and shared responsibility with your students.[120]

Students learn their leadership skills not only from you but also from their peers.[121] Students who have leadership experience can mentor fellow student leaders by motivating them to attend leadership workshops,[122] providing helpful feedback for how to lead,[123] and simply encouraging and supporting their peers to become leaders.[124]

Key attributes of student leadership include *authenticity*, or being honest about what they know and do not know, and *vulnerability*, or being willing to share power and take risks.[125] Student leaders also model good leadership skills,[126] including "establish[ing] clear lines of communication throughout the ensemble and avoid[ing] issues of miscommunication that may occur between teachers and students."[127] Honesty and ethical behavior of the student leader are also important.[128] It is important for students to understand why they are leading and their role as leaders during peer mentoring. Developing *inward* leadership helps student leaders to "become more aware of their own values and competencies,"[129] and developing *outward* leadership helps them to reflect on who they emulate for leadership in addition to reflecting on their own leadership style.[130] From this comes the term *authentic leadership*—self-awareness of being a leader in alignment with the music program's goals and traditions that leads toward development of trust between students.[131] To help students develop authentic leadership, you need to help them be self-aware of their own values, motivation, and feelings; understand how to share their knowledge and experiences without distorting what they know or do not know; act in a manner during peer mentoring that is based on what they consider important and not how they think their peers want them to act; be open to admitting what they do not know; and strive toward building relationships built in trust.

Quick tip: Preparing student leaders

When I prepare student leaders, I remind them to make sure to establish eye contact and have a quick exchange with everybody that's in their mentor group. I advise them to do so at least once a rehearsal. I also stress the importance of just making sure that they've made that contact, and they've let that person know that they matter to them, and that they care about how they're doing.

—*Allison Lacasse, Band Director,*
Belmont High School, Belmont, MA

Servant leadership is the idea that a student leader is at the service of their peers,[132] which includes helping empower the peers they are leading during peer mentoring and putting the needs of their peers above their own. Instilling this notion requires you to focus on the growth and development of student leadership with particular care toward the community of peers in addition to moral behavior.[133] There are eight characteristics of servant leadership: (1) believing in the students they lead and letting them know this, (2) holding both themselves and others accountable for their actions, (3) knowing when to give their peers credit for success, (4) exercising humility, (5) being true to one's self, (6) willing to take risks, (7) practicing empathy, (8) and focusing on the needs of the entire music classroom or ensemble.[134] Combining the servant concept with authenticity provides a more holistic model of student leadership.[135]

Quality in leadership is important,[136] and positive student mentors play an important role in developing effective student leadership. Peer mentoring features diverse groups of students working together. Students need opportunities to lead under the guidance of the music teacher, who provides support and feedback in addition to helping establish and maintain a supporting community of peers that aligns with the goals of the music program. Leadership development also means continually reflecting on how to improve the school music program.[137]

A word of caution is necessary, however, for the same concerns that can develop during socialization, such as sarcasm and peer pressure, can also occur during leadership. Not all students see themselves as equals based upon their levels of musicianship and knowledge,[138] and some students may be hesitant to engage in peer mentoring because of their musical abilities,[139] leading to inequitable relationships between students. In addition, as you learned in Chapter 2, students from dominant populations may not be willing to give up power. Therefore, it is important that you carefully monitor student leaders as they mentor their peers and continue to play an active role in developing their leadership skills.[140]

Leadership summary

- Student leadership and peer mentoring are intertwined.
- Leadership is closely linked to learning, and through leadership students gain confidence and can increase their self-esteem.
- Student leadership can lead to heightened learning for both musical and nonmusical reasons.
- Traits of effective student leadership include demonstrating strong communication skills, engaging in critical thinking, learning from mistakes, and problem-solving. Responsibilities of effective student leadership include helping the music teacher make decisions and helping to set goals and objectives for the music class and ensemble.
- Key attributes of student leadership include authenticity, being honest about what one knows, vulnerability, and being willing to make mistakes.
- Some students can serve in lead mentor or advanced mentor roles. Conversely, all students can engage in lateral mentoring when they rotate leadership roles.
- A primary part of student leadership is the notion that being a leader is providing a service to the music class and ensemble.

Preparing student leaders

Developing students' leadership helps them contribute musical and nonmusical decisions in the music classroom,[141] and you play an important role in creating and maintaining student leadership opportunities during peer mentoring. For example, you can structure mentor and mentee pairings and monitoring their interactions; it is also important for you to continue monitoring leadership once the system is up and running.[142] When creating leadership opportunities, keep in mind that student leadership is most successful when as many students are involved as possible.[143] Maximizing opportunities contributes to the generation of a strong sense of belonging.[144]

When meeting with student leaders, it is important to set clear goals and objectives and create a learning environment that supports their contributions.[145] In turn, student leaders can help their peers co-create musical goals and objectives for learning.[146] Through these processes, ideas generated by students can evolve and help contribute to meaningful learning.[147] Preparing students to engage in leadership during peer mentoring, then, is an important process.[148]

Quick tip: Helping students understand their role as leaders

I try to make sure the classroom environment is safe enough for the students to be vulnerable and to take risks. It is very important for students to understand the weight of responsibility that comes with leadership, and that just because they are a leader, that doesn't mean they are better than their peers. It's an equal playing field, and I instill in the students that effective leaders don't look down on anyone. They're the ones that see the strengths of everybody and how everybody is needed. This creates a sense of community in the classroom that helps a great deal to build leadership.

—*Tiffany Unarce Barry, former Music Teacher at Steindorf K–8 STEAM School, San Jose, CA; current Professor of Music Education at San Jose State University, San Jose, CA*

Consideration of student diversity, including diversity of backgrounds and prior experiences of students, is critical when designing leadership opportunities. It is important to create leadership opportunities that are organic to each learning environment.[149] For example, you can co-create leadership opportunities with marginalized students so they become leaders.[150] Student leaders who are marginalized can help you "initiate difficult conversations about race,"[151] resilience,[152] and inclusion.[153] Through leadership, marginalized students contribute to changing the microdynamics of the music class and ensemble in a way that leads to creating brave spaces for learning, as discussed in Chapter 2. Leadership in this regard plays a significant role that goes beyond elevating comprehension of subject matter and elevating musical performance skills toward helping students understand and value each other's backgrounds, identities, and perspectives.

Six categories of learning provide the basis for developing student leadership and learning: Knowledge, application, integration, valuing the human dimensions of learning, caring, and learning how to learn.[154] As discussed in Chapter 1, *knowledge* comprises foundational knowledge, non-foundational knowledge, tacit knowledge, and explicit knowledge. Because student leaders need to understand these different types of knowledge, they form the basis for leadership during peer mentoring. *Application* refers to the need for student leaders to not only understand knowledge but also be able to explain it to their peers. The next category, *integration*, helps student leaders develop an understanding of how to identify a musical problem and provide a solution during peer mentoring. *Valuing the human dimensions of learning* occurs when students begin to understand their peers' perspectives, value their knowledge and experiences, and tap into that understanding to help lead during peer mentoring. Throughout these categories, *caring* provides a foundation for effective leadership, for when students care about what they are learning, they become passionate about it. Finally, student leaders need to understand the importance of *learning how to learn*. This involves critically reflecting on what they are learning and why they are learning it, which in turn helps them become more effective leaders because they are able to sell what they are mentoring in conjunction with the goals of the music program. In addition, student leaders need to reflect on what went well and what did not during peer mentoring, and you can help guide them through the process of learning how to reflect on their leadership.

Leadership development occurs in a variety of ways.[155] Preparing students to lead involves meetings that span the entire time a student is in the music program. These include meetings outside of and during instructional time, and these range from one-on-one or small group meetings with you to all students learning about leadership during music classes and ensemble rehearsals.[156] You can also include experiences outside of music class, such as drum major camps in the summer months.[157] Holding leadership retreats for students, even once a year, can also help.[158] Your following up after all these experiences is vital to continuing and maintaining effective leadership during peer mentoring.[159]

> **Quick tip: Preparing student leaders**
>
> To prepare student leaders, we did a leadership training academy. This was about developing communication strategies, what it means to be a leader, how you can inspire other students to develop these qualities, and how you can facilitate groups to be successful in achieving the goals of the music program. Because we had a class for leadership at the school, we teamed up with the leadership teacher at the school that was separate from music, and we would often pair up and share strategies and develop new ideas about leadership. Leadership was happening campus-wide, and we had a smaller microcosm of it in the music department.
> —Troy Davis, former Band and Jazz Band Director at Aragon High School, San Mateo, CA; current Director of Instrumental Music and Jazz Studies at West Valley College, Saratoga, CA

Sharing leadership with students

Leadership is often portrayed as either teacher-centered or student-centered, but the two can happen concurrently.[160] You learned in Chapter 2 that you can share in power and authority with regard to learning in the music classroom,[161] similar to how Mr. Ramirez shared authority with the students in Snapshot 4. Working as a facilitator with your student leaders contributes to establishing high-quality leadership experiences during peer mentoring.[162] Thus, it is not always just the students being the leaders all the time. *Shared leadership* or *collaborative leadership* refers to situations, where students provide leadership in conjunction with their music teachers,[163] engaging in "shared governance and collaborative decision making," where "sharing leadership among . . . students of all ages" aids with meaningful learning.[164] Shared leadership occurs, for example, when you and your students work together to plan for rehearsals.[165] Students develop leadership skills not only by participating in the planning processes but also by engaging in repertoire selection[166] and assigning parts.[167] These interactions between you and the students help to create an environment where you and your students share in the learning process.[168] Students can interact with other adults as well, including principals, other teachers, school counselors, and parents.[169] Through the development of leadership in all students, you and your students can "help transform organizational relationships and systems."[170] When you create a learning environment rich in student leadership, many responsibilities are delegated to the students,[171] which aids with strengthening student ownership in the music program. Furthermore, when you do not have to make every decision, classroom and ensemble rehearsal time can be used more efficiently.[172]

Preparing student leaders summary

- You play an active role in creating and maintaining student leadership opportunities during peer mentoring.
- It is important to design leadership opportunities that are organic to each learning environment, for different classes and ensembles have different needs for student leadership.
- Marginalized students can play an important role in helping you to co-create brave learning spaces that help instill leadership skills in all students.
- You can meet with students before, during, and after class and rehearsals to help them develop their leadership skills.
- Students can provide leadership concurrent with your leadership, referred to as shared or collaborative leadership.

Questions for discussion

1. How might you create opportunities for socializing for students to use concrete objects, procedures, and language?
2. What are some musical benefits of socializing that could help your students? What about nonmusical benefits?
3. How might you create opportunities for socializing to help both individual students and groups of students?

4. In what ways might you guide students through learning how to share their knowledge and experiences via verbal and nonverbal interactions?
5. How might you facilitate student leadership opportunities for musical and nonmusical reasons?
6. How might you prepare select groups of students for student leadership positions, such as lead mentor and advanced mentor? How might you prepare all students to engage in leadership, an approach known as shared responsibility?
7. How might you prepare students to reflect while engaged in inward, outward, authentic, and servant leadership?
8. How might you and your students co-create brave learning spaces conducive to discussions about race, resilience, and inclusion?
9. How might you design opportunities to share leadership with students?

Reflection

Socializing involves the interactions between students and is the foundation from which students share their knowledge with their peers. During socializing, friendships develop that are related to social and academic growth, leading to improved attitudes, increased motivation toward learning, self-confidence, and self-esteem. Numerous benefits result from students socializing with each other, including elevated performance skills, comprehension of subject matter, and feeling welcome in the music class and ensemble. Students also develop heightened responsibility when they learn to work together.

As you consider how your students socialize in your music class or ensemble, think about how you can continue to facilitate the development of empathy and trust among your students. This can involve co-creating brave learning spaces with your students, especially those considered marginalized, to create learning environments where students engage in conversations during peer mentoring about racism, resilience, and inclusion so that all students feel safe. In turn, this establishes a learning environment conducive to all students engaging in leadership. When your students socialize with each other during peer mentoring, you will want to continue reflecting on your comfort level with verbal and nonverbal interactions—whether they occur during class or rehearsal and to what extent. As you have already discovered, you will need to carefully monitor student interactions to ensure that sarcasm, negative humor, and peer pressure are kept in check and do not harm the positive learning environment you and your students have created.

Research indicates that peer mentoring and student leadership are intertwined. Any time students share their knowledge and experiences with each other, they are assuming a leadership role. Student leadership is multi-faceted and involves heightened learning for both musical reasons and nonmusical reasons. As you continue to develop and guide student leaders in your music class and ensemble, think about how you can prepare individual students for leadership roles and how all students can assume leadership. As you have likely discovered, student leadership is a flexible endeavor; the ways you structure leadership will vary from class to class and within a music class. For example, at times you may want specific students to engage in leadership, while at other times the learning goals and objectives will necessitate all students take on a leadership role. Using these various structures of leadership can help you and your students to create and maintain a meaningful learning environment. As you learned in this chapter, leadership is often presented as teacher-centered or student-centered, but in reality, you can engage in shared leadership with your students. Not only does this help to make learning more efficient and contribute to heightened student ownership; it also helps sustain a holistic and meaningful learning environment.

Notes

1. Clifford K. Madsen, "Music Teacher Education Students as Cross-Age Reading Tutors in an After-School Setting," *Journal of Music Teacher Education* 20, no. 2 (2011): 40–54, https://doi.org/10.1177/1057083710371441; Hanne Riese, Akylina Samara, and Sølvi Lillejord, "Peer Relations in Peer Learning," *International Journal of Qualitative Studies in Education* 25, no. 2 (2012): 601–624, http://dx.doi.org/10.1080/09518398.2011.605078.
2. Madsen, "After-School Setting"; Riese, Samara, and Lillejord, "Peer Relations in Peer Learning."
3. Warren Gramm, "Peer Mentoring in a Modern Band" (DMA dissertation, Boston University, 2021), ProQuest (AAT 283117250).
4. Gramm, "Modern Band."
5. Andrew Goodrich, "Peer Mentoring and Peer Tutoring Among K-12 Students: A Literature Review," *Update: Applications of Research in Music Education* 36, no. 2 (2018).
6. Goodrich, "Peer Mentoring and Peer Tutoring"; Gramm, "Modern Band."
7. Riese, Samara, and Lillejord, "Peer Relations in Peer Learning."
8. Riese, Samara, and Lillejord, "Peer Relations in Peer Learning."
9. Goodrich, "Peer Mentoring and Peer Tutoring."
10. Riese, Samara, and Lillejord, "Peer Relations in Peer Learning."
11. Gramm, "Modern Band"; Jeff Taylor, "Peer Mentoring within the Middle and High School Music Department of the International School of Kuala Lumpur: A Case Study" (DMA dissertation, Boston University, 2016), ProQuest (AAT 10135020).
12. Andrew Goodrich, "Peer Mentoring in an Extracurricular Music Class," *International Journal of Music Education* 39, no. 4 (2021): 410–423, https://doi.org/10.1177/0255761420988922.
13. John Dewey, *Experience and Education* (New York: Collier, 1938), 25.
14. Alice-Ann Darrow, Pamela Gibbs, and Sarah Wedel, "Use of Classwide Peer Tutoring in the General Music Classroom," *Update: Applications of Research in Music Education* 24, no. 1 (2005): 15–26, https://doi.org/10.1177/87551233050240010103; Andrew Goodrich, "Peer Mentoring in a High School Jazz Ensemble," *Journal of Research in Music Education* 55, no. 2

(2007): 94–114, https://doi.org/10.1177/002242940705500202; Erik Johnson, "Peer Teaching in the Secondary Music Ensemble," *Journal of Education Training Studies* 3, no. 5 (2015): 35–42, http://dx.doi.org/10.11114/jets.v3i5.906; Bernadette Butler Scruggs, "Learning Outcomes in Two Divergent Middle School String Orchestra Classroom Environments: A Comparison of a Learner-Centered and a Teacher-Centered Approach" (PhD dissertation, Georgia State University, 2009), ProQuest (AAT 3371516); Christina Shields, "Music Education and Mentoring as Intervention for At-Risk Urban Adolescents: Their Self-Perceptions, Opinions, and Attitudes," *Journal of Research in Music Education* 49, no. 3 (2001): 273–286, https://doi.org/10.2307/3345712; Taylor, "Kuala Lumpur" (DMA dissertation, Boston University, 2016), ProQuest (AAT 10135020); Richard S. Webb, "An Exploration of Three Peer Tutoring Cases in the School Orchestra Program," *Bulletin of the Council for Research in Music Education*, no. 203 (2015): 63–80, https://doi.org/10.5406/bulcouresmusedu.203.0063.

15. Clifford K. Madsen, David S. Smith, and Charles C. Feeman, Jr., "The Use of Music in Cross-Age Tutoring within Special Education Settings," *Journal of Music Therapy* 25, no. 3 (1988): 135–144, https://doi.10.1093/jmt/25.3.135; Riese, Samara, and Lillejord, "Peer Relations in Peer Learning."
16. Gramm, "Modern Band."
17. Goodrich, "High School Jazz Ensemble."
18. Goodrich, "Peer Mentoring and Peer Tutoring."
19. Gramm, "Modern Band," 198.
20. Gramm, "Modern Band."
21. Gramm, "Modern Band."
22. Gramm, "Modern Band."
23. Goodrich, "Peer Mentoring and Peer Tutoring."
24. Goodrich, "Peer Mentoring and Peer Tutoring."
25. Goodrich, "High School Jazz Ensemble"; Riese, Samara, and Lillejord, "Peer Relations in Peer Learning"; Scruggs, "Learning Outcomes."
26. Riese, Samara, and Lillejord, "Peer Relations in Peer Learning."
27. Michael J. Karcher, "The Cross-Age Mentoring Program: A Developmental Intervention for Promoting Students' Connectedness across Grade Levels," *Professional School Counseling* 2 (2008): 137–143, https://doi.org/10.1177/2156759X0801200208.
28. Riese, Samara, and Lillejord, "Peer Relations in Peer Learning."
29. Goodrich, "Extracurricular Music Class."
30. Goodrich, "High School Jazz Ensemble"; Gramm, "Modern Band"; Scruggs, "Learning Outcomes."
31. Madsen, "After-School Setting."
32. Gramm, "Modern Band."
33. Gramm, "Modern Band."
34. Goodrich, "High School Jazz Ensemble."
35. Cecilia Björck, "A Music Room of One's Own: Discursive Constructions of Girls-Only Spaces for Learning Popular Music," *Girlhood Studies* 6, no. 2 (2013): 11–29, https://doi.org/10.3167/ghs.2013.060203; David B. Fodor, "Critical Moments of Change: A Study of the Social and Musical Interactions of Precollegiate Jazz Combos" (PhD dissertation, Northwestern University, 1998), ProQuest (AAT 9913792); Johnson, "Secondary Music Ensemble."
36. Johnson, "Secondary Music Ensemble."
37. Riese, Samara, and Lillejord, "Peer Relations in Peer Learning."
38. Taylor, "Kuala Lumpur."
39. Karin S. Hendricks, *Compassionate Music Teaching: A Framework for Motivation and Engagement in the 21st Century* (Lanham, MD: Rowman &

Littlefield, 2018); Raymond W. Young and Carl M. Cates, "Emotional and Directive Listening in Peer Mentoring," *International Journal of Listening* 18, no. 1 (2004): 21–33, https://doi.org/10.1080/10904018.2004.10499060.
40. Young and Cates, "Emotional and Directive Listening."
41. Karcher, "Cross-Age Mentoring."
42. Gramm, "Modern Band."
43. Gramm, "Modern Band."
44. Goodrich, "High School Jazz Ensemble"; Andrew Goodrich, "Developing Trust and Empathy Through Peer Mentoring in the Music Classroom," in *The Oxford Handbook of Compassion and Care in Music Education*, ed. Karin S. Hendricks (New York: Oxford University Press, 2023); Hendricks, *Compassionate Music Teaching*; Christa Kiersch and Janet Peters, "Leadership from the Inside Out: Student Leadership Development within Authentic Leadership and Servant Leadership Frameworks," *Journal of Leadership Education* 16, no. 1 (2017): 148–168, https://doi.org/10.12806/V16/I1/T4; Johnson, "Secondary Music Ensemble."
45. Tammy Allen, Stacy McManus, and Joyce Russell, "Newcomer Socialization and Stress: Formal Relationships as a Source of Support," *Journal of Vocational Behavior* 54 (1999): 456, https://doi.org/10.1006/jvbe.1998.1674.
46. Allen, McManus, and Russell, "Newcomer Socialization."
47. Allen, McManus, and Russell, "Newcomer Socialization."
48. Kecia M. Thomas et al., "The Roles of Protégé Race, Gender, and Proactive Socialization Attempts on Peer Mentoring," *Advances in Developing Human Resources* 7, no. 4 (2005): 540–555, https://doi.org/10.1177/1523422305279681.
49. Allen, McManus, and Russell, "Newcomer Socialization."
50. Barry Bozeman and Mary Kay Feeney, "Toward a Useful Theory of Mentoring: A Conceptual Analysis and Critique," *Administration and Society* 39, no. 6 (2007): 719–739, https://doi.org/10.1177/0095399707304119
51. Taylor, "Kuala Lumpur."
52. Thomas et al., "Roles," 544.
53. Thomas et al., "Roles," 544.
54. Georgia T. Chao, Howard J. Klein, and Philip D. Gardner, "Organizational Socialization: Its Content and Consequences," *Journal of Applied Psychology* 79, no. 5 (1994): 730–743, https://doi.org/10.1037/0021-9010.79.5.730.
55. Chao, Klein, and Gardner, "Organizational Socialization."
56. Goodrich, "Peer Mentoring and Peer Tutoring"; Andrew Goodrich, "Peer Mentoring in a University Jazz Ensemble," *Visions of Research in Music Education* 28 (2016), https://opencommons.uconn.edu/vrme/vol28/iss1/7/; Kimberly Van Weelden, Julia Heath-Reynolds, and Scott Lehman, "The Effect of a Peer Mentorship Program on Perceptions of Success in Choral Ensembles: Pairing Students with and without Disabilities," *Update: Applications of Research in Music Education* 36, no. 1 (2016): 37–43, https://doi.org/10.1177/8755123316675480.
57. Lucy Green, *Music, Informal Learning, and the School: A New Classroom Pedagogy* (Burlington, VT: Ashgate, 2008).
58. David B. Fodor, "Critical Moments"; Goodrich, "High School Jazz Ensemble"; Erik Johnson, "Secondary Music Ensemble"; Katherine Strand, "Nurturing Young Composers: Exploring the Relationship between Instruction and Transfer in 9–12 Year-Old Students," *Bulletin of the Council for Research in Music Education*, no. 165 (2005): 17–36, www.jstor.org/stable/40319268.
59. Goodrich, "High School Jazz Ensemble."

60. Goodrich, "Peer Mentoring and Peer Tutoring"; Christine Howe, *Peer Groups and Children's Development* (Hoboken, NJ: John Wiley & Sons, 2009).
61. Strand, "Nurturing Young Composers."
62. Goodrich, "Extracurricular Music Class."
63. Goodrich, "Extracurricular Music Class."
64. Fabiennne d'Arripe-Longueville and Christophe Gernigon, "Peer-Assisted Learning in the Physical Activity Domain: Dyad Type and Gender Differences," *Journal of Sport & Exercise Psychology* 24, no. 3 (2002): 219–238, https://doi.org/10.1123/jsep.24.3.219.
65. d'Arripe-Longueville and Gernigon, "Peer-Assisted Learning."
66. Fodor, "Critical Moments"; Goodrich, "High School Jazz Ensemble"; Lucy Green, *How Popular Musicians Learn: A Way Ahead for Music Education* (Burlington, VT: Ashgate, 2002); Green, *New Classroom Pedagogy*.
67. Goodrich, "High School Jazz Ensemble."
68. Fodor, "Critical Moments."
69. Albert Bandura, "Social Cognitive Theory," in *Annals of Child Development*, ed. Ross Vasta (Greenwich, CT: JAI Press, 1989), 1–60.
70. Lev Vygotsky, *Mind in Society: The Development of Higher Psychological Processes* (Cambridge, MA: Harvard University Press, 1978).
71. Vygotsky, *Mind in Society*.
72. Byrne, "The Give and Take of Peer Review: Utilizing Modeling and Imitation" (PhD dissertation, Kent State University, 2015), 3, https://rave.ohiolink.edu/etdc/view?acc_num=kent143803607019.
73. Bandura, "Social Cognitive Theory"; Fodor, "Critical Moments"; Goodrich, "High School Jazz Ensemble."
74. d'Arripe-Longueville and Gernigon, "Peer-Assisted Learning."
75. Bandura, "Social Cognitive Theory."
76. Green, *How Popular Musicians Learn*.
77. d'Arripe-Longueville and Gernigon, "Peer-Assisted Learning."
78. Bandura, "Social Cognitive Theory," 23.
79. Byrne, "Give and Take," 9.
80. Byrne, "Give and Take," 3.
81. Vygotsky, *Mind in Society*.
82. d'Arripe-Longueville and Gernigon, "Peer-Assisted Learning."
83. Byrne, "The Give and Take."
84. Vygotsky, *Mind in Society*, 86.
85. Vygotsky, *Mind in Society*.
86. David Frost and Amanda Roberts, "Student Leadership, Participation and Democracy," *Leading and Managing* 17, no. 2 (2011): 66–84, https://search.informit.org/doi/10.3316/ielapa.318017162668709; Navalka et al., "Putting Collaborative Leadership into Practice," *Parks Stewardship Forum* 37, no. 2 (2021): 316–324, https://doi.org/10.5070/P537253237; Darrow, Gibbs, and Wedel, "Classwide Peer Tutoring"; Goodrich, "Peer Mentoring and Peer Tutoring"; Goodrich, "Extracurricular Music Class"; Scruggs, "Learning Outcomes"; Taylor, "Kuala Lumpur."
87. Kiersch and Peters, "Leadership"; Navalka et al., "Collaborative Leadership"; Keith D. Richardson, "How High School Band Directors Learn Leadership: The Journey to Transformational Leadership and Autonomous Student Leaders" (DMA dissertation, Boston University, 2022). ProQuest (AAT 28776378).
88. Julie Owen, "Transforming Leadership Development for Significant Learning," *New Directions for Student Leadership* 145 (2015): 8, https://doi.org/10.1002/yd.20120.

89. Jane McGregor, "Recognizing Student Leadership: Schools and Networks as Sites of Opportunity," *Improving Schools* 10, no. 1 (2007): 86–101, https://doi.org/10.1177/1365480207073725.
90. Philip Hallinger and Ronald H. Heck, "Leadership for Learning: Does Collaborative Leadership Make a Difference in School Improvement?" *Educational Management* 38, no. 6 (2010): 654–678, https://doi.org/10.1177/1741143210379060.
91. Julie Owen, "Transforming."
92. Pat Thomson, "Understanding, Evaluating, and Assessing What Students Learn from Leadership Activities: Student Research in Woodlea Primary," *Management in Education* 26, no. 3 (2012): 96–103, https://doi.org/10.1177/0892020612445677.
93. Green, "*How Popular Musicians Learn*"; Goodrich, "Extracurricular Music Class"; Strand, "Nurturing Young Composers."
94. Green, *How Popular Musicians Learn*; Strand, "Nurturing Young Composers."
95. Goodrich, "Extracurricular Music Class"; Green, *New Classroom Pedagogy*.
96. Goodrich, "High School Jazz Ensemble"; Green, "How *Popular Musicians Learn*."
97. David Hebert, "Music Competition, Cooperation, and Community: An Ethnography of a Japanese School Band" (PhD dissertation, University of Washington, 2005), ProQuest (AAT 3163382); Kiersch and Peters, "Leadership."
98. Johnson, "Secondary Music Ensembles"; Scruggs, "Learning Outcomes."
99. Darrow, Gibbs, and Wedel, "Classwide Peer Tutoring"; Goodrich, "High School Jazz Ensemble"; Scruggs, "Learning Outcomes"; Taylor, "Kuala Lumpur."
100. Navalka et al., "Collaborative Leadership," 318.
101. Navalka et al., "Collaborative Leadership," 318
102. David Reed Doke, "Collaborative Learning among High School Students in an Alternative Styles Strings Ensemble" (DMA dissertation, Boston University, 2020), ProQuest (AAT 27955823).
103. Goodrich, "Peer Mentoring and Peer Tutoring."
104. Tamara T. Thies, "Student Leaders as Change Agents: Benefits Emerging from a Curricular Change," *Visions of Research in Music Education* 23 (2013): 1–25, https://opencommons.uconn.edu/vrme/vol23/iss1/4/.
105. Thies, "Student Leaders as Change Agents."
106. Goodrich, "High School Jazz Ensemble"; Hebert, "Music Competition"; Johnson, "Secondary Music Ensemble."
107. Ian Hay and Neil Dempster, "Student Leadership Development Through General Classroom Activities," in *Educating: Weaving Research into Practice* (Queensland: Griffith University, 2004), 141–150, https://research-repository.griffith.edu.au/bitstream/handle/10072/2080/25690_1.pdf.
108. Goodrich, "High School Jazz Ensemble."
109. Scott Rush, *Habits of a Successful Band Director: Pitfalls and Solutions* (Chicago, IL: GIA Publications, 2006).
110. Hay and Dempster, "Student Leadership."
111. John. F. Feldhusen and Mary K. Pleiss, "Leadership: A Synthesis of Social Skills, Creativity, and Historical Ability?" *Roper Review* 16, no. 4 (1994): 292–293, https://doi.org/10.1080/02783199409553602; Barry Z. Posner, "Effectively Measuring Student Leadership," *Administrative Sciences* 2, no. 4 (2012): 221–234, https://doi.org/10.3390/admsci2040221.
112. Hay and Dempster, "Student Leadership."

113. Hay and Dempster, "Student Leadership," 141.
114. Hay and Dempster, "Student Leadership."
115. Karcher, "Cross-Age Mentoring."
116. Connie Tingson-Gatuz, "Mentoring the Leader: The Role of Peer Mentoring in the Leadership Development of Students-of-Color in Higher Education" (PhD dissertation, Michigan State University, 2009), ProQuest (AAT 3381412).
117. Karcher, "Cross-Age Mentoring."
118. Karcher, "Cross-Age Mentoring."
119. Barbara Coeyman, "Applications of Feminist Pedagogy to the College Music Major Curriculum: An Introduction to Issues," *College Music Symposium* 36 (1996): 73–90, www.jstor.org/stable/40374285.
120. Coeyman, "Applications of Feminist Pedagogy."
121. Goodrich, "High School Jazz Ensemble."
122. Goodrich, "High School Jazz Ensemble."
123. Goodrich, "High School Jazz Ensemble."
124. Goodrich, "High School Jazz Ensemble."
125. Navalka et al., "Collaborative Leadership."
126. Navalka et al., "Collaborative Leadership."
127. Gramm, "Modern Band," 286.
128. Kiersch and Peters, "Leadership."
129. Kiersch and Peters, "Leadership," 149.
130. Kiersch and Peters, "Leadership."
131. Kiersch and Peters, "Leadership."
132. Kiersch and Peters, "Leadership."
133. Kiersch and Peters, "Leadership."
134. Kiersch and Peters, "Leadership."
135. Kiersch and Peters, "Leadership."
136. Kiersch and Peters, "Leadership."
137. Kiersch and Peters, "Leadership."
138. Goodrich, "High School Jazz Ensemble."
139. Darrow, Gibbs, and Wedel, "Classwide Peer Tutoring."
140. Scruggs, "Learning Outcomes."
141. Kiersch and Peters, "Leadership."
142. Goodrich, "High School Jazz Ensemble"; Karcher, "Cross-Age Mentoring"; Scruggs, "Learning Outcomes."
143. Frost and Roberts, "Student Leadership."
144. Frost and Roberts, "Student Leadership."
145. Scott J. Allen and Nathan S. Hartman, "Sources of Learning in Student Leadership Development Programming," *Journal of Leadership Studies* 3, no. 3 (2009): 6–16, https://doi.org/10.1002/jls.20119.
146. Navalka et al., "Collaborative Leadership."
147. Navalka et al., "Collaborative Leadership."
148. Karcher, "Cross-Age Mentoring."
149. Owen, "Transforming Leadership."
150. Andrew Goodrich, "Valuing Racialized Student Voices: Transforming Learning Through Peer Mentoring," *Action, Criticism, and Theory for Music Education* 21, no. 1 (2021): 142–171, https://doi:10.22176/act21.2.142.
151. Goodrich, "Valuing Racialized Student Voices," 24.
152. Andrew Goodrich, "Counterpoint in the Music Classroom: Creating an Environment of Resilience with Peer Mentoring and LGBTQIA+ Students," *International Journal of Music Education* 38, no. 4 (2020): 582–592, https://doi.org/10.1177/0255761420949373.

153. Judith Jellison, *Including Everyone: Creating Music Classrooms Where All Children Learn* (New York: Oxford University Press, 2015).
154. Dee L. Fink, *Creating Significant Learning Experiences: An Integrated Approach to Designing College Courses* (San Francisco, CA: Jossey-Bass, 2013).
155. Kiersch and Peters, "Leadership."
156. Kiersch and Peters, "Leadership."
157. Goodrich, "High School Jazz Ensemble."
158. Kiersch and Peters, "Leadership."
159. Kiersch and Peters, "Leadership."
160. Christopher Rhodes and Mark Brundrett, "Leadership for Learning," in *The Principles of Educational Leadership and Management*, ed. Tony Bush, David Middlewood, and Les Bell (Thousand Oaks, CA: SAGE, 2010), 153–175.
161. Rhodes and Brundrett, "Leadership for Learning."
162. Rhodes and Brundrett, "Leadership for Learning."
163. Hallinger and Heck, "Leadership for Learning."
164. Carol A. Mullen, *Mentorship Primer* (New York: Peter Lang, 2005), 4.
165. Hay and Dempster, "Student Leadership."
166. Hebert, "Music Competition."
167. Hebert, "Music Competition."
168. Johnson, "Secondary Music Ensembles."
169. Hallinger and Heck, "Leadership for Learning."
170. Mullen, *Mentorship Primer*, 87.
171. Mullen, *Mentorship Primer*.
172. Mullen, *Mentorship Primer*.

Part II
Narrative portraits of four music teachers

5   Dana Monteiro

The first four chapters of this book describe how peer mentoring and student leadership contribute to meaningful learning in the music classroom and ensemble. Peer mentoring involves the sharing of knowledge and experiences by the students themselves, and these initial chapters point out some of the valuable supplementary benefits of peer mentoring in the classroom. Peer mentoring supports the development of student social skills, self-esteem, motivation, and ownership in the music class and ensemble, and it works in a diversity of settings in a variety of ways.

Chapter 5 narrows in on how peer mentoring and leadership become essential parts in learning a musical style—in this case, samba. The setting for the discussion is Dana Monteiro's samba program at the Frederick Douglass Academy in Harlem, New York. In 2021, Dana's students nominated him for the "Flag Award for Teaching Excellence," and he received his award during a live performance with one of his samba ensembles on *Good Morning America*.

The samba program at Frederick Douglass Academy replicates how samba is learned and performed in the samba schools in Rio de Janeiro, and the way that Dana and Frederick Douglass and the Rio samba school connected makes an interesting story. The added value to the narrative, however, is the realization that samba heightened student ownership and commitment at Frederick Douglass, thereby elevating performance levels and nurturing student enthusiasm for lifelong participation in music.

Introducing Dana

Most people remember where they were on 9/11. They recall being glued to their television sets as they watched the horrific events of that day unfold. As time went by, they began sharing their stories of where they were and what they were doing when it all happened. Each story is a bit unique. For Dana Monteiro, the terrorists took down the Towers on his fourth day of teaching. Having completed his undergraduate degree in music education at New York University in the spring of 2001, he had just begun teaching in the New York City public school system at the Evander

DOI: 10.4324/9781003243618-8

Figure 5.1 Dana Monteiro.
Source: Photograph provided by Dana Monteiro.

Childs High School that fall. According to Dana, Evander Childs is "a humongous school of 5000 students in the Bronx," but what he remembers most about it is the fact that "9/11 was his fourth day at work."

Dana is a classical trumpeter and a native of Providence, Rhode Island. At Evander Childs, he was one of four music teachers, two of whom had many years of teaching experience, and the third was not much older than he was. As Dana remembers it, the other music teachers mentored him and "helped me quite a bit to find my footing." As what was going on in the outside world grabbed the headlines, Dana's personal world centered on his new job. "Evander Childs was a rough, rough high school, but it did help provide me with skills for dealing with classroom management and discipline." He remained at Evander Childs for two years and then took a teaching position at the Frederick Douglass Academy in Harlem, where he has been ever since. In 2007, he completed his master's degree, also in music education, at Teacher's College, Columbia University. He eventually earned his Doctor of Musical Arts degree in music education from Boston University in 2016.[1]

At Frederick Douglass, Dana "was more or less the only music teacher." He began by teaching "the traditional band curriculum," which included middle school and high school marching band. Frederick Douglass, he points out, "is one of the only schools in Manhattan with a parking lot." To pick up some practical insights about teaching, Dana also "spent a lot of time sitting on the floor of the dance room watching the school's dance instructor teach." These observations helped Dana improve his skills in "classroom management and learn how and when to speak to students and when not to speak to students." He concluded that these two elements of teaching were more important than "the actual music," for "you have to have control of who's in front of you and earn their trust that you're going to provide a good environment for them to get the content you're trying to teach." Even as Dana fine-tuned his teaching approach, however, he encountered an issue that faces most music teachers: How to get students to practice. In Manhattan, for example, the "kids come in on public transportation, and some travel over an hour. Getting them to carry a tenor sax home was impossible, and if you did get them to take it home, more than likely they did not always bring it back for regular rehearsals."

New York State has a policy requiring that "high school students have credits in the arts to graduate," so Dana had to design his program to accommodate the students who needed to meet the requirement. At Frederick Douglass, it "was one music teacher and one art teacher, so one or the other of us ultimately had every kid in the building. I didn't have time to teach middle school because I had so many high school students working to get their credit." Dana admits that "it sounds great that every kid is required to have art or music," but he also points out that in New York City, "with its high number of students and its low number of music teachers," the requirement "actually destroys instrumental music in a lot of our schools because there's just no time for it."

For Dana, these challenges are further compounded by another problem shared by music teachers: The scheduling of classes. He notes:

> Scheduling was a big barrier for band. You may have a group of 40 ninth-grade band students, but there's no guarantee that those 40

kids are going to be in your class for tenth grade. Every year, I lost an entire section. You know, they decided to have precalculus during the same period, so I lost this whole group who just by coincidence all played the same instrument. So now, the first couple months of the year, we have to convert someone to a new instrument. You might get half of them, or you might lose the entire trombone section, you know. You can't quite have band if you, say, lose your trombone section. You can't just go to flute players and say, "Hey, come on over here, you're playing trombone," in tenth grade.

The solution Dana was looking for was one where he could teach music and not deal with attrition due to scheduling. Enter samba.

Discovering samba

Dana discovered samba in 2004 on a trip to Brazil. He jokingly recalls wanting to go to Hong Kong, but his wife wanted to go to Brazil, "and she won." Dana took his trumpet with him, thinking that he would get into something there and play. Good thing he did, for once he was in Brazil, a saxophone player recommended he go to a samba school. They are not actually schools; they are community spaces in various neighborhoods. These community organizations parade in the Rio de Janeiro Carnival and also serve as a social/nightlife event every Saturday night. Dana attended a "rehearsal" one night with what he estimates was around 3000 other people playing in various groups. Without prior samba experience or any time playing drums, he went to samba school, where he "saw 275 people playing in one group" and quickly noticed "another one with 275 people also rehearsing late on a Saturday night." He ultimately discovered "there are 75 of these groups just in Rio alone."

As Dana observed the "275 drummers playing at the same time," he realized that the samba might be a good fit for his school, for "I had a lot of students back in Harlem who wanted to drum." When he returned home, he went to his principal and announced, "This is what I want to do, okay?" With the principal's approval and a dozen instruments, Dana began the samba program at Frederick Douglass Academy. At first, "it was an after-school club," but fortunately, "the kids were really into it." Over the next two years, he continued to buy instruments until he had 50, at which point he could offer samba during all his music classes for he "had enough instruments to go around." There are now four classes per day that often include 40 to 50 students plus an advanced group of 20 to 30 students. In the initial years of offering samba, Dana was "still pretty teacher centered" in his approach. He taught the samba just as he had taught band classes, where "all the information was coming from me." What made it less than satisfactory was that by his own admission, "I had very little information because I was a trumpet player and not a percussionist, so I was learning things and just trying to stay about two weeks ahead of the students."

At Frederick Douglass, "every single student is with me for one full school year," Dana recalls. And hurrah for samba. As time progressed, all the problems with large class sizes and attrition were "solved by the samba." All "350 to 400 kids a week" were playing drums, and their parts were interchangeable," he explains, which "allowed us to weather the problem of kids coming and going" due to scheduling from year to year. For example, you have "this kid who is a really good player, and he leaves, or you have an advanced class and here comes somebody that's never touched an instrument before. If I had a concert band, these are things that would be a much bigger challenge than with samba."

The flexibility of samba helps Dana deal with "occasional issues with scheduling," and for students who do have scheduling conflicts, especially if they "have AP classes," the students can still come to samba "during lunch periods and help me out. That is a big way of how those students stay involved." It also helps that the advanced ensemble, which plays in parades, events around town, and school concerts and assemblies meets the last period of the day. Dana says that the advanced ensemble "often hangs over after school, so sometimes players can catch a few minutes by running down to class as fast as they can and get in a few minutes" of playing time. Students who cannot participate in samba due to scheduling conflicts can still perform. When the advanced ensemble performs, "I invite students who are not in the class to participate. Most of the time it's students who have taken the class before, and I can still find a place for them somewhere in the group so that they can stay connected." Dana quickly discovered that when students were able to return to samba class, either as registered students or during lunch or catching the last moments of the advanced ensemble, they could help lead the group newcomers learn how to play the samba.

Genesis of student leadership and peer mentoring

It was the school lunch period that was instrumental in helping Dana realize that he no longer needed to be the sole authority of knowledge in the classroom. As the samba groups "got more experience," his students began taking on more leadership responsibilities through peer mentoring, and Dana was "able to capitalize on the all-important student lunchtime."

Due to the large student population at Frederick Douglass, the administration schedules "seven lunch periods for all but the first two periods of the day." Soon, Dana realized that except for those first two periods, he "could ask some students who had a little bit more experience and didn't want to sit in the very crowded and loud lunchroom to come down and help me teach my class." In fact, "in most cases, I didn't have to actually ask them; they just would wander in." Initially, Dana thought the students should be at lunch, but "eventually they wore me down. Through their insistence," he explains, they "became part of my teaching. I always had someone who had at least a minimum amount of experience. Maybe they were not an especially fantastic player in the beginning, but at least they had heard this lesson before."

"One of the things about samba," notes Dana, "is the players don't have to read music." Of course, "I do eventually teach them to read music, but we don't read music and play samba at the same time." In samba, "the focus is on each other. It is on modeling how to play, so the students are getting everything verbally and musically." When the students learn samba, "they have to memorize everything, for everything's been taught by rote." For Dana, the student helpers "who are embedded in the group and are playing along" provide him with opportunities to become a facilitator in rehearsals, where all students have "to listen to me and to the ringers in the group who by their playing are serving as correct examples." Dana realized that when he transitions to the role of facilitator, the learning process becomes more efficient; it "goes a lot faster when I have students helping me." For example, "I may ask for something, and I know there is at least one person in the sea of people that is doing it correctly. You can see it spread very, very quickly through the group as the model plays with somebody else." In tandem with peer mentoring, Dana finds this method very helpful because the "beginning students are getting help from students who are advanced students." In a samba class, then, peer mentoring plays an important role because "when I have 60 students playing, ten of them are there during their lunch period for the sole purpose of helping me with the beginners."

Teacher as facilitator

As Dana transitioned into his role as facilitator, he began to "see within five minutes of the beginning of a class" that his students "were picking up everything much faster" than he had seen before. Dana realized that "what happens in that moment is I get to shift from being the expert to being the kid on the end of the line who doesn't get it when everybody else gets it!" In addition, "I am completely comfortable with having my students be better than I am." He knows that learning to be a samba drummer does "not come easily." When he was learning samba, for example, he "did not get it right away. Back when I was just trying to stay two weeks ahead of my students, I wasn't presenting samba to them as an expert, admonishing them to do as I say. It was always an exploration of this thing that we're going to do together."

That said, Dana still understands he is the teacher. "I know that I work here, and I'm getting paid to be here," he says, but this does not eliminate the fact that he and his students are also learning together. When he began the samba program, peer mentoring provided him with opportunities for them to learn together. "I'm going to struggle," he admitted to the students, "and I'm going to watch your hands to learn something." He finds this approach beneficial, for "I think if all students realize that oh, here's the teacher, and look how lost he is, and look how he's looking to get extra help," it communicates that we never stop learning and "that we learn not from only the person who's up in front, but also we learn from each other."

As Dana continued to use more peer mentoring in his program and settled into his role as facilitator, he became aware that peer mentoring was adding another layer of sound to the class. Peer mentoring is "messy, very messy," explains Dana. "It's messy because each of those 50 kids is holding something that makes a lot of noise, and they're never going to stop tapping on it.

Now, we're going to introduce into the chaos students who know the answers and who are going to be talking when I'm talking. It's productive talking, but it's messy." Initially, Dana "was resistant to that mess," and he admits that in the beginning he was opposed "to not being the only voice in the room and yielding control to other people." Then he just told himself that "this is going to be messy and to just go with it and see where it leads." Using this approach, "our program got a lot further than I thought it was going to go."

Peer mentoring and samba

With the peer mentoring system gaining traction in the samba classes, it was also becoming an extremely important part of how students learned samba. Dana recognized that "the type of learning they were doing really was rooted in the samba. We were recreating a miniature oral tradition within our school building." With peer mentoring, the students learn "a lot closer to the way that people in Brazil would learn this music—by coming into a rich environment and absorbing what they can for a set amount of time." Although Dana "knows what order all of the rhythms should be played," the peer mentoring that occurs between students in class makes it evident that it is "better for students to just be thrown in and learn from somebody that isn't always me." For Dana, the student leadership exhibited in peer mentoring is an important factor in the success of the samba program. "I don't think they really grasp that what they're doing is hugely responsible for the strength of the whole program."

Student leadership

Student leadership in the samba classes is multi-dimensional due to the peer mentoring embedded in the structure of learning. In the samba classes, the advanced students engage in leadership by helping their peers acclimate to playing samba and modeling commitment. Student directors also play a vital role in leadership.

Strength in numbers

Dana teaches samba in the auditorium because "we outgrew the band room a long time ago." Part of the structure of samba is that "the music itself is built to increase the number of participants." In Brazil, "everyone learns the music by just getting together, picking up what you can, and over time—because the music is repetitive—you have enough opportunities to keep trying out what you learned the moment before." Dana also reassures beginners that "if you mess up, it's coming back around again. You can try the pattern again and again. All you have to do is hang out with a partner every day. Just come in; don't worry about making any mistakes." Through peer mentoring, chances to refine samba rhythms are always there. "You have an almost unlimited amount of time to apply what you just learned from your partner, and you're doing it in real time."

Knowing that students will mentor their peers in learning their parts has influenced how Dana teaches samba. "Now, when I am rehearsing something new, I only look for a minimal amount of understanding from the group. After that first pass," he explains, "I've got two or three kids who get it. And then the next pass through, maybe I'm up to five. Finally, the kids who don't get it are now surrounded by people who do." As he continues to use new rhythms in class, "I really depend on the rest of the group to carry the lesson over the next time as we warm up with this rhythm or warm up with this particular piece of information." Dana feels comfortable with this approach for the advanced students who are "really, really strong. They can play everything that's being played in Rio de Janeiro. They can handle anything."

Peer mentoring provides opportunities for beginners who have typically "never seen a drum before" to "hang out with somebody that knows what they're doing and will every five minutes or so give you a tidbit of information." When advanced students mentor beginners on "how to hold the sticks," for example, the advanced students will problem solve to help the beginners. "Hey, try this with your right hand," they might suggest, or "Try doing a rim shot," or "Fix this elbow." The advanced students are also good at breaking down the process of playing complex rhythms and sequencing instruction. Dana rarely meets with these students to discuss leadership "unless there's an issue or unless I think that there's a way that they could maybe help me a little more." He notes that "they know how to do it because they remember watching somebody else do it." For example, "with an instrument like the *caixa* . . . it's like a snare drum . . . so if in the rhythm that they're playing, most of the accents are on the right hand, the partner can show them just the accents. If they're not able to alternate hands yet, they can play just the accents." For Dana, "the important thing is that the kid within that first hour is going to pick up something, and they're going to feel like they're contributing."

Peer mentoring allows Dana to focus on pacing instruction in the class, for when class begins, "I do not slow anything down." He wants to maintain the pace of learning because "I don't want to lose the attention of the advanced kids. I don't slow anything down for the new students either. They will get everything from their partner and from the other students in the room." On the other hand, Dana explains, "I'm not throwing them in the water and then leaving them there to drown," so to speak. "In the long run, many of the beginning students go on to be really important members of the ensemble, and in the end, they play really well." Dana attributes this to peer mentoring because "they never really went through the experience of my writing Rs and Ls on the board, or my trying to show the pattern, or my showing things at a slower speed. They learn all that from each other."

Samba lends itself to verbal mentoring, and peer mentoring does not become a distraction because "you have the space within the group, and it's so loud nobody's gonna hear you. You have that strength-in-numbers thing." He adds, "if you are having trouble learning a particular rhythm or technique, you can do that with everybody else. That's the fastest way for students to learn. From each other."

Students modeling behavior and commitment

Peer mentoring in the samba classes extends beyond the students who share their knowledge to help their peers elevate their performance skills and beyond "modeling good musical behavior" to include what Dana terms a "discipline thing." Since some of his "classes are rough . . . students that come in and show how they should carry themselves in a class" have saved him from having some of the "significant discipline issues other classes in the school suffer." The advanced students, "kids that spend a lot of time with me," help Dana with classroom management by communicating that "what this guy is saying is important." During rehearsals, the advanced students help their peers "focus on what I'm saying. And if there is some kid who's maybe talking in the back, those kids will not hesitate to turn around and say, 'Hey! Stop talking. We're doing something here!' " Dana appreciates the help of the advanced students, for "there are a lot of kids in front of you, and that is a lot of order to keep. That's a lot to handle."

Dana appreciates the examples set by the advanced students. By showing up before school and during lunch periods, they show their peers the importance of coming to class. Dana "sees the progress in the beginners and observes that kids in those classes who have a lot of support from others tend to be more serious in their study." He said this is especially apparent when a samba class of beginners meets at the same time as a class that the seniors have to take, such as economics or government. When he does not "have that older set of people to come in and help, the classes move a lot more slowly. As a result, by the end of the school year, that one class could be several months behind another class." The advanced students demonstrate a "certain attitude of responsibility to younger students who may end up doing this kind of work in the future; they make sure that they're leaving the group with somebody else to come in and replace them later."

Student directors

Dana began using student directors approximately a decade ago when he was doing fieldwork in Rio as part of his dissertation. "I was in one of the samba schools and having an interview, and I was asking about their method of teaching and whatnot. And the master drummer there, who's the director of this big group of 275 people with one person in charge and 12 directors below him, asked me, 'Well, how many people do you have working with you?' I said, 'It's just a small 30-person ensemble! Like, I don't have anybody; I do it all.' And he was so confused by why I would try to do all of it by myself. Why would I conduct alone? Why would I choose to do that? So, he gave me the following advice: 'You need to have other people teaching with you at all times.' And so as soon as I got home, I started thinking about which two kids I was gonna deputize here."

Once Dana began using student directors, "it made a tremendous difference." Each year, he appoints two student directors, which he views as being like drum majors in a marching band. "They don't have to be the best players, but they have to be good enough to have the respect of their peers." Communication skills are important, and "we've definitely had students who are fantastic players but poor communicators."

The process of selecting student directors is not part of a formal process at all, for Dana uses interactions between students to evaluate who has potential for leadership. "There are some that you can just see that other students are already starting to gravitate toward, already kind of looking to them for information." In addition, Dana adds, "you can hear the students talking among themselves and already referring to somebody in the future tense as being a director." Therefore, Dana maintains, "the choices have been obvious, both to me and to the students. You can see who really wants to do it and values its importance."

Diversity and inclusion

In the samba classes at Frederick Douglass, "we've had racially diverse students. We've had gay students. We've had as wide a range as we can have in our school building. We have had pretty much every group represented." Likewise, Dana adds, "we have a diversity in who is going to be the student director." Sometimes, though, it does not work out the way he expects it. He recalls a moment "about ten years ago. We had an assembly, and it was one of those times I stood in the back, and they performed without me. I looked up and I saw that the group was, with one exception, all boys. And I was just horrified. I wondered what message this was sending to the entire student body right then. That girls don't play drums? It was the wrong message to send. I had to convince some girls to join the group."

Soon after the assembly, Dana "named a female student to be the director for the first time." He recalls that when he told her, "she looked shocked," but Dana told her he had confidence in her leadership skills. "She was a really good player who didn't quite believe that she was as good a player as she really was," so he "put her in charge." "The next time we had a big assembly like that," recalls Dana, it was "still a mostly boy group, but there was a female student in charge and standing up in front. That spread the message of 'maybe I should join the group for the girls in our school.'"

"In the next couple of years, having a female student director swung the group to one dominated by girls." According to Dana, the female students were "definitely the better students, the better players, and the ones responsible for logistics and organizing everything," and "I absolutely believe that it was a female up in front of everybody" that led to this transformation. Dana notes that now ten years later, samba ensembles are populated by "mostly female leadership," and "five out of six of the last student directors were female."

Preparing student directors

Once the student directors are selected, Dana meets with them before, during, and after school to talk about how to conduct the samba ensembles. He calls these meetings "conversations" and considers them crucial, for these are the kids who are "going to be leading the advanced group." These conversations cover "how to conduct, different ways of counting rhythms, and what to keep track of while leading the group." For example, "I'll say things, like, 'Hey! Yesterday when we were playing this arrangement, I could see that this area of the class, this instrument group, is a little bit weak,' or I could say, 'Hey! Pay close attention to this one student because they're really getting lost.'"

During these conversations, Dana remembers what it was like to not know anything about samba drumming when he first started. "I can remember what it felt like not to know what to do," he says. "When I'm teaching, I can still remember the limitations I had or still have in some cases." This reminder informs his instructions to the student directors: "Remember what it's like to not know how to do something," and they do remember when their hands just don't work like they're asking them to, for example. "They also remember being completely confused inside this very lesson last year. In many ways, they are able to better explain what it is that I want in that moment because they have had this experience of not knowing."

Leading warm-ups

Dana considers students ready to lead the samba class "once they're good at conducting." One of the first things he has them do to practice is "warm the group up before the lesson starts." Student directors begin the warm-ups with "call" patterns to "get responses out of everybody and get people to snap into place very quickly." The student directors then run through all the routines, followed by the catalog of music comprised of 15 years of material that everybody has learned. "They'll start to just play that stuff for about ten minutes, just to work through everything."

Allowing the students to run the warm-ups gives Dana time to take care of his administrative tasks. His office is next to the stage in the auditorium, so even while doing something else, he can still pay attention to what is going on in the class. For example, while Dana takes attendance, he can "peek out from the doorway" to see who is in class. He can also finish sending emails. Sometimes, "I may just close the door and listen to see what's going on." Dana feels more comfortable in his approach about halfway during the school year, for "it takes a long time to get the students to be able to conduct and be able to count correctly."

Leading the samba class

Once Dana feels confident that the student directors can lead the warm-ups, "once they've practiced that and we've practiced conducting," he considers them ready to direct rehearsals. Samba, though, is different from other types of ensembles, such as concert band, "where you're starting from silence until the conductor raises their arms to conduct." In samba, the "room is full of sound, and it's going, and then you're using a hand signal and calling for a particular arrangement to start when everything is already in progress." Dana models his samba classes at Frederick Douglass on what he learned during samba ensembles in Brazil: He conducts, and the student directors "stand next to me and copy what I'm doing." Dana describes how it works in Brazil: "There's the main director, which is the *mestre*, which means master, and then there are usually 10–12 directors below him. The directors control either an instrument section or a geographic region within the street block-long ensemble, which is called a *bateria*. A full bateria can include up to 275 drummers in the bigger samba schools, and since the ensemble is so large, several conductors are needed. Dana explains that "one of the reasons for this is that the person in the back can't see the front." This emphasizes why it is important for Dana and the student directors to spread out and "be able to conduct together."

Conducting samba with multiple directors requires "a different way of thinking," Dana explains, "because you have to know where you are." Student directors need to "keep track of when to call certain things, because in samba you're asking for something to happen when something's already happening." In addition to keeping track of when to call certain rhythms, "you also have to keep track of the beat and make sure it doesn't speed up or slow down." Breaks are an important component of samba, and student directors need to know when a "break might be ten seconds long . . . or a minute long, where the rhythm is altered." Student directors also need to know when breaks "happen at particular points in the song." As a result, "the conductor has to know the song, has to be singing the song, and has to know where to call the timing for certain breaks that are happening based on the song form." To help the students learn how to direct the ensemble through these breaks, they imitate Dana as he is directing the song; he models directing for the student directors when he serves as the primary director. Once they are comfortable with directing the samba class, "then we reverse it, where they're leading the group, and I'm conducting along with them." In conducting these breaks, Dana and the students use hand signals as part of their directing. For example, "[making a T with the fingers of one hand touching the palm of the other hand] this means something. And this means something [fists closed with knuckles touching, palms facing forward]. And the different numbers mean something [counts to four, starting on his index finger]. And there's an endless number of hand signals that we have that will tell the group different changes to make."

When conducting, Dana may be in front of the entire ensemble, and a student director "might be with one set of instruments." Therefore, it is important for the student directors who are in front of a particular instrument group to be able to use their "hands, face, and whistle for the people that are in their neighborhood." They must be able to "give specific instructions for what's coming up or what's happening." Ultimately, "a big part of their job is to really know the material of the group and to know what the others are doing." When the student directors and Dana successfully coordinate their conducting, "you can hear that level of detail being given by the conductors—plural. You can hear the group play differently because they have confidence." Dana recalls playing in Brazil and watching the director immediately in front of him. "I didn't have to worry about the macro view. I could just worry about what was in front of me and what it felt like to get that translation for my instrument." At Frederick Douglass, Dana has set up a system replicating how directors lead samba ensembles in Brazil. "Recreating that technique has really helped us push the level much higher in our school."

Once he is confident that the students know how to lead the samba class, Dana turns all the rehearsal conducting over to the students. "It's important," he believes, "to remove myself as much as possible." He values the opportunity that having the student directors allow him to "leave the front of the room to walk around, do quality control, and spot-check issues. Even if I pull a kid aside, the lesson doesn't have to stop."

The student directors also lead the samba ensemble for performances at school and outside of school. "If there's a school assembly," for example, "I usually prefer to be in the back of the auditorium rather than up on the stage participating. Sometimes, I'll grab an instrument and just be one of the players." The samba ensemble also does gigs. People call and say, "We're going to have a show in Jersey City. Can you come?" And the students "will come pick up the drums and go perform the gig. They don't need me to go and perform with them."

Alumni leadership

Dana notes that in addition to having advanced students mentor the beginners, "we often have alumni who come in to play with the advanced class, and I also have some alumni who come in and just play all day. They'll play with all the beginning classes." Some of the alumni who return to Frederick Douglass are "now 30 years old!" According to Dana, this drop-in mentoring is informal, for he has no idea "who's going to come in when the door swings open."

Although the mentoring is informal, it collects an added dimension with alumni participation, for in addition to playing with the kids, they also serve as tacit role models. Dana views the role of the alumni as an extension of the role played by the seniors, who model commitment by coming in to play during their lunch hour. Dana notes this dedication is even more significant when it is exhibited "by someone who's 26 years old, who called in sick from work to come be in band for the day." This has had quite an effect on current high school students, for they realize that if they continue to practice, "they'll always be able to come back and play here." Dana considers this understanding very important, for it helps the current high school students realize that playing samba "is not just for high school. This is something that while I'm here every day doing it, I need to get as good as I can now so that when I come back, I'll be good at playing." The alumni then are responsible for encouraging current high school students to "understand that they're not playing music just in high school. This is not a school activity; this is an ensemble that you can be in as long as you want to."

In addition to inspiring current high school students to perform at a higher level and to take their participation in the samba classes seriously, alumni participation "helps me maintain the group memory, the institutional memory. All the material that we play is locked into the group. It's in everybody's mind. Everybody remembers all the repertoire." This ensures that each year when Dana introduces new repertoire to the samba ensembles, "we can still play everything from when we started samba back in 2006." To be sure, "some things leak out, and when we forget to touch it for a while, people forget, and I have to kind of reteach it, but for the most part, all of the rhythmic materials are locked in the group mind." In addition, if Dana has to reteach some material, he has the alumni to help. "That 28-year-old former player may make an extraordinary contribution in showing us some of those smaller details that we may have forgotten." Alumni leadership, then, helps Dana maintain the group memory of repertoire. "When the alumni come back, they help me continue that group memory," for "when the door swings open, and it's a former student who graduated in 2010, and we all switch what everybody's playing to the 2010 version so that they can participate, it helps us to stay really sharp."

Not only do alumni return to Frederick Douglass to play in the samba ensembles, but their participation also feeds their desire to keep playing. This has led to the creation of a new community ensemble outside of the school. Dana created "a nighttime adult class" that meets in an elementary school near Frederick Douglass. "It's mostly my former students who still want to play, but it also includes people from outside the community." The adults who are not former students "go all the way up to age 70." The community ensemble "never has shows of its own," for the focus is on "trying to make sure that they know all the most current stuff." When the community ensemble does perform, Dana combines it with "my school group. Mixing everyone together with people from high school age up to age 70" provides new opportunities for current high school students to "have the experience of playing" with alumni and community members. In this combination, mentoring takes on the added value of "the younger people learning professionalism and how to do a gig from the older people, even though the best players in that ensemble are my current students who play with me five days a week."

The alumni who participate in samba also mentor area music teachers who want to learn about the style. Dana says that some former alumni "work for me, too" in a non-profit that he started called "A Life with Drums." Through this program, "we've put samba into 11 other schools in New York." The alumni help Dana mentor current music teachers in a six-week program. The music teachers who participate are "like me, who once upon a time didn't know what to do at school the next day." They sign up for the program and learn in a samba ensemble comprised entirely of teachers. Then, "they go back to their schools, and they get instruments." The learning does not end in the ensemble, however. Dana points out that "they're not necessarily ready to do this by themselves, so some of the former students that I have hired go to the different schools to mentor the other teachers as they teach samba." In these mentoring situations, the alumni occasionally teach an entire lesson, but "in most cases, they're just there to serve as examples. The teacher is still in charge of the class." Each situation is different, though, for "some teachers are more comfortable letting control go to somebody else than others are, so you have to figure out which is best for everybody." Typically, though, "my former students are floating around, just helping the students, just playing along, and just serving as those examples within those classes."

Questions for discussion

1. When should you serve in the role of a teacher, and when should you serve in the role of a facilitator of learning in your music class or ensemble?
2. How might you use peer mentoring in teaching a specific musical style?
3. What is your comfort level going to be when students engage in verbal mentoring during class or rehearsals?
4. When will you use peer mentoring? Concurrent with your leading instruction? During designated times in class or rehearsal? Or in a combination of these two activities?
5. Based upon what you have read about Dana and his students, how might you structure peer mentoring so that your students help each other continue the traditions of the music class or ensemble?
6. How can you design leadership opportunities for all students so that they can contribute to meaningful learning in the music class or ensemble?

Reflection

Peer mentoring in the samba program at Frederick Douglass Academy grew out of what Dana had observed in practices in the samba schools in Rio de Janeiro. From a continent away, these routines provided a foundation for student leadership in a Harlem high school. In addition, Dana was looking for a solution to the problem of class scheduling and student retention at Frederick Douglass, and samba classes presented a viable option. Upon his return to Harlem, Dana revamped his music program with a focus on samba.

Roles of teacher and facilitator

As the samba program became more and more established at the Frederick Douglass Academy, Dana's teaching evolved from a teacher-centered approach, where he was the sole deliverer of knowledge, to a role of facilitator for student leadership and peer mentoring. This transition was somewhat fluid. While Dana was aware that he was still the music teacher and ultimately in charge of the samba program, he also allowed his students the autonomy to lead and mentor their peers and thereby elevate learning. Chapter 1 points out the importance of the facilitator in enabling peer mentoring and leadership in your students. As you reflect on your dual roles as deliverer of information and facilitator of learning, think about the times when you are the sole leader of learning and the times when you are the facilitator of learning for your students. Although you likely serve in each role at times in your teaching, reflecting on *when* you serve in these roles may provide insights into new opportunities for you to be a facilitator of student leadership and peer mentoring. For example, reflecting on your roles as teacher and facilitator can aid with establishing decentralized learning,[2] where you and your students share in guiding the learning that occurs in the music classroom or ensemble. Not only does this help with the sharing of knowledge and experiences by students, but it also helps create new knowledge[3] in the music class and ensemble, which contributes to meaningful learning experiences.

Peer mentoring and learning a musical style

One of the unique features of peer mentoring at the Frederick Douglass Academy is that the learning is structured based on how musicians learn samba in Rio de Janeiro. This includes peer mentoring that is based in aural learning (by ear) and oral learning (verbal directives). As Dana notes, learning and performing samba are not necessarily about reading music but rather involve student leadership for mentoring each other musically and verbally to learn the rhythms. This type of peer mentoring creates opportunities for meaningful learning,[4] for the students engage in active learning to help each other understand and reinforce the rhythms in the samba ensemble.

Peer mentoring can be used with many musical styles. As you reflect on why and how Dana uses peer mentoring, think about the musical styles you teach, such as jazz and popular music, and how peer mentoring is part of how that musical style is learned. For example, in the early days of jazz, musicians did not attend school to learn the form. Instead, to pass on the nuances of style, harmony, and improvisation, and to learn songs,[5] musicians shared their knowledge and experiences in what today would be characterized as peer mentoring. When Joe "King" Oliver mentored young Louis Armstrong in New Orleans and later in Chicago,[6] for example, he was peer mentoring. Although musicians in the early days of jazz mentored each other in a non-academic environment, the aspects of peer mentoring presented in Chapters 1–4 are still applicable to jazz ensembles. For example, students can mentor each other individually in dyads or in groups, including a section (e.g., trumpet) or across sections (e.g., lead trumpet player mentoring members of the saxophone section for articulations).[7] Students can mentor each other in musical content, such as style, articulations, and phrasing, in addition to nonmusical objectives, such as classroom management.[8] Another musical style that involves peer mentoring in the learning process is popular music. Popular musicians have historically mentored each other to elevate their knowledge about performing, such as how to tune their instruments. Today, students continue to learn to play popular music by mentoring each other. They help each other learn the fundamentals of music, such as playing scales and chords, and may even branch out beyond the fundamentals to form bands.[9] Through peer mentoring, students in popular music ensembles or general music classes can play an active role in learning by coaching each other while they learn songs by ear from recordings. This may lead to arranging songs and even composing original music.[10] Tapping into these peer mentoring experiences based on how the musical style was originally learned can provide meaningful learning experiences for your students. Jazz and popular music are but two examples. Dana capitalized on peer mentoring in teaching the samba; think about how you can create peer mentoring opportunities for your students that reflect how musicians learn a particular musical style.[11]

Preparing student leaders

Applying peer mentoring to the practice of learning and performing samba led to the development of student leadership at Frederick Douglass. In Rio de Janeiro, leadership is built into samba. The mestre, or lead director, performs the routine for subordinate directors. This model easily translates into the practice of having students serve in leadership roles as student directors. Dana considers the student directors a consequential part of the learning process. Although he does not necessarily consider them the best players, he selects students he considers good communicators, those who have the respect of their peers. Think about the selection of your student leaders and how you prepare them to become leaders. Think about Dana's preparation of his student conductors, which is a sequential process. First, he meets with student conductors to talk about how to lead the ensemble, including how to conduct and how to give verbal directives to their peers. Then, he has the students lead opening warm-ups. This student leadership provides him with opportunities to take care of administrative duties, such as taking attendance. The next activity in learning student leadership for Dana's students involves having them conduct rehearsals. This requires knowing when to call the next rhythm and keeping track of the beat. In conducting samba, students need to know the music and how to communicate proper performance procedures to the ensemble. When Dana sees his student directors become confident in directing the rehearsal, he leaves the front of the ensemble and lets the student directors do all the conducting. As you continue to reflect on how you prepare student leaders and compare your experiences to Dana's, think about what works best for your music class or ensemble. What is the appropriate time for your students to run parts of classes or rehearsals so that meaningful learning takes place? In your music program, you may use a similar approach with section leaders and/or drum majors in marching band who serve in a role subordinate to your position as ensemble director. Based on how Dana uses student leaders in conjunction with his role as primary leader, think about how you could use students to conduct while you conduct or even lead the music class or ensemble rehearsal. This could even morph into having students conduct in school music program concerts or ensemble performances.

Dana believes student leadership opportunities should also provide marginalized students the chance to become leaders as well. He noticed early on that the leaders in the samba program were all male. To address this issue, he created opportunities for female students to become leaders in the program. He began selecting student directors who were female, based on his assessment of their leadership skills combined with student input. Chapter 4 reminds you that you play an important role in creating and maintaining student leadership opportunities and that student leadership is most successful when you and your students engage in leadership together, along the lines of how Dana prepares his students to conduct.[12] Think about how you co-create leadership opportunities with your students and how you might be able to refine what you do based on how Dana prepares his students to conduct, for example. Dana has found success in having his student directors direct alongside him[13] and involves students in selecting their own leaders. This creates opportunities for marginalized students to lead the learning in the music classroom and ensemble. Chapters 2 and 4 point out that marginalized students who become leaders learn how to avoid giving up power to dominant groups. In addition, marginalized students help create learning opportunities in the music classroom and ensemble.[14] As you co-create learning goals and objectives with your students, marginalized students can help you and the rest of the class in understanding racism,[15] resilience,[16] and inclusion.[17] As Chapter 2 points out, marginalized students play a significant role in changing the dynamics of the classroom, and musical objectives are augmented by a greater student understanding of each other's backgrounds, identities, and perspectives.

Modeling and imitation

Students who could no longer participate in samba classes due to scheduling conflicts still showed up and played during their lunch breaks. In the early days of the samba program, these students served as a catalyst for peer mentoring because they just automatically began to share their knowledge with the beginning students. They engaged in verbal mentoring to explain, for example, how to play rhythms and in modeling, to demonstrate how to hold the drumsticks. Chapter 2 explains that modeling is an important part of peer mentoring because it helps students learn new information as well as refine what they already know.[18] This helps all students elevate their performance skills:[19] The mentors reinforce their own knowledge when they explain musical concepts to their peers,[20] and the mentees are on the receiving end of the new information.[21] Modeling, then, fortifies desirable behaviors, which includes everything from performance skills to classroom management.[22]

As the samba program at Frederick Douglass Academy grew more and more popular, and Dana saw more and more of the benefits of peer mentoring, he also realized that students were not only learning from the students who came in during their lunch breaks. He noticed that students regularly enrolled in the samba class were picking up rhythms very rapidly and in turn could mentor their peers in playing the rhythms correctly. It was at this point in the development of the program that Dana realized his students learned faster and retained more knowledge when learning from each other—whether by modeling, imitation, or verbal mentoring—instead of from him. Research confirms his observation that students retain information more easily when they have learned it from their peers.[23] As Dana became more convinced that his students were learning samba rhythms at a faster pace than they had before, he modified his teaching approach. Instead of trying to get every student to master a particular rhythm, Dana counted on the students who were playing it correctly to mentor the rest of the class by modeling. Peer mentoring allowed Dana to move at a fast pace because the students who were getting it could help their peers who were struggling to learn their parts. And, because of this sharing of leadership, Dana was free to go on leading the rehearsal. Chapter 2 defines this as differentiated instruction—a situation where there is more than one leader in the music classroom or ensemble, and the additional person can help you share knowledge with all students.[24] In turn, this leads to the more comprehensive learning experiences that result in meaningful learning.

Although these learning experiences take place in a musical setting in a samba class, students are learning more comprehensive lessons as well. They may mentor for classroom management, for example, when they make sure their peers understand that when Dana is speaking, it is important, and they need to listen to him. Peer mentoring then becomes multidimensional, for the students who seem for all intents and purposes to be mentoring for musical reasons may also be serving as positive models of behavior and classroom expectations. For example, the students who came to rehearsals during lunch modeled commitment for the beginner students.

Teachers themselves also learn as peer mentoring is going on. Watching his drum students engage in peer mentoring, Dana remembered his own struggle learning how to drum, and how as students shared their knowledge, the teacher–student roles were reversed. Dana became a student of his students. Not only do students share knowledge they learn from you, but they also share knowledge they learn from their other teachers (both music and nonmusic), from participating in ensembles outside of school, and from their private teachers.[25] As you reflect on how students mentored each other in the samba ensembles, think about what knowledge you have learned from your students. Based on Dana's experiences, how can you develop new learning opportunities for your students so they learn and you learn, too? You can then use their knowledge—and your new knowledge—to continue providing meaningful learning experiences from year to year.

Although the benefits of peer mentoring and student leadership are well worth the effort in the samba program, they are often achieved by way of a "messy" process. In samba rehearsals, not only do the students play their instruments, but they also engage in verbal instruction that contributes to additional noise. For example, verbal cues are often lost in the volume of the drums. Therefore, one of the early decisions music teachers have to make is the extent to which peer mentoring will be used. What is your comfort level for how often students engage in verbal mentoring and modeling? As Chapter 2 points out, when practicing differentiated instruction, it is helpful to determine ahead of time what your comfort level will be. As you reflect on this, think about whether you are okay with students' peer mentoring while you are teaching the class or directing the ensemble. Do you want to set up peer mentoring so that students have designated times to mentor, times when you are not directly leading instruction? Or perhaps you want to use a combination of these approaches. If you have the space, you may also want to consider having students mentor each other in an adjacent room while you lead a class or rehearsal.

Consider the Frederick Douglass Academy alumni who return to school to play with the samba ensembles. In addition to mentoring current students as they learn to play the correct rhythms, these alumni model a commitment to playing and to the samba program for all the students. Dana finds this nourishes the notion that playing samba is not just a high school activity but rather a lifelong pursuit. The alumni also help to continue the traditions of the ensemble, including peer mentoring, which is one of the benefits of student leadership. Dana also credits the alumni for the maintenance of institutional memory, for they remember rhythms learned in prior years and are able to mentor the current students in learning them. As you reflect on how the alumni contributed to meaningful learning in the samba program, think about additional ways you could create mentoring opportunities for your students. Similar to Dana's experiences, could you have alumni return to school and mentor current students in your music class or ensemble? You could invite alumni back to school when they are home on break or have a day off from work. As you reflect on this, remember that the term *alumni* in this context does not necessarily refer to adults. You may want to consider using cross-age mentoring, where high school students mentor younger students at the junior high school, middle school, and elementary school levels. In these cases, mentoring opportunities could potentially occur during lunch periods or during before- or after-school rehearsals. Including alumni and/or older students in your program could provide opportunities for meaningful learning experiences for your current students. Alumni could help with easing the understanding of subject matter and the elevation of performance skills, as well as help continue the expectations and traditions of the music program. The alumni in these instances could also help plant the notion in current students that participation in music does not end upon entering high school or even upon graduating from high school.

As you reflect on student leadership and peer mentoring in the samba ensembles at Frederick Douglass Academy, think about the similarities between Dana's approaches to peer mentoring and yours. Then, think about how you could implement what you have learned from Dana into your program.

In the next chapter, we move across the country for a visit to an elementary general music program led by Kara Ireland D'Ambrosio in East Palo Alto, California. Her experiences will broaden our understanding of how students can share their knowledge to contribute to meaningful learning.

Notes

1. Dana Monteiro, "Samba: The Sense of Community in Participatory Music" (DMA dissertation, Boston University, 2016), ProQuest (AAT 10193022).
2. Antoni B. Valori, "Meaningful Learning in Practice," *Journal of Education and Human Development* 3, no. 4 (2014): 199–209, https://doi.org/10.15640/jehd.v3n4a18.
3. David Jonassen and Johannes Strobel, "Modeling for Meaningful Learning," in *Engaged Learning with Emerging Technologies*, ed. David Hung and Myint Swe Khine (Dordrecht: Springer, 2006), 1–27.
4. Richard Mayer, "Rote Versus Meaningful Learning," *Theory into Practice* 41, no. 4 (2002): 226–232, https://doi.org/10.1207/s15430421tip4104_4.
5. Andrew Goodrich, "Utilizing Elements of the Historic Jazz Culture in a High School Setting," *Bulletin of the Council for Research in Music Education* no. 175 (2008): 11–30, www.jstor.org/stable/40319410.
6. Andrew Goodrich, "The Social Language of Jazz," in *Teaching School Jazz: Perspectives, Principles and Strategies*, ed. Mike Titlebaum and Chad West (New York: Oxford University Press, 2019).
7. Andrew Goodrich, "Peer Mentoring in a High School Jazz Ensemble," *Journal of Research in Music Education* 55, no. 2 (2007): 94–114, https://doi.org/10.1177/002242940705500202; Goodrich, "Social Language."
8. Goodrich, "High School Jazz Ensemble."
9. Lucy Green, *How Popular Musicians Learn: A Way Ahead for Music Education* (Burlington, VT: Ashgate, 2002).
10. Lucy Green, *Music, Informal Learning, and the School: A New Classroom Pedagogy* (Burlington, VT: Ashgate, 2008).

11. Goodrich, "High School Jazz Ensemble"; Andrew Goodrich et al., "Comentoring in a University Jazz Ensemble," *Visions of Research in Music Education* 25 (2014), http://www-usr.rider.edu/~vrme/v25n1/visions/Goodrich_Comentoring_University_Jazz_Ensemble.pdf; Green, *How Popular Musicians Learn*; Green, *New Classroom Pedagogy*.
12. Scott J. Allen and Nathan S. Hartman, "Sources of Learning in Student Leadership Development Programming," *Journal of Leadership Studies* 3, no. 3 (2009): 6–16, https://doi.org/10.1002/jls.20119.
13. Chandni Navalka et al., "Putting Collaborative Leadership into Practice," *Parks Stewardship Forum* 37, no. 2 (2021): 316–324, https://doi.org/10.5070/P537253237.
14. Andrew Goodrich, "Valuing Racialized Student Voices: Transforming Learning Through Peer Mentoring," *Action, Criticism, and Theory for Music Education* 21, no. 1 (2021): 142–171, https://doi:10.22176/act21.2.142.
15. Goodrich, "Valuing Racialized."
16. Andrew Goodrich, "Counterpoint in the Music Classroom: Creating an Environment of Resilience with Peer Mentoring and LGBTQIA+ Students," *International Journal of Music Education* 38, no. 4 (2020): 582–592, https://doi.org/10.1177/0255761420949373.
17. Judith Jellison, *Including Everyone: Creating Music Classrooms Where All Children Learn* (New York: Oxford University Press, 2015).
18. Albert Bandura, "Social Cognitive Theory," in *Annals of Child Development*, ed. Ross Vasta (Greenwich, CT: JAI Press, 1989), 1–60.
19. Bandura, "Social Cognitive Theory."
20. Christine Howe, *Peer Groups and Children's Development* (Hoboken, NJ: John Wiley & Sons, 2009).
21. Andrew Goodrich, "Peer Mentoring and Peer Tutoring among K-12 Students: A Literature Review," *Update: Applications of Research in Music Education* 36, no. 2 (2018), https://doi.org/10.1177/8755123317708765.
22. Kathryn Byrne, "The Give and Take of Peer Review: Utilizing Modeling and Imitation" (PhD dissertation, Kent State University, 2015), https://rave.ohiolink.edu/etdc/view?acc_num=kent1438036070.
23. Goodrich, "Peer Mentoring and Peer Tutoring."
24. Diana Lawrence-Brown, "Differentiated Instruction: Inclusive Strategies for Standards-Based Learning That Benefit the Whole Class," *American Secondary Education* 32, no. 3 (2004): 34–62, www.jstor.org/stable/41064522.
25. Richard S. Webb, "An Exploration of Three Peer Tutoring Cases in the School Orchestra Program," *Bulletin of the Council for Research in Music Education*, no. 203 (2015): 63–80, https://doi.org/10.5406/bulcouresmusedu.203.0063.

6 Kara Ireland D'Ambrosio

Kara Ireland D'Ambrosio teaches TK through eighth-grade general music in a school on the west side of Bay Area Peninsula, California. In addition to this full-time position, she is on the music education faculty at San Jose State University. In 2002, Kara was awarded a Grammy Gold for excellence in music education, and she has also received two awards given by the California Music Educators Association: The Peripole-Bergerault General Music Educators Award and the Outstanding Classroom General Music Award. For Kara, peer mentoring serves as a platform for building a community of learners in the music classroom. For her students, it represents a pathway to figuring out what they know and what they do not know. Through a process of working together, Kara and her students produce an environment of meaningful learning.

In Kara's classroom, learning is holistic and multi-dimensional. She believes that knowledge sharing is accomplished through a trusting partnership between the teacher and the student, and she uses teaching methods that value student voices. As a result, her students feel empowered to make meaningful contributions to learning by sharing their musical interests and knowledge.

Introducing Kara

As with most experiences in life, growing up a church deacon's kid has its virtues as well as its challenges. For Kara Ireland D'Ambrosio, one of the main advantages of being the daughter of a husband–wife team of church musical directors meant she was immersed in music almost from the moment she was born. By the time she was three, she was singing in the Billy Graham Crusades, and she also tagged along with her parents on missionary trips and sang in the choir in services. At home and at church, she explains, her mom "rehearsed the songs for the church service they were leading that week, and my dad would play piano or organ." Throughout her childhood when her dad played piano, she would provide the vocals, and "while I was studying voice, he would

DOI: 10.4324/9781003243618-9

Figure 6.1 Kara Ireland D'Ambrosio.
Source: Photograph provided by Kara Ireland D'Ambrosio.

help me practice opera, gospel, folk, and classical vocal literature and learn the music."

Kara's experiences learning music from her parents and singing in the church choir gave her the confidence to share her knowledge with others. As early as the fourth grade, she taught songs to her classmates—songs that she made even more interactive by stepping to the beat and clapping rhythms. Kara loved to lead her peers in song. She found the whole process lively, direct, and engaging, and it was not long before she realized that "this is what I want to do. I want to be a music teacher."

When she got older, Kara sang in the choir and played the piano and the violin. She even "went the orchestra route for a little while" and ended up playing the viola as well. During this time, Kara's parents continued to have an active role in her learning and cultivated in her the belief that studying a new instrument did not necessarily mean abandoning your old ones. One of her favorite memories of middle school was when band and orchestra members from the high school reached out to encourage the younger students to continue playing and join band or orchestra the following year. These connections she made with the older students during these visits and the cross-grade concerts that followed left a mark on Kara: She was motivated and "awestruck" by the high school students who loved the same things she did. She remembers that "the older kids taught the younger kids the songs, taught them how to harmonize," and "the younger kids couldn't wait" until they were the ones in high school and could share music with the middle schoolers. Kara also remembers how good it felt to be the high schooler working with the younger students, and of all the music teachers she has had over the years, her high school music teacher remains her "favorite of them all."

Kara went on to earn her Bachelor of Music Education degree at the University of New Hampshire, Durham. When she graduated in January of her senior year, she found it difficult to find a music teaching position in the middle of the school year, so she took a job at a Boston company that created technology for medical organizations. She was the trainer for nurses learning the medical records software and mobile hardware. As she looks back at this time, she says "that the position allowed her to hone her skills of presentation."

Kara next moved to California, where she held positions at six different schools. "The K–6 classroom teacher in California . . . *is* the music teacher; general music is not often taught by a credentialed music teacher." Her schedule included studio lessons, children's choirs, and performing groups at music schools in the area. In time, Kara realized she "needed more education to be a better teacher," and so she began classes at Holy Names University in Oakland, earning her Master of Music Education degree, with a concentration in Kodály's experience-based teaching method. Kara also began teaching in East Palo Alto, California, where she "taught amazing students from diverse backgrounds." Over time, however, the "school started going more of an after-school instrumental way" and "preferred to have bands and orchestras taught after school, instead of the choir, drama, and general music . . . that I was doing during the school day." She next moved to a position at a public school on the west side of the Bay Area Peninsula, where she taught TK through eighth-grade (TK–8) general music and choirs. This school hired two full-time credentialed music teachers who were supported and encouraged to develop and sustain a "fully integrated spiral curriculum of general music, which was a joy and a dream." Kara partnered with the band director to develop a meaningful transition between fourth-grade general music and fifth-grade band, a collaboration that resulted in "a 95% retention rate, where the kids chose to stay in music and loved it."

Kara soon realized that she wanted to learn more about teaching and research, so she became a doctoral student at Boston University, earning her Doctor of Musical Arts in Music Education in 2015.[1] While working on her degree, she began teaching graduate-level courses in music education for elementary teachers at San José State University. Finally, with her doctorate in hand, Kara began teaching music research classes and advising master's-level music research projects. She is now the Field Placement Coordinator for the secondary credential program in the Department of Education. In addition, she continues to teach preservice elementary music teachers as well as maintain her TK–8 teaching position.

Early experiences using peer mentoring as a music teacher

Kara's early experiences with peer mentoring from fourth grade through high school provided her with opportunities to be a student mentor and lead instruction and also to be a mentee. "Because of my own background," Kara explains, "I knew that teaching is a partnership between the student and teacher, and this interaction allows each to learn from the other. There were times when a student's experience and sharing taught me, and I was receptive [to] and engaged in these moments. My recognition of student knowledge was just a natural thing."

When Kara began teaching, she was a Caucasian girl from New Hampshire, and the population of the school in which she was going to teach was "80% African American and 20% Hispanic. Over the years I was there, the demographics flipped to 80% Hispanic and 20% African American. Many kids were English-language learners, and their background experience was very different from my own. My goal was to be open and learn from my students and their community." She especially "did not want to go in with the attitude that I knew everything, and you have to do it my way," so she used "music from the kids, from their homes, and from their own experiences and their loves," and she brought their musical interests into "class right away." As the students introduced the music that they enjoyed to their classmates, Kara used it as an opportunity "to help them share these interests and what music means to them, and then I used their musical interests to teach music concepts."

To further develop community and engage more students in the learning, Kara tapped into the school-wide program "Buddies." In this program, which lasted the entire year, fifth graders were buddies to second graders, fourth graders were buddies to first graders, and third graders were buddies to TK/K classes. Older buddies led and supported reading, art projects, SEL, and many other activities. In her classes, Kara arranged for older buddies to help younger buddies learn music. She considered the "older brother–older sister mentality" a big help in maintaining "good classroom management."

At first, the older students focused on control: "We're older, we're wiser, we're going to help you." As a result, Kara had to spend some time working with the older students to make sure they realized "it's not about your being in control of the younger kid. It's about your modeling and supporting them." She discovered this arrangement also provided opportunities for younger students to see what was next and begin developing a growth mindset as "older students were able to process and perform music that the younger students couldn't do yet." The "behavioral changes were unbelievable," Kara observed, as both the older and younger students really enjoyed working together.

Using peer mentoring

Kara used peer mentoring for more than instructional purposes. Another program at her school scheduled eighth graders to serve as monitors at recess. Why not have the eighth graders monitor during music, she wondered. Her students "came from really tough backgrounds, where gangs sometimes invaded our campus . . . [and] it was really scary at times." She began adding a couple of eighth graders to each music class, one class per grade level, "just . . . to sit in the class and play with the kids. Behavior and engagement noticeably improved." For example, "it wasn't just me telling them to sing *Little Sally Walker*." The eighth graders led the instruction and added their experiences "and then we were able to explore new ways of playing and singing the song with beautiful rhythms and body percussion . . . more meaningful and culturally relevant to our community of learners."

Peer mentoring also contributed to the success of the spring PTA celebration, an annual fundraising affair at the school. Established nearly a century earlier, the event maintains the tradition of the third graders performing traditional folk dances for the town each year. In Kara's opinion, "the May Day Dances are actually a pretty difficult, challenging experience" for third graders, as the dances involve "a ten-minute performance with many transitions. They are one big, massive act of theater dance!" Kara immediately "planned to bring the fourth-grade students in to help the third graders learn the folk dances." For her, having the older, "experienced" students work with the third graders was a no-brainer. Because the fourth graders had learned the dances the year before, they would still remember them and get a kick out of coaching the younger students. From the viewpoint of the third graders, these fourth graders were their helpful "mentors who could successfully perform the complicated steps, and this made [the steps] seem less challenging."

One thing that surprised Kara was how well the fourth graders broke the dances down and explained the steps. "I feel like I am pretty good at breaking down learning into chunks with scaffolding, but it was amazing the difference in how quickly the third graders were learning the dances with the fourth graders demonstrating for them. Teaching the steps without the fourth graders would have taken me a month. But with the leadership of the fourth graders, it was fast. All I could think was, 'this is awesome.'" It was an "aha" moment of realizing how important peer teaching is. At the same time, Kara also acknowledged that she was not feeling anxious or frustrated in these teaching sessions. She was neither demanding nor controlling the learning; rather, she was able to coach, guide, and offer support while her third graders received one-on-one instruction from their older peers. It was a great experience for everyone. When the third graders presented their dances, the fourth graders were their biggest fans. They were the loudest supporters in the crowd, and the community was thrilled by this display of community spirit and peer-to-peer support.

Preparing students for peer mentoring

Kara begins peer mentoring with students as soon as they start school. Kindergarteners play games to develop in-tune singing, beat awareness, and other essentials of music. She also uses strategies for SEL, such as *pair/share*, which she integrates into the peer mentoring that she begins in the early years of elementary school. "Students pair/share to teach each other an instrumental part or the lyrics to a song or melody line," she explains.

Preparation for mentoring and being mentored can begin as soon as students start what the California Ed Code calls transitional kindergarten. Students who turn five after the school year begins make up TK, and the number of students varies from year to year. At the elementary school, it typically ranges from 5 to 18 students; the average enrollment is around 12. Kara views TK as having "completely changed my kindergarten program," for the students who participate in TK are able to become mentors the following year in kindergarten. TK graduates are able to model community learning. They are peer educators who help the other kindergarten students follow the learning plan and sing, dance, and play instruments in a responsible way.

For the older elementary students, to figure out where her students are in terms of prior knowledge and music experience, Kara uses social–emotional tri-fold assessments and short exit ticket surveys. The tri-fold assessments are a way for students to share how they feel, set feeling and musical goals, and determine what tools will help them achieve their goals. "Through this exercise, I can learn if a student is struggling emotionally or musically in preparing for a concert, for example. I can offer support, check in with parents to offer help, and pair them with a peer to practice with or get support," Kara describes. This activity informs Kara about her teaching practice so that she can tailor her next lessons to the needs of her group. The short exit surveys ask the students to write their names, instruments they play, how many years they have been playing, and what their private teacher's name is or if their parents (or someone else) are teaching them. "When I learn a student is taking private lessons, I can invite them to share (model) their learning in class. Their music background helps me in pairing peers," says Kara. She adds that "the biggest thing I have ever learned in my teaching is how important it is to get to know your students. I try to never assume what they know or don't know. I assess their musical work in class and talk to my students to develop a safe learning environment with trusting relationships. This atmosphere is what allows peer teaching and mentoring to happen."

Student interactions

Kara uses SEL to structure student interaction. She often begins by having the students sit in a large circle in the music classroom. She then has a smaller number of students sit in the middle of the large circle and peer mentor. The activity, which is called *fishbowl*, gets underway as "the kids in the big circle stand up and watch, getting a bird's-eye view" of the middle circle of students. Kara then motions to the inner circle and says, "Let's watch them peer mentoring and see how this group works together, how they speak to each other properly, and when." She also asks the students to reflect on what they have seen and asks them how the mentors taught and how they shared information. For example, "Did they read, then assess? Did all the steps get followed through on?" Of course, Kara continues, "it's all about knowing the roles and every part, but it's also about watching it happen, about their modeling it." For Kara, practicing how to engage in peer mentoring is "just like learning an instrument," and "you have to practice the setup." With peer mentoring "you don't just hand out a list of learning goals and say, 'Go do it.' They have to see it happen a little bit before they are ready to use it."

Kara also evaluates how she is making use of peer mentoring. "I intentionally stop and think, 'Where am I in the process of peer mentoring? What do I need the students to learn? How can I use the peer mentors to help?'" Reflecting on her use and adjustment of peer mentoring, practice is ongoing.

Once peer mentoring is up and running, Kara continues to guide students through the process of how to interact with each other. When disagreements begin between peers, "I usually call them to me and step outside to talk to them one-on-one. I offer them SEL strategies or a break." She finds this effective, for "a lot of my kids, when they get angry or frustrated, they [have trouble articulating it]. They need time to recover." Students can let Kara know they need a break by giving her a hand sign or asking for a time out. Then, they can go to the sensory integration cabinet and pick a tool to help calm them down, "maybe it's a sharp spiky ball, soft piece of Velcro, or squishy ball" that they play with.

Once they have calmed down, they put the tool away and rejoin class or talk out their concern with their peer. To help students understand this coping strategy, "we practice it when they're not upset. Everybody gets to go and feel the spiky ball or one of the other coping tools to figure out what tool is going [to] help them." Kara summarizes it this way: "I try to help the peer mentors take responsibility for the mentee's emotional state. The emphasis is on making your peers feel valued and safe and feeling good when they are playing and hearing feedback from you. We don't want your friends to feel frustrated. We want them to feel as if they are able to do it, and you're willing to help them."

Kara knows when students are upset "when they're peer mentoring, and if I hear negative comments, I intervene. I don't ever leave them alone." To support students in these moments, Kara models behavior for them: "I notice when a group is having challenges and ask the kids how it's going. Usually they answer, 'You know, Johnny's really being rough right now. He's not showing me how to do it.' Then, I'll ask Johnny how's it going, and he will probably respond that 'they're not getting it, they're not getting it!' And I'll say, 'Yeah, mentoring is really hard sometimes. Do you want to step back and watch me do it once?' And then I'll model mentoring and ask Johnny to try again."

For Kara, the connections established between the students, and between her and the students, is "what I love the most" about peer mentoring. She views these interactions as opportunities for students to learn how to work together toward a common goal, which she considers an important skill that they will call on throughout their lives. When sharing their knowledge with each other during peer mentoring, the students in Kara's classes learn how to enjoy the good times and "have an incredible tool to make it through the hard times that life is going to bring them." She also sees peer mentoring as a chance to establish "a lifelong love of music and show kids how to be good patrons of the arts, which keeps the door open for future ways for them to make music in their lives."

Kara has also found that student leadership helps during peer mentoring, especially in the areas of diversity and inclusion. In one case, Phil,[2] a third grader, was not interacting well with his peers in music class, and he "was really struggling," remembers Kara, who also learned that Phil "didn't really like school" and was getting into a lot of disagreements and arguments on the playground at recess. "He and I checked in, and I discovered that this past year of COVID has been miserable for him." She continued to ask him how she could help him in class, and "eventually he volunteered that he loved K-Pop and this artist and that artist.'" Kara then saw the opportunity to empower this student:

> Why don't you help me lead a unit on that? I'll help you lead it, but you have to find songs that have school-appropriate themes and lyrics. You have to find me three songs that you really like and that are

positive. Then, he felt special because he was able to use his phone as a research tool, and he saw this as an exception to the school rule that kids are not allowed to use phones in school. He thought that was really cool! He found his three songs and led the class in learning about the songs, and I actually tied it to our curriculum focusing on Asian American composers and performers.

After Phil taught the lesson, he participated in music with a more positive attitude.

Student initiative

Once the students are comfortable with peer mentoring, they begin taking initiative and "doing it on their own." They learn their music ensemble part, "teach it to someone else, and soon they are practicing together." Since Kara has worked with peer mentoring for so many years, she calculates that students "do it on their own" by middle school. And while she emphasizes the importance of student initiative in peer mentoring, she confesses that in the early stages it is sometimes difficult for her to just stand back and watch. She wants to jump in. Then, she "takes a deep breath" and lets the students do it so they will be able to "build independence and relationships." This is the way they learn how to share their knowledge with each other.

To help students get used to peer mentoring, Kara explains to them, "Now it's your job to practice and your job to reach out to your peers and get peer feedback, get peer help yourselves, and then give it to someone else." Kara tells students the knowledge they share is "their gift to give," and that sharing is an important part of peer mentoring.

Kara has learned that the middle school-age level does present some challenges "because middle schoolers are harder on each other. Or they are the opposite and are too worried to give honest feedback or coaching." In addition, Kara has discovered that students who would normally not interact with each other tend to do so during peer mentoring. "Sometimes in middle school, students cling to their friends and no longer hang out with everyone as they do in elementary school. In music class though, they still support one another in the common goal of learning a piece of music." In one case, a young vocalist needed help with pronunciation/diction and vowel formation, and "one of her choir peers helped her with that." Kara realized that "peer mentoring really connected them. These are really, really wonderful moments."

Kara also uses cross-age mentoring to help student leaders mentor their younger peers. In fourth grade, the students learn soprano recorder by sitting in a band-ensemble format to prepare them for fifth-grade band. As third graders, they are invited to the fourth-grade concert to get a preview of what fourth-grade music will be like. They get to see the formation and hear the songs on the recorder, which helps prepare them for "sitting in a band formation and following the conductor." At the end of fourth grade, fifth graders visit music classes where they are introduced to band instruments to get them ready for the next year of music. The fourth graders "watch the fifth graders demonstrate how to play and take care of their instrument, and the fifth graders can ask the younger students what they like about their instrument."

During this fifth-grader peer mentoring of the fourth graders, Kara is careful not "to give away answers and interrupt the fifth graders." She stands back to give the fifth graders full responsibility and space to share. In a pinch, Kara might break in to help by saying, "What else is important about cleaning your instrument? Would you share another way you articulate on your instrument?" These things, Kara notes, prepare fourth-grade students to move on to band with the confidence and readiness that the band director appreciates. Peer mentoring has been very helpful in these grade-level transitions.

Rotating peer mentoring roles

Kara regularly rotates peer mentoring roles. For example, at times, she has the students break into "teaching stations," where small peer groups each has a role in the learning and peer mentoring SEL concepts are "integrated naturally." This routine helps provide a safe, consistent environment for student learning. The task of a station might be to learn the alto xylophone part of a song, for example, and "a peer mentor offers support after a student has taken a turn playing the xylophone. Before the mentor hands off the mallets, "they make sure the next person playing knows what to do. The peer mentor watches the next friend and gives them feedback to make sure they are playing the xylophone part correctly."

The role of the peer mentor rotates in these teaching stations. "There's a timekeeper, there's a note keeper, peer mentor, engagement leader, and researcher." Kara describes the roles: "The timekeeper makes sure the project gets done on time. The note keeper writes down the music or notation of the work. The peer mentor leads the academic work [subject matter] and helps teach the concept or technique if needed. The engagement leader makes sure everyone is heard and participating. The researcher asks questions and follows up with the teacher when the group needs help."

When the groups meet, Kara assigns roles to her students, "so that we make sure everybody has an experience in each role." As the project progresses, the student who served as the previous peer mentor becomes the peer learner. Rotating the jobs gives everyone an opportunity to build leadership and responsibility, and throughout these processes, "care and compassion are integrated into the entire setup." These are important "because I want everybody to grow. This means everybody gets to be the leader, everybody gets to give support, everybody gets to share their assets and their needs, and SEL is intentionally integrated and part of that process." Kara has found that peer mentoring has helped her students learn that "everybody has strengths, everybody has areas of growth, and we are all responsible to help one another learn."

Questions for discussion

1. Do any of Kara's early experiences with peer mentoring remind you of your own? If yes, how do you incorporate your prior experiences into your teaching? If no, based on your prior experiences, in what ways could you tweak your use of peer mentoring so that it would contribute to meaningful learning in the music classroom?
2. Based upon Kara's teaching, what are some ways you can create a welcoming and supportive learning environment conducive to peer mentoring?
3. How might you prepare students for the roles of mentor and mentee in your general music classroom?
4. How can you tap into students' musical interests and use these interests to guide learning in the music classroom?
5. In Chapter 1, you learned about hierarchical structures (a more-knowledgeable peer sharing knowledge with a less-knowledgeable peer) and nonhierarchical structures (peers of similar abilities sharing knowledge with each other) mentoring structures. Based upon what you learned about Kara's use of peer mentoring, how might you use these structures in the general music classroom?
6. What are the ways you can monitor how peer mentoring is going for your students?

Reflection

Kara partners with her students to provide meaningful learning experiences. In her general music classes, her students engage in peer mentoring by helping each other with singing and dancing and learning how to play instruments. Students also share their musical interests with each other when they are working on songs together. Peer mentoring begins for students when they begin TK and continues through the grade levels in the music program. By the time the TK students enter kindergarten, they can serve as mentors to their peers. For Kara, peer mentoring is ultimately about working together with the students in creating shared learning goals. Chapter 4 pointed out that co-creating learning experiences with students leads to improved attitudes about learning, increased motivation for learning, heightened ownership in the music program, and meaningful learning.[3] Kara's school anchors its instruction in SEL, with care and compassion integrated into all peer mentoring experiences. This emphasis creates an environment where students understand that they all have strengths, but they also have areas for growth. The bottom line is they are all responsible for helping each other learn.

Sharing knowledge

For Kara, peer mentoring begins with establishing a supportive learning environment for students to share their knowledge. This includes helping students understand what they know and what they do not know, and that learning is a joint activity involving contributions from everyone. Kara's desire to establish a welcoming atmosphere for learning was inspired by her early experiences with peer mentoring and leadership experiences; these included mentoring her peers in fourth-grade general music class, being mentored by high school orchestra students when she was a middle school student, and then mentoring middle school students when she was in high school. These peer mentoring experiences helped strengthen Kara's conviction that teaching is a partnership between the teacher and students. As you reflect on Kara's early experiences with peer mentoring and how they inspired her current use of it, think about how you were mentored, or how you mentored your peers, when you were in school. What experiences from your past are similar to the ways in which you use peer mentoring today with your students? Are there experiences you have not considered that could be of use to you today? Reflecting on your prior experiences with peer mentoring is important because it can help set the foundation for how you facilitate peer mentoring with your students.

In conjunction with creating a welcoming atmosphere for learning, an important part of co-creating learning opportunities with students involves understanding what knowledge they have before they begin to mentor their peers. Kara uses emotional tri-fold experiences and short exit ticket surveys for these evaluations. Emotional tri-fold experiences show Kara where her students are emotionally and help her and her students set musical goals for what they want to learn. Students also provide basic information in exit surveys, which reveal prior musical experiences, including whether they have taken private lessons. She uses this information to prepare students for leading instruction and also for pairing them up for mentoring. She also draws on students' musical interests and encourages them to use songs they like to sing when they are leading learning. In turn, she has found this leads to heightened ownership in the music class and improved attitudes about learning. These processes help Kara understand what knowledge her students possess. How do you determine what knowledge your students have before they begin peer mentoring? Chapter 2 detailed how students have knowledge they learn from you, prior music teachers, other music teachers in the school, private music teachers, and teachers and conductors in ensembles outside of school.[4] Kara values student input and creates learning opportunities for students to share their knowledge with each other. As you reflect on how you use student knowledge, revisit where you think they have learned it and how you guide them through the process of sharing it with their peers. Also, think about what you have learned from your students and how you might use that new knowledge to enhance learning in the music classroom.

Once Kara has an understanding of what knowledge her students have, she provides opportunities for them to share what they know during peer mentoring. Researchers have found that students do bring in knowledge from outside of the music class or ensemble;[5] this information becomes a functional part of co-creating in the classroom. Chapter 1 shows how students can share their knowledge and experiences with each other and how, with your guidance, they can also contribute to the creation of learning goals and objectives. This input from students helps establish ownership in the learning that occurs in the music class and ensemble. Co-creating goals and objectives also helps build trust between students and between you and your students.[6] In addition, you and your students can work together to co-create brave spaces for learning.[7] Brave spaces provide opportunities for marginalized students to lead learning in the music classroom[8] and are a leap beyond the safe spaces that reassure students they will not be discriminated against or harassed while they are participating in a dialogue or conversation. Brave spaces not only help with integrating social justice issues in the music classroom;[9] they also aid in providing marginalized students a comfortable place to share their knowledge and experiences. Kara and her students create learning objectives for their classroom; the students acquire ownership in their learning; and finally, the students feel safe when sharing their knowledge and expertise with their peers. Think about how you can co-create brave learning spaces for your students so they feel comfortable sharing their voices to help lead instruction.

Using school resources for peer mentoring

Existing mentoring programs at her school also help Kara accommodate peer mentoring. The Buddies program, where older students mentor younger students, and the recess monitors, where students monitor behavior on the playground, provide good structure for peer mentoring in the classroom. The Buddies program helps with learning in the music classes, and the recess monitors help with classroom management. Think about the existing mentoring-type programs at your school and how you can tap into these programs for peer mentoring in your music classroom. Because students in these programs already have an understanding of how to mentor each other, you can use them to upgrade the effectiveness of peer mentoring. Another thing you may want to consider is setting up a program that operates in conjunction with peer mentoring in your music classroom.

Structuring peer mentoring

Using both hierarchical and nonhierarchical mentoring structures in her music program helps Kara provide effective learning experiences, where students not only share their knowledge but also learn the skills to effectively convey their knowledge to someone else. Examples of hierarchical peer mentoring include cross-age mentoring with fifth-grade students helping fourth graders learn the recorder and with fourth-grade students mentoring third-grade students for the annual May Day dances. Not only did Kara discover that the older students were a tremendous help to the younger students; she was also surprised at how well the fourth-grade students explained how to do the dance steps when mentoring the third graders. She realized that students could share their knowledge in a way that mentees can sometimes comprehend more easily than by listening to the music teacher. You read in the last chapter how Dana Monteiro came to understand the same thing: Students learn from each other more rapidly than they do from the teacher. As you reflect on Kara's use of cross-age mentoring, think about how you could have older students come in and mentor younger students in a general music program, and consider how you can use hierarchical peer mentoring structures to aid with more efficient learning.

Although peer mentoring is largely hierarchical in Kara's music classrooms, she does emphasize rotating the roles of timekeeper, note keeper, peer mentor, engagement leader, and researcher in her learning stations. Rotating student mentoring roles requires them to learn musical concepts, as well as develop a diverse skill set of musical tools. Students sometimes mentor each other to learn lyrics, while other students mentor their peers to learn the melody to a song. Chapter 2 shows how both hierarchical and nonhierarchical peer mentoring structures are effective in music learning. Think about how you use both hierarchical and nonhierarchical structures in your own music classes. What learning scenarios warrant the use of hierarchical or nonhierarchical structures or both? If you only use hierarchical mentoring structures, for example, think about how you could incorporate nonhierarchical structures. Using both structures—as Kara ultimately does—provides more holistic and comprehensive approaches to meaningful learning.

Modeling and monitoring peer mentoring

Chapter 2 emphasizes how important modeling peer mentoring is, for it shows students proper behavior that includes how to mentor and how to be mentored.[10] Kara often models peer mentoring for her students. She is very specific with targeted goals when modeling, and she finds this really helps the students understand their roles in peer mentoring. Kara continually evaluates how she uses peer mentoring and whether it is meeting the needs of the students and the objectives for learning. Kara finds that behavioral issues do arise during peer mentoring, and she continually monitors student behavior. In turn, she uses these opportunities to continue modeling behavior for the students. In this way, she creates a cyclical process for checking the success of peer mentoring. Modeling can also include modeling improper behaviors, such as using sarcasm and peer pressure, so that students understand what not to do.[11] Think about how you model peer mentoring for your students and how often you do so. Based upon what you learned about how Kara models peer mentoring for her students, think about whether you can make any modifications in how you model for your students and what this might entail.

For Kara, peer mentoring begins with establishing a welcoming and supportive environment for learning in her music classes and continues with consistently monitoring it. Understanding what knowledge her students have and then co-creating goals and objectives for learning are preliminary steps to using peer mentoring to provide meaningful learning in the classroom. Kara's use of hierarchical and nonhierarchical learning structures allows her to engage in a partnership with her students to establish this meaningful learning. The next chapter features Sharon Phipps, a middle school band director in Boxford, Massachusetts. You will learn how Sharon uses peer mentoring and student leadership on a daily basis, and how they make learning more enjoyable for her and her students.

Notes

1. Kara Elizabeth Ireland D'Ambrosio, "The California Music Project Teacher Training Program as an Intervention in Poverty and Income Equality" (DMA dissertation, Boston University, 2015). ProQuest (AAT 3686092).
2. Pseudonym.
3. Andrew Goodrich, "Peer Mentoring and Peer Tutoring Among K-12 Students: A Literature Review," *Update: Applications of Research in Music Education* 36, no. 2 (2018): 13–21, https://doi.org/10.1177/8755123317708765.
4. Richard S. Webb, "An Exploration of Three Peer Tutoring Cases in the School Orchestra Program," *Bulletin of the Council for Research in Music Education*, no. 203 (2015): 63–80, https://doi.org/10.5406/bulcouresmusedu.203.0063.
5. Andrew Goodrich, "Peer Mentoring in a High School Jazz Ensemble," *Journal of Research in Music Education* 55, no. 2 (2007): 94–114, https://doi.org/10.1177/002242940705500202; Andrew Goodrich, "Peer Mentoring in an Extracurricular Music Class," *International Journal of Music Education* 39, no. 4 (2021): 410–423, https://doi.org/10.1177/0255761420988922; Webb, "Exploration."
6. Andrew Goodrich, "Developing Trust and Empathy Through Peer Mentoring in the Music Classroom," in *Compassion and Care in Music Education*, ed. Karin S. Hendricks (New York: Oxford University Press, 2023).

7. Brian Arao and Kristi Clemens, "From Safe Spaces to Brave Spaces: A New Way to Frame Dialogue around Diversity and Social Justice," in *The Art of Effective Facilitation: Reflections from Social Justice Educators,* ed. Lisa M. Landreman (Sterling, VA: Stylus Publishing, 2013), 135–150.
8. Andrew Goodrich, "Valuing Racialized Student Voices: Transforming Learning Through Peer Mentoring," *Action, Criticism, and Theory for Music Education* 21, no. 1 (2021): 142–171, https://doi:10.22176/act21.2.142.
9. Arao and Clemens, "From Safe Spaces."
10. Alice-Ann Darrow, Pamela Gibbs, and Sarah Wedel, "Use of Classwide Peer Tutoring in the General Music Classroom," *Update: Applications of Research in Music Education* 24, no. 1 (2005): 15–26, https://doi.org/10.1177/87551233050240010103; Goodrich, "High School Jazz Ensemble"; Andrew J. Hobson, "Fostering Face-to-Face Mentoring and Coaching," in *The Sage Handbook of Mentoring and Coaching in Education*, ed. Sarah Fletcher and Carol Mullen (Thousand Oaks, CA: SAGE, 2012), 59–73.
11. Erik A. Johnson, "The Effect of Peer-Based Instruction on Rhythm Reading Achievement," *Contributions to Music Education* 38, no. 2 (2011): 43–60, www.jstor.org/stable/24127190.

7 Sharon Phipps

Chapter 2 describes how individualized and differentiated instruction allows music teachers and students to share knowledge in a music class or ensemble. One of the most effective ways to enable that exchange of information is by peer mentoring. Sharon Phipps, who is a middle school band director in Boxford, Massachusetts, is an enthusiastic supporter of peer mentoring and believes the more students engaged in it, the better. According to Sharon, the best student mentors are not always the best players and vice versa; therefore, devoting time to learning what her students know and do not know and how they interact with each other is critical to setting up successful peer mentoring experiences. In Sharon's band classes, peer mentoring serves as a conduit for in-depth learning and comprehension of subject matter, and she is convinced it makes learning more enjoyable for the students.

Introducing Sharon

Sharon's relationship with music got off to an inauspicious beginning. When she wanted to learn to play the violin, she failed the required music aptitude test. As it turned out, however, aptitude was not the problem; Sharon was "more than 50 percent deaf." While she had struggled with hearing all her young life, it was not until she was in the third grade that experts figured out the extent of her hearing loss. Before that, when she participated in a school music program, she "had to find people to help [her] along because [she] couldn't always hear the teacher."

Two years later, after undergoing corrective surgeries, Sharon finally got to play the violin. And while this meant she had to work double time to catch up with her fifth-grade peers, by the end of the year, she had "moved to the front of the violin section." About this time, she also participated in a summer music camp, where she was mentored by older campers who helped her with her violin playing. As she became more and more confident, she began playing other instruments as well, including the oboe.

These early musical experiences impressed upon Sharon the importance of being mentored, for she had "always needed help from mentors

DOI: 10.4324/9781003243618-10

Figure 7.1 Sharon Phipps.
Source: Photograph provided by Sharon Phipps.

to catch up." She admits that in her early years of learning to play an instrument, she "didn't always know what was going on and was always looking for *those* people." Sharon remembers that when she entered Wakefield High School in Massachusetts, she "had a great band director, who was a role model for me. I had a lot of great friends. I played sports and I did music, and I had mentors in both sports and music." In addition, she continued to attend summer music camp until she eventually became a mentor for the younger kids there. After high school, Sharon majored in music education at the University of New Hampshire and became a drum major in the University of New Hampshire band at the end of her first year. "I'd always been in these leadership/mentorship-type roles from the very beginning. And I don't know, people just like to come ask me questions. I am just that person."

Following graduation, Sharon attended the Bowdoin International Music Festival in Bowdoin, Maine, where she remembers feeling like "a fish out of water," for "it's where all the Juilliard kids go, but I got into it for some reason." At the festival, she stayed "in a house with a bunch of people from all over the world that she didn't know" and learned from good mentors there, people her own age, people who "knew that I didn't know what I was doing."

With continuing help from players around her, Sharon kept working on her music. At one point, virtuoso oboist and teacher Ronald Roseman encouraged her to "go play the oboe professionally." Initially she was hesitant, for she "wanted to be a teacher," but Ronald assured her she could do both: Play professionally for a while and then go teach music. Sharon knew she should listen to this type of advice, for when a person like "Ronnie Roseman looks at you and says, 'You need to go play,' you probably should go play for a little bit."

Sharon decided that pursuing a master's degree was a great way to "go play" her oboe and help improve her performing skills at the same time. Soon, she matriculated at the University of South Carolina, and although she was a performance major, she did some private teaching and even "ended up teaching Gordon's Music Learning Theory with Ed Gordon." She valued these teaching experiences because she always "wanted to learn more." While she was in the degree program, she also recognized that she "had more teaching experience than some of the other graduate students, for they might not have done any student teaching prior to graduate school. Because I had been teaching in different places such as the summer music camp, the Bowdoin festival, and internships during my music ed degree, I ended up as their peer mentor at that point, just through my experiences."

After returning to Massachusetts and teaching in Franklin for a year, Sharon went back to South Carolina to teach for three years. In South Carolina, she found the "climate really good for peer mentoring." She was able to "have the kids volunteer to be on different committees, such as setting up for concerts and helping put together the programs, those types of things." Sharon also taught marching band and found South Carolina "a different world" from Massachusetts; "they use peer mentoring all the time."

Sharon had over 100 students in band, and with a learning environment rich in student support, she introduced chamber music. She also recalls that she "started putting the kids together in terms of their performing abilities—strong and not so strong—in different groups. Sometimes, they chose what group to play in, sometimes I placed them in groups, and sometimes it was my coaxing or saying, 'I want all the trumpets together!' I didn't really want them all together for musical reasons, but it wasn't always about a performance; it was about somebody there learning from somebody else."

Following her time in South Carolina, Sharon moved back to Massachusetts where she taught middle school band at Chenery Middle School in Belmont for 18 years. Now, she teaches in the Boxford Public Schools in Boxford, Massachusetts.

Philosophy of peer mentoring

For Sharon, peer mentoring is "an important part of education. You just don't know what students might be when they grow up, and peer mentoring especially teaches you how to be an adult, how to get along with people, and how to develop the skills you need for life." Sharon also confesses she does not "know how you teach without it, [for] you're always going to have a lot of kids, and there is no way that you're going to get to every kid in that room; it just doesn't happen."

Sharon's philosophy of peer mentoring grows out of her realization that "sometimes teachers talk *at* the band, and the students don't get anything from what the teacher is saying to them." According to Sharon, this is "when a teacher needs to admit that the students are not getting it and let the students be the teacher." Her invitation to her students sounds like this: "Can you help me out and tell me how to explain that to the band?" She also acknowledges that "when I ask kids to teach other kids, I've served more kids than I could have that day."

Sharon believes this also makes learning more enjoyable for her students because "who the heck wants to sit there and just watch me conduct the whole time? That's not fun." Instead, she recommends "having kids help lead the ensemble. That's peer leadership, and before you know it, on the next day, you have kids coming up and asking, 'Ms. Phipps, can I do that again?'" Sharon then asks, "Do you have something to share with them?" And then they become leaders because they want to get back up on the podium. "They're now sitting back in their seat, being a leader for other people around them. It's just contagious. Get it started, light the fire, let it go."

Sharon recalls that using peer mentoring in her first music teaching position in Franklin was difficult because she was "just getting through every day and trying to survive." She did not know the kids well enough and did not know the staff well enough, either.

> You can't just walk into a situation that's chaotic and have peer mentoring happen. It's not going to work because the kids don't feel comfortable, [and] you don't feel comfortable. And if they can tell

you're not comfortable, then they're not comfortable asking questions about peer mentoring. The kids don't know you; they don't know what you would consider good mentoring of somebody else. You need to believe in it first. You have to trust yourself, trust the kids, and be convinced that if you start it going, you will be light years ahead in a little while. It doesn't take long. In one year, for example, the kids in Boxford were volunteering to do things.

There will be bumps in the road, however, Sharon warns. "A kid reacts wrong in rehearsal, and you get an email from a parent. But if you get on the phone with that parent and talk to them and explain what you're trying to do with peer mentoring, and say, 'I would really like your son to try this next,' a lot of parents agree that it's a good way to learn." For Sharon, a significant goal is "having fun" with peer mentoring and "making sure you tell the students to have fun with it. There's no right or wrong; you just have fun."

Mentoring the student mentors

Although Sharon encourages students to have fun, she also makes sure mentors and mentees are clear on what they are trying to achieve in the process. To help guarantee this, she does her own preparation, carefully selects student mentors, sets goals for peer mentoring, and constantly monitors how the mentoring process is going.

Preparing mentors and mentees

For Sharon, selecting students who can mentor and guide students through learning how to be mentored is an important part of the process. She points out that "you have to know your student body pretty well. There are some kids who can't handle peer mentoring . . . you've got to know you have some prickly types, and you need to be careful. Often, the kids have other issues that they're dealing with in school."

Peer mentoring for Sharon then is a multi-leveled process involving different roles for different students. She is aware that "some kids are only up to the task of walking a kid down the hall to the bathroom. That's where they're going to be a peer mentor. But other kids can step up a lot faster and mentor for musical reasons." You do "have to find somebody you think is capable and knows enough about music to help their peers."

Sharon does not use an established leadership curriculum but rather "guides students toward leadership," for she is "a leadership-by-example person." When Sharon observes a student demonstrating effective leadership skills, she passes her observations along: "You know, Johnny, you have a lot of good leadership qualities." For Sharon, "these kids are natural leaders. When they lead, people follow them; they're just naturally good at it." Sharon has also discovered that with other students, she needs to encourage them to be mentors. "I think there are many other kids who are good peer leadership people who aren't the ones you notice or that you would pick out immediately." To help determine the leadership capabilities of students and with an eye toward possibilities for peer mentoring, Sharon might approach a student and say, "'You know what? Get your music and sit down, and let's watch how many other people follow what you do.' At that point, some are puzzled and wonder, 'why does she think I can do that?'" During this activity, Sharon is "testing kids to see if they think they have the confidence to mentor." Another tactic she uses involves doing a "scramble" with the students in rehearsal, telling the "kids they can change their seat to anywhere in the room and take their stand and the chair anywhere." Although "it is a mess," she acknowledges, "you quickly find the one kid who is standing with a bunch of kids who can't play at all. And as the students gravitate toward that student, I've got an idea about who can mentor. The scramble makes it a little easier for me to see the kids who can do it. They're not embarrassed at all to be helping their peers. In fact, they are proud to be able to do it."

Sharon considers student accountability very important during peer mentoring, for she knows she is helping prepare "the next generation of leaders." Even when Sharon identifies students as effective leaders or begins working with them to see if they are capable of leadership, she sometimes still encounters issues. Student leaders sometimes exhibit inappropriate behavior, such as "running down the hall," for example. Then, she has to put on her in-charge hat and confront them: "Hey, come here. Are you being a very good leader if you're demonstrating how to run down the hall?" Or, in the case where five kids are in the corner talking while John's trying to teach band, she has to remind them that they are the leaders. "You are the mentors here," she emphasizes. "You can't be doing that. Get your instruments and do what you're supposed to be doing." Sharon "often meets with the kids before class, especially if I feel things aren't going well." For the most part, though, Sharon strives to "meet one-on-one with the kid who's mentoring because I don't want that mentor to lose confidence."

Sharon works with students on how to be mentored as well as on how to mentor. She emphasizes how important it is "to talk about how they're going to receive knowledge from their peers." As part of these discussions, which often occur during rehearsal, Sharon models how she would like them to receive advice. For example, she will model how to share knowledge and then ask them to tell her how she did it incorrectly. She makes this fun for the students, acting "like an idiot in front of them." Ultimately, however, she depends on how the students "tell her who those kids are that are able to mentor because they're the first to come up and tell me how I explained it wrong. That way, I can tell how students are responding to being mentored."

Setting objectives

Having settled on which students are probably good candidates to be mentors and which students should probably be mentored, Sharon establishes daily mentoring objectives. She uses a variety of approaches to accomplish this important part of the process. For example, she asks them what they think the objectives should be for a particular rehearsal. And to help make every minute of the band rehearsal more productive, Sharon projects the objectives for the day's rehearsal on a screen for the students to see when they enter the band room. These include "what we're going to do for the day. It's telling us some objectives, and there might be some directions for later in the week." She also uses a separate screen for the mentors that varies with each rehearsal, where she "puts as much or as little on that slide as I need to for them." Although "all the kids sitting there are going to see it, they may not understand what I wrote to the mentors because I've already talked to the mentors at some point before the rehearsal."

Sharon also provides objectives for the student mentors verbally. "Sometimes, I don't write the objective," she explains, "but I tell them a goal or a couple of goals to get to." Helping their peers "make sure they know all of the notes of the B-flat major scale in today's class" is a good example of a daily mentoring objective. Sharon asks the students for input on how they can share their knowledge with their peers, asking the mentors if they have "some ideas for how to teach the correct notes of the B-flat major scale." As she seeks their input, she also asks them if they need any materials, such as a "fingering chart." This process helps Sharon understand what the students understand and what they do not, and this helps her to "see if they've got some idea" about how to share their knowledge. As a result, "I know they understand, and sometimes, just the way a kid puts it [is] different than how I explain it, and this is good," because "I don't have to do all the teaching."

Another thing Sharon watches out for grows out of her not wanting "to have two kids sitting awkwardly in a room for 20 minutes," with the mentor having no idea of how to share knowledge and help the mentee. This typically involves asking students to engage in peer mentoring about musical questions. Sharon might explain that Susie is[1] having trouble with the B-flat major scale, and then ask a mentor: "How would we show her how to do that?" Through this exercise, Sharon discovers the individual leadership and mentoring styles of her students. For example, students will use "a variety of ways to mentor. Some kids will get up and walk over. Another kid might hold up their instrument, another kid might explain it verbally." As a result, peer mentoring becomes layered in that "one kid might explain it and the other doesn't get it, so then one kid helps, and then the other kid helps the kid who's trying to help." Although Sharon does provide some structure for peer mentoring by guiding them through how to share their knowledge, she prefers a more organic approach and does "not put a time limit on how long kids are together."

Pairing students together

Understanding what knowledge students possess and what their individual mentoring and learning styles are helps Sharon pair students for successful peer mentoring experiences. "Sometimes, peer mentoring can just be putting a strong player next to a not-so-strong player," which Sharon refers to as putting "strong–weak next to each other." Among the advantages to this approach is it helps motivate students to engage in peer leadership. Sometimes, the strong player "might not be the one who volunteers to peer mentor" but is someone who "I think could do it, and after they do it for a little bit, they might come up to me after class and say, 'Ms. Phipps, that was fun, can I do that again?'" An additional advantage to this approach is that it can help the weaker students play at a higher level. When Sharon senses that students are having problems playing their parts, she finds that by "putting a support right next to them helps them get through the rehearsal." She often uses these opportunities to challenge a weaker player, "giving a third clarinet player a first clarinet part and seating them next to somebody I know is going to be a good peer leader and help them." During this process, "I haven't said anything to the stronger student about peer mentoring; I haven't said a word to them about it. I just put them in the position to do it if they want to." She finds that giving students the chance to self-select opportunities for mentoring ultimately leads to greater ownership in learning.

Sharon remembers one year when "the sixth-grade band was huge." She and her co-director at the middle school "were just not enough for that many sixth graders," so she created a chamber music program to help mitigate the issue. "I wanted a way to challenge some of the kids who needed to be challenged," she says, "and I wanted a way to help the lower-level students. But I didn't want to say, 'Oh, you're the best kids, here, you're going to go play this quartet,' so I let the kids pick. They basically sent me an email that said, 'I'm really interested in doing chamber music,' and we talked about it. Then, we concluded, 'It's fine if you're not high level!' And we also told them there would be a concert, and they were going to have to stick with chamber music for a few months. I also purposely grouped the kids in high- and low-level pairs." For Sharon, this took a lot of effort and time "because I knew I'd be putting them in a room by themselves, and someone had to figure that out." However, "it just took a little creativity to make it work." Then, she adds, "a lot of teachers are afraid to use peer mentoring like this because they know it takes a lot of work." And while Sharon would agree with them, she also believes that "in the long run, it truly doesn't because there's so much student-leading going on peer-wise that teaching actually becomes more efficient."

For Sharon, the time and effort did pay off, and she soon concluded that "this was the best thing we ever did," for "it ended up being all about kids mentoring and helping each other." The students were excited about playing chamber music. "Every day they would ask me, 'When can we go to our group? When can we go to our group? When can we go to our group? We wanna work together! Oh, can we do this after school now?'" Interestingly, Sharon finally had to rein in the excitement and rotate groups "because there were so many groups, they couldn't always do it once a week. I couldn't always have the same group out of band, so I had to be careful what days they played chamber music."

Continual monitoring of peer mentoring

Problems do surface with student mentors from time to time, and Sharon has to redirect them through the process of mentoring. A fine line is all that exists between their verbal mentoring during rehearsal and their becoming a distraction. "Sometimes, you get into rehearsal, and your mentors are distracting," Sharon notes. "They're not on task; they have attitude. It's as if they are walking examples of what not to do. They communicate the idea, 'Oh well, we're the mentors; we can talk. We can do this; we're the big shots.'" In fact, Sharon laments, "sometimes kids think it's even okay to holler across the class to Johnny or Mary or whomever." When this happens, Sharon helps the mentors understand when and how it is okay to talk during band rehearsal. "We have conversations about how you're not supposed to talk during band rehearsal, but if you can help a neighbor quietly, then yes, let's do that." In these moments, Sharon asks the students "how many people are sitting in a chair with good posture?" Sharon also teaches students how to use an appropriate speaking voice when peer mentoring. "When student voices get too loud," she said, "I try to teach them the skills for communicating correctly so when they get with a couple of kids, they're not going to be just yelling at somebody."

Sharon also seeks input from the students on what proper peer mentoring behavior is for the classroom. "If somebody's messing up the same thing over and over, which happens all the time, I'll ask if somebody will raise their hand and tell me how we might help our classmate with that. If we were going to teach them, how would we tell them? Not the way I tell you, how would you tell them?" Sharon stresses that "the mentor should be walking around, making sure people have music, making sure they know how to put their instrument together." She finds it important to remind the students "they are mentors and are supposed to help their peers, rather than just being students in band." Continuing, she adds, "If a kid really is having trouble, then I'm going to have a chat with them personally. I really don't try to do it in a group."

There are times when Sharon does meet with multiple mentors at once, especially "if we have a lot of kids together. Then, I'll stop and talk with them." Sharon solicits feedback from the student mentors to get a sense of how things are going in band. "I like to ask them if there is something [they] think we should be doing that we're not doing." Sharon finds this helpful, for "the mentors come up with ideas that I don't know about. I'm not sitting in that chair!" She also shows them how to share their knowledge with their peers. For example, "if [a mentee] can't get a sound, I'll quickly take [the mentor] out of the room for a moment and show them different ways to help their peers improve their performance." She considers this continual monitoring important, for "[mentors] need to have an understanding of how it is different for them to be that person, rather than just a student in band."

Learning appropriate mentoring behavior during rehearsals is also part of Sharon's curriculum. "I lead them into good behavior" by guiding them through the process of "learning how to help each other," she explains. She models "ways for them to help each other without being intrusive. That might include a quiet 'shh' to their neighbor if their verbal directives are too loud and interrupt the rehearsal." Through modeling, "I'm just trying to show them how you help people." Sharon "reminds the students that they have an expertise now and can help each other learn." Sharon considers the rehearsal time spent modeling proper mentoring behavior to be worth it, for it helps make certain that when she begins rehearsal, everyone is ready to play, and when students engage in peer mentoring, "I can trust them."

Student initiative with peer mentoring

Sharon finds that students assume leadership roles when they initiate peer mentoring. She recalls a time when "a group of three student saxophonists were preparing to play "America the Beautiful" for a Memorial Day assembly. Two of the kids were really good, and the other kid was just okay." As the students prepared to play, "one of the kids, who's a good mentor kid, asked, 'Ms. Phipps, can we all just play that same line with him so we can help?' 'Yeah, go ahead,' I responded. 'Why don't you count it off?'" The outcome was positive, as Sharon "just stood there and watched" the two musically stronger students help the weaker student. She noted that for this to happen, the students "have to be comfortable enough to ask me that. I'm not offended if a kid thinks they can do it. Go ahead, let's try!"

For Sharon, student leadership and initiative are important. "If the kids are together in a room and I'm not there, and I'm asking them to mentor somebody the same age as they are, I need to know they have some idea of how to do it. They've watched me do it, but have they picked up what they need? This is the thing that is most important about peer mentoring, realizing they're not afraid to come up with an idea of how to teach something and then do it." Sharon is aware that this is counter to what many music teachers do, for "they feel threatened on the podium and whatnot. They say, 'No, no, I'm the one who's going to tell you.' And there are times where I need to be that way, right? But I just don't teach that way."

Students can also take on leadership by creating their own peer mentoring program, as Sharon's high school students did one year. The students "wrote a handbook" that included "a schedule for students. About 30 kids showed up after school to meet with high school mentors who came back just to help out the kids." This mentoring program was set up for the middle school students to "get lessons." Although the program was student designed and led, Sharon "helped them figure out groupings of students." Which students would mentor which students? Which students would mentor students who played different instruments than they did? Other than that, Sharon's participation involved her "opening the doors, and calling home if needed to make sure the kids that were there were supposed to be there." The whole project was to the credit of the high school kids who wrote the handbook, contacted the parents to set up the program, and everything else that needed to be done." Sharon was just available in case the students needed guidance.

In addition, according to Sharon, one of the high school students who was a "great clarinetist" and who "was doing peer mentorship out the wazoo" recently "created a YouTube channel." She also created a website that has YouTube videos that show kids how to do things." Allowing students to design and run the peer mentoring program provided opportunities "for the kids to figure it out on their own" and is one of the primary reasons the program has been successful.

Peer mentoring and students with disabilities

Throughout her teaching career, Sharon has found that peer mentoring in band helps connect students with disabilities with typically developing students. Through these connections, Sharon has watched many typically developing students who normally do not offer to mentor step up and help their peers with disabilities. This includes typically developing students connecting with students with autism spectrum disorder or Down syndrome. At Chenery Middle School, these connections were supported by programs, such as Best Buddies, a part of the LABBB program[2] specifically designed to connect typically developing students and students with disabilities. Encouraging these connections is important to Sharon, and she emphasizes the importance of them in band. "We can support that connection with somebody they feel safe with already."

One time, when she was teaching a guitar class, one of her students was "a kid with Down syndrome." Although she knew the student "couldn't play the guitar," she commented that she "didn't care, nor did the other kids, and I always invited him into the class." She was amazed in retrospect that a "group of eighth graders who are really snarky, who didn't really want to be there" would instantly change their attitude when the student with Down syndrome entered the room. "The class became a totally different group of kids and would suddenly shout out, 'Can I help? Can I? Can I? Can I?'" In addition, because all the typically developing students wanted to mentor the student with Down syndrome, she had to "switch which kids could mentor each day because so many kids wanted to do it." This process reaffirmed Sharon's belief that "there are a lot of kids who'd like to be peer mentors but really don't want to admit they're doing it." Continuing, she said, "There are a lot of shy, quiet kids who do it, and you have no idea." She concludes that these students remain quiet because "they don't want the acknowledgment and be embarrassed by it at all. But they like to do it, for it makes them feel good." In addition, Sharon acknowledges, "They may not be my best players. In fact, some of the best players aren't the best mentors. It's just like musicians. Some of the best musicians aren't good teachers."

Sharon shared another story about "a clarinet kid who was not a very good clarinetist. He was never going to go over the break, even by eighth grade. He was that kid who wanted to be in band but wasn't really going to excel," but he was in Best Buddies and "would always volunteer to sit near" a student with severe autism. "Band was the only class the autistic student came to that was outside of the LABBB program." Sharon marveled at how the student clarinetist "got such pride out of sitting there and helping him every day." She also noticed that the student clarinetist and the autistic student formed such a strong connection that if the clarinetist were absent, "the autistic kid would be very nervous that day." At the end of the autistic student's eighth-grade year, Sharon wanted to give him an award for his participation in band at the LABBB program graduation. To no one's surprise, it was the student clarinetist who wanted to give the award to the autistic student, and Sharon agreed that it was a wonderful idea. She recalled that it was a "cry-your-eyes-out moment watching this kid who had befriended this other kid give him his prize. That's ultimate peer mentorship!"

Questions for discussion

1. Based upon the various reasons (e.g., walking a peer down the hallway to the bathroom) and ways (e.g., student mentors help peers learn their parts) Sharon uses peer mentoring, how might you use peer mentoring with your students?

2. Leadership in Sharon's band classes ranges from students helping each other with correct fingerings to serving as good role models for behavior. Considering how Sharon uses student leadership, what are the various reasons you could use student leadership and peer mentoring for meaningful learning?
3. Sharon devoted time to modeling peer mentoring and leadership for her students. How might you use modeling with your students, and when should you use it?
4. How might you effectively communicate mentoring goals and objectives for your students engaged in peer mentoring?
5. Based upon how Sharon monitored peer mentoring, what are some ways you can monitor peer mentoring with your students?
6. For Sharon, peer mentoring takes a significant amount of time to establish and maintain throughout the school year. How much time do you devote to the establishment and maintenance of peer mentoring, and how might you make this process more efficient?
7. How might you set up peer mentoring for typically developing students and students with disabilities?

Reflection

Sharon sets up peer mentoring so that as many students as possible can be engaged. She shifts the focus away from only teacher-led instruction to allow students to provide input into learning that occurs in rehearsals, but she maintains an active role facilitating these experiences for her students. Sharon finds that when students peer mentor, they comprehend what they are learning on a deeper level. From her perspective, peer mentoring and student leadership are closely related, and they help make learning more enjoyable for her students. To ensure that they remain productive, Sharon continually monitors peer mentoring and its student leaders. By setting goals and objectives with her mentors and meeting with them before and after peer mentoring and leadership experiences, she is able to reflect on what went well and what did not go well during learning.

Creating peer mentoring and student leadership opportunities

Sharon plays an active role in creating peer mentoring and student leadership opportunities for her students. Because peer mentoring may range from helping a peer walk down the hallway to the bathroom to working with each other in rehearsals to elevate performance levels, she has to be realistic in her expectations for her mentors and mentees. Chapters 2 and 4 explain how the selection of mentors and mentees is critical to creating successful peer mentoring and leadership experiences for your students.[3] For Sharon, effective peer mentoring begins with getting to know what knowledge the students have and whether they demonstrate any potential for leadership.

She stresses the importance of understanding her students' levels of knowledge and skills so that when she puts them together, she pairs them toward success. Understanding what your students know is an important part of meaningful learning. As you think about how Sharon emphasizes the importance of knowing the capabilities of her students, consider how you gain insights into what knowledge your students know and how you use their knowledge to contribute to learning in the music class or ensemble. In addition, think about whether any of Sharon's experiences remind you of your own, and if so, how you might modify the selection of your student mentors and mentees. While doing so, you may want to reflect on different ways you could learn what your students know, such as using a survey similar to the one Kara discussed in Chapter 6. These strategies can help you create more effective peer mentoring experiences for your students.

Once Sharon has a handle on what her students know, she observes her class to see who would make effective leaders. As Sharon assesses students and their capabilities, she carefully considers the roles they will play. Leadership is multi-dimensional in Sharon's band classes; some students take on leadership for musical reasons, such as working on fingerings, while others lead for nonmusical reasons, like being good role models for behavior. Sharon also places strong musicians next to weaker musicians. When this occurs, the strong musicians serve as silent mentors, who are responsible for modeling how to play the music properly without giving any verbal directives. Leadership then is an important part of how Sharon shores up peer mentoring. Based on her informal assessment of student knowledge and student interactions in rehearsals, she selects students she considers natural leaders but also cultivates leadership in students she sees as having potential. Although Sharon believes student leadership is important, she considers it informal in nature and uses a lead-by-example structure in class. She models leadership for her students in how to share (mentor) and how to receive (mentee) knowledge—an approach she calls leading them into "good behavior." Throughout the modeling process, she reminds students they are there to help their peers. Sharon models effective leadership, but she also models ineffective leadership and asks the students to identify what she is doing wrong. The student responses provide insights into who the effective leaders are.

In addition to modeling leadership, Sharon continually monitors behavior, for issues do arise, especially in verbal interactions. To resolve any issues or avoid them entirely, she works with students during rehearsals to explain proper behavior; she also meets regularly with students before and after class to debrief about leadership. In these meetings, she seeks student input on what is going well and what is not going well in rehearsals, and she provides specific directives to guide them through the process of being a leader. When meeting with students, she finds that they have ideas and are aware of musical issues that she is not aware of. Sharon underscores the importance of not singling out students who are having issues during rehearsal; instead, she meets with them on an individual basis. Think about how you devote time to monitoring peer mentoring with your students. Based upon how Sharon monitors peer mentoring, think about how you can continue to devote time to meeting with students and what you can continue learning from your students during the process.

Setting goals and objectives

Chapter 4 emphasizes how important it is to set expectations for and with your students about what you want to accomplish with peer mentoring and leadership. These expectations include working with your students to set goals and objectives for learning as well as creating a supportive atmosphere among the students so they value their peers' leadership.[4] Sharon considers student input important, for she finds it both makes learning more enjoyable for them and leads to increased ownership in the learning process. She also considers it highly important to make sure students understand the importance of why they are mentoring. To facilitate the learning goals and objectives for peer mentoring, Sharon projects the objectives on a separate screen in the rehearsal room in addition to verbally stating the objectives in class. As you reflect on how Sharon communicates the objectives that she and her students created, think about how you communicate objectives to your students and whether you could use tactics similar to Sharon's, if you are not doing so already.

Stepping up to leadership: Student initiative

Although Sharon invests a significant amount of time and energy in making peer mentoring and student leadership a natural and productive part of her classroom, she finds the time devoted to really getting to know her students in terms of what knowledge they have and what their potential for leadership is provides the most return on her investment. Through this effort, she also discovers students who exhibit leadership on their own volition, recalling the quiet student who stepped up and took the initiative to mentor his peer with disabilities. Chapter 2 mentions times when peer mentoring can provide an opportunity for typically developing students to demonstrate leadership and mentor their peers with disabilities. In turn, this helps students with disabilities feel like they are part of the class. In Sharon's guitar class, both the typically developing student and the student with a disability benefitted from a mentoring relationship. Think about any times you have set up peer mentoring for typically developing students and students with disabilities, and whether any students stepped up to a leadership role on their own. Or as you continue to reflect on these mentoring relationships, think about how you could set up these opportunities in the future. Consider how you could get support from your administration, staff, and students at your school.

Not only has Sharon discovered that students will occasionally engage in peer mentoring on their own, but she has also learned that once the peer mentoring network is up and running, it can make learning in rehearsals more efficient. Once students understand the goals and objectives for learning in addition to understanding how to mentor and why they are mentoring, the structure almost runs on its own. Sharon knows that even though the process of peer mentoring is self-perpetuating, she still must maintain an active role in monitoring peer mentoring activities. This pays big dividends in improved attitudes toward learning, increased motivation, heightened ownership, and elevated performance skills. Perhaps most importantly for Sharon, students learn how to interact with each other, a lifelong skill they can carry into adulthood. In her view, this gives her students the ability to succeed in life.

In the next chapter, developing student leadership and peer mentoring continue to be explored with a visit to Vince Cee, orchestra director at the ISKL, in Kuala Lumpur, Malaysia. Vince creates formal student leadership opportunities for his students and instills in them the idea that leadership is ultimately about service to their peers.

Notes

1. All student names are pseudonyms.
2. LABBB refers to Lexington, Arlington, Burlington, Bedford, and Belmont. These five communities in Massachusetts have schools that use this program designed for students with disabilities.
3. Andrew Goodrich, "Peer Mentoring in a High School Jazz Ensemble," *Journal of Research in Music Education* 55, no. 2 (2007): 94–114, https://doi.org/10.1177/002242940705500202; Andrew J. Hobson, "Fostering Face-to-Face Mentoring and Coaching," in *The Sage Handbook of Mentoring and Coaching in Education*, ed. Sarah Fletcher and Carol Mullen (Thousand Oaks, CA: SAGE, 2012), 59–73.
4. Scott J. Allen and Nathan S. Hartman, "Sources of Learning in Student Leadership Development Programming," *Journal of Leadership Studies* 3, no. 3 (2009): 6–16, https://doi.org/10.1002/jls.20119.

8 Vince Cee

Having zigzagged back and forth across the United States, you will now travel to Southeast Asia to learn about Vince Cee's orchestra program at the International School of Kuala Lumpur, Kuala Lumpur, Malaysia. Vince, who provides the final portrait on peer mentoring, believes student leadership provides the platform for him and his students to engage in meaningful learning. Prompted by the success of student-led learning in his classes, Vince began using student leadership and peer mentoring in his teaching. Among the strategies he uses to help build this leadership—which he feels is of primary importance to the success of peer mentoring—is modeling for his students the values of integrity and energy, and the importance of doing what you say you are going to do.

Introducing Vince

When Vince was ready for college, the Cee family found themselves in a common standoff. Vince wanted to major in music at the University of Utah, while his parents really wanted him to attend pharmacy school. "Then," they reasoned, "at least you'll be able to make a living." In a fortunate turn of events the summer after his first year of pharmacy school, he "got an offer for a scholarship to study music" at the University of Alaska Fairbanks (UAF). There, he would be able to pursue his dream of becoming a professional musician. His parents "relented and let me be a music major," recounts Vince, but there was one hitch in their agreement: "I had to be a music *education* major." That way, they figured, he would still be able to support himself.

Vince felt all right registering as a major in music education. After all, he thought, "I can still perform as much as I want." As time went on, however, Vince discovered that "when I listed my major, the school started putting me in education classes, for they viewed me as a preservice teacher and started giving me teaching opportunities." One of those opportunities was working with one of the youth orchestras in Fairbanks, which Vince knew had a "very strong youth orchestra program." What Vince did not know at that time was how the orchestra members "would

Figure 8.1 Vince Cee.
Source: Photograph provided by Vince Cee.

just blow him away." He discovered the students "were so smart, they were so clever, they would play jokes, they would say the wittiest little things," and before long he began thinking that someday he "would bring about a shift to where the student would be taking a bigger part, to where the student is not just this passive receptacle waiting for knowledge to be poured into it but rather an actual catalyst in the whole learning process."

After completing his degree in music education at UAF, Vince went on to Arizona State University in Tempe to pursue a master's degree in music

166 *Narrative portraits of four music teachers*

education with a jazz concentration. After finishing his master's degree, he taught for five years in the Mesa Public Schools.

Noticing students helping each other learn

In Vince's first year of teaching at Porter Elementary School in Mesa, the sixth-grade strings were scheduled right after lunch, and "even though people told me not to do it, I let them eat lunch in the music room." After the class had finished lunch one day, they asked him if they could play the piano, and although Vince had "seen other teachers close their piano or lock it," he let the sixth graders play it "as long as they washed their hands." Then, Vince went on, "after watching them mostly teach each other 'Heart and Soul,' I realized that they were teaching each other faster than I could teach them." As Vince reflected on this, he had to admit that they likely learned the song faster because "if they were to come in and learn 'Heart and Soul' from me, I would say, 'Okay, sit down with your feet flat on the floor. No, no, feet have to be here. No, move that foot. No, your foot needs to be there. Okay, now have your back straight. No, change your feet. Look let's go back to your feet. Now, you need to open the piano, go ahead and open it. Wait, your feet have shifted.' And before you know it, the lesson is over, and they haven't even begun 'Heart and Soul'."

The more Vince thought about it, the more frustrated he got. "When the students walked in with each other, they would just sit down and start playing it and teaching." He discovered "they were better teachers than I was." Vince "learned to watch" what was happening and would think to himself, "If you let them do this, they're going to take it, and they can go and pass and teach faster than you could ever, ever teach."

Beginning to develop student leadership

Near the end of Vince's first year of teaching, a position in orchestra became available at Skyline High School in Mesa. His colleagues warned him that "nobody gets a high school job in this district without experience," and during his interview, Vince was convinced that the committee was "not interested in anything I was saying." Near the end of his time, however, Vince mentioned the subject of "student leadership" and noticed that suddenly "they all changed their posture and sat up and started to smile; at that point, they were interested in everything I had to say."

After the interview as Vince "walked out of the room, I was hit with the realization that I didn't know anything about student leadership," and later when he did get the job, he recognized he was going to have to really explore this subject that had landed him the position. He "bought every book on leadership you can imagine." People also gave him more leadership books over the years because they knew he was interested in the subject, and these even included books on army ROTC leadership. "I've even got ones called *Leadership and the New Science*[1] and on chaos theory. I started reading and asking a lot of questions about leadership."

Although Vince characterizes his teaching style as that of "a control freak—I would have all the bowings written on the wall and say, 'Copy these, it's my way or the highway,'" he was also fully aware of the potential for student input in learning. Vince decided the best way to encourage student leadership was to create an orchestra council. He asked "every teacher I knew for information, and they used to give me their syllabi. I scattered them all out on the floor and combined many of the ideas for my council." Vince told his students about the orchestra council and explained he was putting it together "to form lines of communication between you and the conductor." Vince pointed out that he could not "just walk in and say we're only going to play Bach, Beethoven, and Brahms, or here's our concert attire. It's to really have open lines of communication." Vince recalls the orchestra council was "informal at first," and he told the students, "If you have a problem, just write an anonymous note to me and slide it under my door. And the kids would do it. The notes were hilarious and were not always about problems. At first, they would write notes just to be funny and always sign them *anonymous*. Eventually, things settled down though, and I got some really pertinent notes. For example, one said, 'how come for every good kid who quits, we get another crappy bass player who's a beginner?' Wow, I thought. That's a problem." So it worked.

Refining his ideas about teaching

During his fourth year of teaching, Vince decided he needed to go back to school himself, believing that "if I didn't go back to school and ask the right questions, I would become the worst teacher in the school." Then, after five years of teaching in the Mesa Public Schools, Vince enrolled at the University of Massachusetts Amherst to pursue a PhD in music education. He made this move for two reasons: "One was to ask the right questions, and the other one was to kind of figure out why people teach music in the first place." An unexpected benefit was "meeting Christopher Small and studying with Roger Rideout. Seeing those brains together really helped me to advance my thinking about how to teach music."

Upon completion of his doctorate in 2008,[2] Vince landed a teaching position in music education at his alma mater, the UAF. "It was a crazy year to apply for a job," he remembers, "because it was 2008, and at the same moment that jobs were opening, they were also drying up before anyone was interviewed." On the other hand, he added, "I was able to build the program to about 40 music education majors, and because almost everybody in the district was retiring at that time, my students were getting jobs."

Allowing students to take the initiative with their learning

At UAF, Vince began to realize the importance of letting go of the control at times in the classroom and allowing students to take the initiative with their learning. Initially, Vince "was having a terrible time getting students to engage in group discussions," even though he had watched numerous videos on how to facilitate them, some of which even featured "Harvard professors telling you to do this or that." In addition, he attended workshops and seminars. Despite his preparation, Vince still did not consider himself effective at inspiring student discussion in the classroom. "No matter what I did, whether I'd show them the most provocative video or the most profound reading and follow it up with an enthusiastic 'Okay, let's have a group discussion,' it wasn't happening. Student A would look at me and say, 'Blah blah blah blah blah, this is what you want to hear.' And then Student B would look at me and say, 'Blah blah blah,' and the two students wouldn't even look at each other. They wouldn't participate at all in a group."

Then one day in class, Vince showed an episode of *This American Life*. "It's the Ira Glass thing, where they clone the bull. The whole reason I was showing it was allegorical, to say you can't copy someone else's teaching necessarily, you've got to become your own teacher." Near the end of the video, Vince panicked as he "looked at the whiteboard and realized there was not a single marker on the tray." Just as the video finished, he panicked again and thought "Oh no, I can't teach because I can't teach without writing on the board." Trying to cover what he was going to do, Vince said to his students, "All right. Video's over. Discuss." He "walked out of the room, ran to his office, retrieved the markers, and ran back." When he opened the door, they were all talking to each other, having a group discussion. "And I just slinked into the room, closed the door, sat down with the markers in my hand, and didn't say a word. The whole thing had happened without me." For Vince, this "was another light-bulb moment that revealed *I'm* the one getting in the way." He recognized that he "just needed to leave the room and let the kids go to it. And they had a beautiful discussion; it was appropriate, it was within the confines of what I thought they should be talking about, and it had nothing to do with my leading it."

Another major learning experience occurred when Vince taught at a science camp run by "MIT guys" in Fairbanks during the summer. Although the camp "really exposed the soft underbelly of my lack of knowledge about how the scientific world works," he felt qualified "to help the students learn about sound," which was what he was supposed to do. Vince enjoyed the experience in part because with "eight to twelve kids to every two teachers," it was "the best student-to-teacher ratio I'd ever had." Another plus for Vince was that "there were no bells there; there were no tests." The mandate was to "let the learning be fun, and the rest will follow." In Vince's mind, "watching those kids learn without having to teach to the test or dictate what should be known was one of the most beautiful things I've experienced."

One circumstance that did frustrate Vince at first was the requirement that "we had to eat lunch with the kids." This created a problem for him because "I'm an introvert. I need that time to myself. I need to think about what we're going to do in the afternoon. And so I wondered how I was going to do this." When Vince went to his first lunch, however, he made another discovery:

> It was cool because the kids who like you sit by you, the kids who don't, go sit by someone else. And eventually you have this informal group where you don't have to say, 'you have to be with this person, this person, this person.' And the lunches became so enjoyable, I found myself going to breakfast. And then the teacher I was teaching with, he and I, would even stay for dinner. Then, we would stay for the activities just to be around the kids, and often it would seem like we were playing soccer, but before you knew it, we'd all be back in the lab doing science again, even though it was 9:00 p.m.

In one of these late-night sessions, Vince once again saw the importance of letting students take the initiative in problem-solving and taking the lead with their learning. "One of the MIT guys looked at a kid and said, 'How does a speaker work?' And the kid said, 'Well, there's a wrap of wire around a magnet, and it gets an electrical signal that's negative and positive.' And the MIT guy just screamed at him, 'You'd be great at the SAT! Go make a speaker now! With whatever's in this room!' And he got all the kids to make a speaker. We did not have our speaker done until midnight, but when we were finished, we were so proud of it." And Vince learned from this experience. "It was just letting the kids find their way instead of dictating so much, and then watching them mentor each other, and help each other, and support each other."

Even though Vince enjoyed his position at the UAF, he left in 2014 "right before more budget cuts happened again." His next position was in Malaysia at the ISKL.

Current teaching position

Vince describes ISKL as "a true international school . . . which is completely non-profit and has student test scores high enough that students can choose to go to whichever college they want." The student body is "about 1,700 to 2,000-ish, with about 155 from the U.S. Embassy, so we are the U.S. Embassy school." The music programs "are based on the large ensemble format, and they expand outward to include experimental music, DJ music, songwriting, things like that." Vince admitted that he had never "been to a school like this, where the academic focus is so high." The students are "extremely motivated; when they come into the room, they're not talking about who they're going to go on a date with or what they're doing that weekend. What they do discuss is which private courses they will take on the weekend to help strengthen their portfolios for college admissions."

At ISKL, Vince conducts five orchestras ranging from middle school through high school. The sixth-grade orchestra is "for anyone in sixth grade who wants to take orchestra," which includes students who "are all the way from very beginner on their first day opening the case to some kids who've been playing for ten years." At the middle school, he also teaches a combined seventh- and eighth-grade orchestra, and at the high school he teaches three orchestras that are ability based. One is an entry-level no-audition ensemble that often caters to students who want to begin playing a stringed instrument and will take it "as a breather or some enrichment" because "this is a high-pressure school, and they're under a lot of academic pressure." The other two high school groups are auditioned; one is an intermediate group, and "the top group is definitely advanced and competitive." The top group, which Vince calls the "elite group," is extracurricular. This ensemble is "a team of eight students, and they work with Singapore, Jakarta, Manila, Taipei; all of our sister schools are in this group." The elite group "performs in that circuit each year." These performances involve every student "preparing a solo with accompaniment. They play in an octet, so they're getting a chamber experience, and then each school's octet combines into a large group, so they get the large group ensemble experience as well."

Student leadership

At ISKL, Vince wanted to be more proactive in implementing peer mentoring in his teaching, so he began a peer mentoring program using a student leadership model. In this model, student leadership is the conduit for peer mentoring, and Vince chose this method "because I had some interest in it and experience with it." Vince believed peer mentoring at ISKL would encourage student interaction, for "we've got around 60 different cultures represented at this school." In addition to the numerous cultures, "we definitely have a humongous mixture of the world religions." Vince has seen how the varied backgrounds of the students "sometimes determines how they treat each other and how they hold the group together or how they kind of push the group in different directions." His observations then made more perceptible "how different cultural ways of being were impacting the ways that group did everything."

Qualities of effective student leadership

Vince believes effective student leadership includes integrity, energy, and trust built from the belief that it is important to do what you say you are going to do. He often draws upon figures in the business world, such as Warren Buffett, to generate ideas for student leadership, even wishing at one point that he was "Warren Buffett, because he said it best; at Berkshire Hathaway, Buffett looks for people who have integrity and energy and smarts. And you've got to have integrity first because if you have energy and smarts and you're not a very ethical or moral person, you're going to move the orchestra in the wrong direction." One angle of leadership that Vince has "always held the closest is *you always have to do what you say you're going to do*. I'm looking for kids who do what they say they're going to do."

Vince helps students understand what these leadership qualities mean by referencing the college admissions process. "I work with kids who are all going to have perfect ACT scores and perfect SAT scores and perfect 4.0s." In their discussions, Vince and the students "talk a lot about how a college decides to accept you or not. And I would say integrity mixed with energy and brightness is one way." Vince also draws inspiration from "Harry R. Lewis, former dean of Harvard College, who in his book *Excellence Without a Soul* declares that Harvard looks for who has done the most with what they have," so Vince and his group "talk a lot about how you do the most with what you have when you already appear to have everything."

Vince reminds his student leaders that "people may forget what you do, people may forget what you say, but people will always remember how you made them feel." He considers this important for them to keep in mind, for it clarifies the responsibility leaders carry when they interact with their peers. "There have been times when people are just power hungry or rude or unaware that they're intimidating or oblivious to the fact that they're making people feel bad." Vince says that in rehearsals, "we talk a lot about how you make other people feel. Let's say you have a really clear objective. Let's say you really know that viola players can do these things better. How do you get to know that person enough; how do you get them to trust you enough so you can finally help them perform at a higher level?" In one instance, he "had a student who simply just gave up and couldn't even lead. The orchestra was never going to be as good as she wanted, which seemed really weird. One day, she was in tears and sobbed, 'I used to think it was your fault, and now I realize it's us. We just can't get along, and we can't do this.'" In moments like this, Vince helps students through the process of solving these issues when they arise. "You have to continually help them in learning how to lead." On a personal note, Vince explains how his teaching approach has changed: "Now my teaching time is spent not just in saying, 'Well, do this note with high third finger,' or 'Shift to fifth position,' or 'Try this bowing,' but in building in and scaffolding how to deal with things which are not perfect and how to always be aware of how you make other people feel."

Having an awareness of how his students make others feel is a primary training principle for Vince, and he works with his student leaders on understanding the benefits of treating each other with respect. This includes talking "a lot about how we treat other people and how we gain the respect of other people." Vince admits that he "probably doesn't really understand respect fully and doesn't know if anybody does," but "most people I meet say I value respect more than anything, and the idea of earning respect and earning trust just takes so long." Respect is important, Vince points out, for "in a leadership position, everybody is watching what you're doing, so if you're going to be a leader these days, you've got to be so good." Pinning the issue down even more, Vince adds, "If you make a mistake, you've got to know how to apologize, and you have to know how to show people you're human at the same time you're maintaining that high-end professional level. In the end, this is not rocket science, but there is an art to doing what we do when dealing with humans." To illustrate the importance of admitting their mistakes, Vince confesses "he's a very nervous guy." He tells them not to "watch him all the time," because he has a lot of anxiety. "I've sometimes had to admit my own flaws[3] in order to help some students see theirs. I don't care if a student has flaws. I'm just mostly concerned that they're working on them."

To set the groundwork for effective student leadership in the orchestra programs at ISKL, Vince began by creating a welcoming atmosphere, or "family" as he calls it, in the octet, his smallest and most advanced ensemble. This family "dimension is also woven into the peer mentoring program." He created an orchestra council to enable a small group of students to begin demonstrating and modeling leadership for all students. Vince then collected student input about nonmusical objectives at first, such as selecting concert attire, and then transitioned into musical objectives, such as identifying musical errors. "I feel like if I had any strength," Vince explained, "I would be able to convince students to at least believe in the logistical aspects of the orchestra before I could get them to believe in the musical aspects." Of course, peer mentoring extends beyond nonmusical and musical objectives, but Vince promotes student leadership opportunities to develop student individuality.

Eating lunch together

To build a foundation for collaboration, Vince considers it important for the students to understand the distinction between a class and an ensemble:

> I write on the board CLASS. And then I say, 'Well, is there anything else that we could be?' And somebody will usually say, 'Yeah, we're

an ensemble.' And I'll say, 'Well, how is an ensemble different from a class?' Now, the kids know me well enough, especially since I have them from the sixth grade on, so they'll say, 'Well, in a class we can't collaborate. We have to do our own work most of the time. Here, you give us the test immediately, and we start collaborating.' So that's one of the rules, too, I say. In math class, they hand out the test last, and you don't look at each other. In orchestra, I hand out the test first, and everybody has to work together.

While Vince does not remember which teacher said it, he does remember the point made. "You don't come to rehearsal to learn your part; you come to rehearsal to learn everybody else's." And so, "after the students realize that there is a difference between the class and the ensemble and have more or less figured out what the term *ensemble* means," Vince explains that "an ensemble is a team." As a final shot, Vince writes "family" on the board and remarks, "You're not a family if you don't eat together."

The octet eats lunch together at least once a week on Saturdays during the rehearsals that last approximately three or four hours. According to Vince, the idea for eating together came "from a book called *The Culture Code*,"[4] in which the author "reports that what successful groups have in common is that they eat together." For Vince, it is relatively easy to encourage students to have lunch together, for "most people don't have family in Kuala Lumpur. Everyone's 3,000 miles away from their families. Creating families in school probably wouldn't happen if the students lived with their families." When Vince and the students eat together, they sit in a circle, and "the rules are simple: I only ask them questions about themselves, and I usually just let them talk." When the students began eating together, Vince would occasionally sit outside the circle, but soon the students demanded Vince eat in the circle with them. The lunches were set up by the students, who "chose to do that." Vince also seeks "student input on how to interact with each other" above and beyond the discussions during their lunches together.

Vince has no "peer mentoring lesson plan," nor does he "pair this kid with that kid." Instead, "I kind of just do it Vince Cee style, where I put them in the room and let it happen." For example, students select a guest artist from the local symphony to come in and rehearse the octet. Vince adds that "you'll hear them coming up with the musical problems and solutions for how we fix the errors."

It took time for Vince to allow the students to make decisions and provide their input for learning. When the octet was first formed a few years ago, he would choose the repertoire. "I would tell the students, 'This is what we're doing.' I would tell them how we're doing it; I would have the musical ideas." Now, in a total 180, "it's just open-ended. I sit down with them—or I don't even sit down with them—and they choose the repertoire."

Orchestra council

Drawing upon his experiences with the orchestra council at Skyline High School in Mesa, Vince decided that an orchestra council of four or five students could help provide a core for developing student leadership at ISKL. The council, which Vince admits should be called a leadership council, meets weekly for an hour, and it is here Vince gathers student input. "I cannot keep my finger on all the repertoire and the changing trends," he explains, "and now that I'm getting older, I'm farther apart from what they often want to do."

Vince made it clear to the students that "the orchestra council is not a popularity contest." It does have a president, but they do not have a vice president "because as I explained to the students, I don't know what the vice president does on these councils." The roles are fluid from year to year depending upon need, but they typically include a president, a media relations representative, a public relations person, and a secretary. Marketing is important to both Vince and his students because "they need to make sure the school understands what they do." Vince concedes that having a president "is a throwback to the idea that the concertmaster is still dealing with the conductor type of thing. That might be a flaw in the way I've done things, but we've also borrowed some strength from age-old tradition."

To be considered for orchestra council, students submit an application to Vince. "Everyone writes a perfect application because everybody has great dreams at the outset." To help him select council members, Vince asks "the following questions: *What do you want to do?* And the next question is *how do you plan to accomplish it?* And then the next question is *what do you see as obstacles?* or *what do you think's going to bother this plan?* And then the final question is *how do you plan to get around that?* or *what are you going to do to get around these problems?*"

The answers to these questions assist Vince in "spotting an application that stands out above the others, where someone's actually honest about what the problems are." For example, Vince often receives applications with statements, such as "I want to change the orchestras. I want us to all be playing Grade 5 repertoire and playing all scales in three octaves with arpeggios by the end of the year." Vince does not consider these types of answers to address actual problems in the orchestra; he is looking for "the students who can be honest and say, 'I'm not going to be successful my first time,' or 'I'm going to have to deal with resistance,' or 'I'm going to have to build my capacity for change.'" For Vince, "these are the kids I'm really interested in, the ones who can actually start to think of the dream and help other people get to it. And I've been lucky to have some of those."

Vince typically receives 12 to 15 applications per year for one or two open positions in the council. In the beginning, he reviewed the applications alone, with no input from the students, but now he lets the orchestra council members read the applications and provide input on whom to select. Even with student opinion, however, Vince likes to maintain control of the process because he does not "believe membership is a reward, it's a service position." Vince really drives home this point to the students because I want them to realize "they're serving their orchestra. My theory is that the greatest leadership is through service." For Vince, the service component is important for the students to recognize; otherwise, "it's a thankless job, and they're doing it because they're aware that if they don't, one teacher can't do everything that they want to do." The positives of service are further championed by ISKL as well because the school requires the students to engage in some type of service. "There are incentives to do projects like this where the students can also get credit in other areas."

Once the orchestra council was organized, Vince "let the students find a problem" to get to work on. "For some reason," he explains, "it was way easier for me to let students find a nonmusical problem than to let them find a musical problem," So he asked, "What's the biggest problem in the orchestra?" Even as he asked it, he realized that "it's kind of a hard question for them," but "finally somebody said, 'Well, we don't like the concert attire.'" Not quite expecting this response but happy to have something to work with, Vince then said, "That's perfect." Together, they began the process of selecting new concert attire. As Vince looks back on it, "We got to successful concert attire, we showed everyone that we did it, we publicized it, we made everyone happy, and yes, we got a win." For Vince, this was an important first step, for "the orchestra council had documented a problem, they fixed it, and they were successful."

Expanding leadership

Once the council was functioning, Vince began to expand leadership roles in other parts of the orchestra program. "The other students see the leaders being successful and accomplishing things, and that's how the idea of leadership trickles down. We've opened everything up for more people so we have section leaders." In addition to section leaders, "we also have auxiliary members," students who become part of an ad-hoc committee that is developed for a single project depending upon the needs of the ensemble. Occasionally, Vince "calls a group meeting" of all students in leadership positions, although finding a common meeting time is nearly impossible because "everybody's doing some extracurricular something." Sometimes, it is just easier to have only the core council of four or five students meet.

With leadership expanding throughout the orchestra program, Vince continued to encourage students to take on more responsibility for creating learning opportunities. The students "didn't always get along," Vince remembers, "and they also didn't play that well together." In all honesty, Vince admits, "That's something I just can't handle," so he told the students that they "needed to figure something out to change that." What the students came up with was the creation of a chamber concert called the "String Fling," where everyone performed solo and ensemble pieces on stage. For this concert, "each group made a poster for their composer or their piece, and then we had food afterwards." The students "had to plan the whole thing," and although "we still don't get along, and we don't play that well, we did find a way to fix it, and after that, a way to document it." During this whole process, "all I really have done in terms of working with peer mentoring is shift the emphasis from logistical problems to musical problems." Many times, the students "are in charge of making the whole thing happen, even though there are adult conductors."

The transition from logistical problems to musical problems also helps Vince encourage student input during rehearsals. This process is not easy, however, and "it was very, very painful at first. It was only through frustration" that the students began taking on more leadership. "We've got all these minds in here, and all these individuals in here, and they need to become a group, so I told them to run the rehearsal. I would just observe." The students immediately began mentoring each other. "Students who had never said anything to anybody began commenting on something as simple as a wrong note." They "started demonstrating bowings for each other or showing them a different way of doing something with their left-hand technique." Vince also pointed out that students were no longer "circling forte or writing eyeglasses because I yelled at them to do it," but instead "they're actually writing in the name of another student they need to make eye contact with or one that has a pattern with them or that they're handing a phrase off to." This is a thing of pride for Vince. "You look at their music, and they've written in all the different directions for the ensemble that they need to have. So much different than my announcing, 'Everybody, measure 34, mark it up.'" In addition, "now in the groups, we decide on the bowings together, and we have a rule that the bow only goes two ways. We talk about the consequences of each different bowing. We listen to a lot of peer groups, we try a lot of different things, and now I can say that in my group, even in the most stringent audition, they will break into discussion automatically first. That took some time to get it to where they now make musical choices before they wait for any authority from me."

Student reflection

Reflection on learning during rehearsals is an important aspect of student leadership, and Vince spends considerable time leading students through the process of learning how to reflect and contribute to learning. "They certainly didn't have it when we started, and that was something we just had to build through countless rehearsals where they worked on reflection." Sometimes, "after a tough rehearsal, Vince would have them do a reflection-on-action by prompting them to write a one-page reflection on a shared doc." His directions remind them, "You're all going to see what you're writing, so be kind to each other. Or write it just to me or write it to yourself. But, go ahead and think about what happened." Vince considers reflection an important part of his conversation with students about learning. When he thinks about it, he recalls a clinic at a festival where "the teacher came out and did a clinic with the violists. And she said, 'Okay, the fingering for the Dvořák is 4, 3, 321, 1, 3, 3, 4 4 4, 3, 3, 32, 4 4 4, shift 4, shift, shift, shift, 4, 4,' and then she asked, 'Got it? Does anyone need it again?' And I thought, Wow, that's such a fast pace, and she really knows her stuff, but we can't learn like that. That's not a conversation."

Vince's method is different. "Every time I see them learning, we think about whether this was the best way for them, whether this is what works in this ensemble right now." As they reflect in action, Vince reminds them about the importance of critical listening. "We might say, 'Well, wait a minute, what should we do here?' Or sometimes we say, 'Well look, there are probably at least three ways to do this. Let's try all three and see which one we like best.'" During these moments of reflection-in-action, "sometimes we vote, and if we don't reach consensus, sometimes I do say, 'we are doing it this way,' but that's very rare." Interestingly, "many times, it's their decision, but I believe it's actually a choice before it turns into the decision. As long as their choice is cohesive with how they believe the piece should sound, I'm okay with their choice. These students are way brighter than you think. Give up some of the control. We'll just see what happens, see how clever they are, see how creative."

Although Vince encourages the students to be active participants in their learning, he has also heard the criticism that "he's not teaching; he's just letting the kids do it." At these times, Vince draws on scholar Christopher Small, who "brought that up, too, where he said he was teaching the kids to teach themselves." For student input to happen, Vince acknowledges that "you have to have an administration who is aware of it and values it; you've got to have other teachers who are willing to let something like that happen."

Student identity

As the students were working through the process of mentoring each other on musical issues, peer mentoring began to take on added dimensions. Student leadership and interaction during peer mentoring convinced Vince that he was "seeing the students for who they are, not for who he wants them to be," and he told the students about his feeling.

"Yeah," they told him, "we want you to see us for who we are, and not just that we have tons of potential or you should be able to do that." As Vince sees it, "the way the music classes have changed under student leadership and peer mentoring is more about the adults' understanding who the students are and about the students' understanding who they are. And not just who they are in terms of what fashion they like or what's in style but really who they are as musicians, and who they want to be as expressive individuals. You've really got to get to know these kids, and beyond just a superficial level. When I can make that happen, I get energy from them. I like being around them."

Peer mentoring for lifelong participation in music

One of Vince's hopes is that peer mentoring will help instill a desire for lifelong participation in music in the students. Vince has "never met anybody who doesn't love music," yet "at best, only 12% of students play in a school-offered ensemble, and most kids quit once their senior year starts." Vince, then, hopes "that peer mentoring will empower students to consider music making a lifelong pursuit" and remarks that he "would love it if a kid would write in ten years and say, 'Mr. Cee, you might not remember me, but I'm a CEO at this company. I was in Jakarta this weekend, and I played duets with someone from high school.'" With student input and leadership, "the kids should be able to do that," for "I've told them many times 'I'm not going to be there your whole life. You're going to need to do this yourself someday.'"

Vince views peer mentoring as an opportunity for students to gain skills that will serve them well into adulthood. He points out to the students that "the first thing you're going to do in your first job is you're going to get put on a committee, and you're going to have to go work with people. We might as well start practicing how to work with people now." For Vince, peer mentoring and student leadership provide the opportunity "to make a lot of mistakes in how they deal with people and how they work with people. The bonus is that this type of involvement and participation provides them with the strategies to fix it."

Questions for discussion

1. As you observe instances of peer mentoring and leadership, how might you incorporate what you see and what you have learned from Vince into your future teaching?
2. Vince admitted it took time before he was able to take a step back from being the authority in the rehearsal and give students opportunities to provide input into the learning. Based on Vince's story, what are some ways you could allow students to guide their learning?

3. How might you instill in your students the notion that leadership is service?
4. What are some ways you can use student leadership to encourage a heightened ownership in the music program?
5. How might you use reflection-in-action and reflection-on-action with your students?
6. As you encourage student leadership and peer mentoring, how could you also introduce or reinforce the idea that music is a lifelong endeavor?

Reflection

Early in Vince's career as a music teacher, he noticed that the students who engaged in peer mentoring were effective leaders in learning and was amazed at how quickly the students learned from each other. He reflected on these experiences and wondered how he could incorporate them into his own teaching. His first step toward nurturing student leadership was to introduce the idea of an orchestra council. Vince then made sure he had a welcoming and supportive atmosphere conducive to student input. The orchestra council and supportive learning environment provided a foundation for students to take initiative for their learning by peer mentoring in the orchestra program.

Creating opportunities for student leadership

Vince created formal leadership opportunities as the gateway to peer mentoring in the orchestra program. To develop student leadership, Vince framed a multi-dimensional atmosphere that included an orchestra council with formal leadership positions, a welcoming learning environment that included the notion of being part of a family, and communal eating so that students could bond during lunches. Leadership in the orchestra council initially dealt with nonmusical objectives before Vince guided the students toward leadership for musical objectives. Reflect on how Vince's orchestra council worked, think about what nonmusical and musical goals and objectives you and your students have for learning, and consider how student leadership can help address these needs. In addition, as you think about the family-type environment Vince created at ISKL, think about the ways you might develop a similar atmosphere and whether any of Vince's approaches could work for you and your students.

Chapter 4 went into the important role a music teacher plays in setting up student leadership opportunities.[5] Vince actively works with students on their leadership, including helping them understand what makes a good leader and promoting the belief that leadership is service. Service, or servant leadership, focuses on the idea that student leaders are helping their peers in some capacity.[6] Vince expanded leadership from orchestra council to include section leaders and additional students on ad-hoc committees to help with specific projects. How do you structure leadership in your music program and how is it related to service?

Vince also guides students toward leadership opportunities to heighten ownership of their learning in the orchestra ensembles at ISKL. Increased ownership is an important part of leadership and can help make learning more efficient because students take on greater responsibility in making decisions in rehearsals.[7] Vince teaches his students that leadership includes considering how you make other people feel, and this concern is an important aspect of developing respect as a leader. This aligns with aspects of Chapter 4, where you learned that students must be willing to admit what they know and do not know (authenticity) and be willing to share power and take risks when engaged in leadership (vulnerability).[8] Reflect on how you use the concepts of authenticity and vulnerability with your students when developing their leadership.

Leadership and reflection

Reflection is an important responsibility of student leadership. After learning how to learn, it is important to think about what went well and what did not go well during peer mentoring,[9] for example. Vince realizes the importance of student reflection and uses reflection-on-action,[10] asking his students to write an individual, one-page online assessment to be shared by him and his students so they can determine how an activity went. Vince also uses reflection-in-action,[11] where the students engage in critical listening to determine how they perform in rehearsals and concerts. Reflecting on peer mentoring and leadership is important; it provides a basis for students to take initiative in their learning. For example, Vince's students began taking the initiative for their learning by coming up with their "String Fling," where they perform solo and ensemble pieces to help elevate performance quality. Other students ran rehearsals with Vince as a facilitator. Vince views these initiatives as opportunities for students to gain confidence that they can take responsibility for their learning, which will ultimately lead them toward participating in music into adulthood. Peer mentoring, therefore, becomes a conduit for lifelong participation in music. In addition, Vince considers peer mentoring a mechanism for teaching students to learn how to interact with each other and how to make a lot of mistakes and grow from them. Think about the key moments in your teaching experience when you allowed students to lead learning, and how you helped them to reflect on any disappointments that may have occurred. While doing so, consider ways you can enable reflection-in-action and reflection-on-action with your students. How does Vince's experience provide insights into additional ways you can prepare student leaders to assume responsibility for their learning in your music classroom?

For Vince and his students, reflection plays an important part in the learning process, and it provides the basis for successful student leadership and peer mentoring experiences, both of which are intertwined in the orchestra program. Vince maintains an active role working with students to select members of the orchestra council, giving students space to create opportunities for learning and guiding them through the process of reflecting on their leadership and mentoring. Vince believes the interactions embedded in student leadership and peer mentoring are the gateway for his students to learn how to work with people into their adult years.

Notes

1. Margaret Wheatley, *Leadership and the New Science: Learning about Organization from an Orderly Universe* (San Francisco, CA: Berrett-Koehler Publishers, Inc., 1994).
2. Vincent Cee, "Christopher Small and Music Education, 1977–2007" (PhD dissertation, University of Massachusetts Amherst, 2008), ProQuest (AAT 3336978).
3. During the interview, Vince jokingly stated—but with a hint of seriousness—that his chapter should be called "Leadership and Mentorship Through Mistakes."
4. Daniel Coyle, *The Culture Code: The Secrets of Highly Successful Groups* (New York: Bantam, 2018).
5. Christa Kiersch and Janet Peters, "Leadership from the Inside Out: Student Leadership Development within Authentic Leadership and Servant Leadership Frameworks," *Journal of Leadership Education* 16, no. 1 (2017): 148–168, https://doi.org/10.12806/V16/I1/T4.
6. Kiersch and Peters, "Leadership."
7. Carol A. Mullen, *Mentorship Primer* (New York: Peter Lang, 2005).
8. Chandni Navalka et al., "Putting Collaborative Leadership into Practice," *Parks Stewardship Forum* 37, no. 2 (2021): 316–324, https://doi.org/10.5070/P537253237.
9. Ian Hay and Neil Dempster, "Student Leadership Development through General Classroom Activities," in *Educating: Weaving Research into Practice* (Southport: Griffith University, 2004), http://hdl.handle.net/10072/2080.
10. Donald A. Schön, *Educating the Reflective Practitioner: Toward a New Design for Teaching and Learning in the Professions* (San Francisco, CA: Jossey Bass, 1987).
11. Schön, *Educating the Reflective Practitioner*.

Blended progression
Peer mentoring and student leadership

This book explores ways music teachers and their students together engage in peer mentoring and student leadership and create opportunities for meaningful learning in the music classroom and ensemble. Part I shares observations about the nature of peer mentoring and student leadership, including an explanation of the role of the student and the importance of brave spaces in the development of meaningful learning. Depending on the objectives for that learning, peer mentoring and student leadership structures are flexible in terms of whether they occur before, during, or after class or rehearsals.

The organic processes of peer mentoring and student leadership

Part II provides snapshots of how the method works in the classrooms of Dana, Kara, Sharon, and Vince, who chronicle their experiences with, and their passion for, peer mentoring and student leadership in their music programs. The narrative of these four professionals likely resonates with you as you reflect on how you structure peer mentoring and student leadership with your students. You may even have nodded your head in acknowledgment as you read about the amount of time these four invested in creating, implementing, and sustaining peer mentoring and nurturing student leadership. Yet, Dana, Kara, Sharon, and Vince developed peer mentoring and student leadership depending upon the learning needs of their students. Sharon, for example, stressed that peer mentoring and student leadership do not just happen; you have to work at it. She also argued you have to trust the process and trust yourself and your students as well. As their stories reveal, the extra time spent developing peer mentoring and student leadership has paid dividends for Dana, Kara, Sharon, and Vince, and they are the first to admit it. As a result of their thoughtful effort and planning, their students have assumed greater responsibility for their learning. Although Dana, Kara, Sharon, and Vince are only four in number, they provide some common experiences in developing peer mentoring and student leadership that you may find

Blended progression: Peer mentoring and student leadership 183

helpful in your own music classes and ensembles. An important takeaway from reading about their programs is that they and their students create peer mentoring and student leadership opportunities depending upon what is needed at the time. An organic process, it pivots on what the particular learning needs of students are at any given moment.

Peer mentoring is student leadership

By way of peer mentoring and student leadership, Dana, Kara, Sharon, Vince, and their students were able to make learning more interesting and productive in their music classes and ensembles. A first step for all four of them involved figuring out what their students already knew. Kara, for example, used emotional tri-fold experiences and exit surveys, while Sharon met with her students. Dana tapped into what his students had already learned about playing samba and then had them pass it on and mentor the beginner students, and Vince used orchestra council to get a sense of what knowledge his students already had. Once Dana, Kara, Sharon, and Vince had a good understanding of what their students knew, they consistently and carefully monitored how their students shared this information in sessions of peer mentoring and student leadership. Think about how you determine what knowledge your students have, and compare how you go about doing so with how Dana, Kara, Sharon, and Vince figure out what their students know. Their stories will hopefully provide you with some additional insights into understanding what knowledge your students bring to the music class and ensemble.

In some cases, modeling was also an important tool for helping students navigate the process of peer mentoring. Sharon used a do-this/don't-do-that approach as she demonstrated to her students how they should interact with each other. For her, the importance of guiding students toward good behavior was a priority. Dana's modeling replicated how samba is learned in samba schools in Rio de Janeiro, demonstrated particularly when he called on student conductors to help lead the samba class. Modeling in peer mentoring, then, can partner in teaching a process or serve as a template in structure. For example, you and your students can engage in modeling during music class or ensemble rehearsals to teach the process of how to be a mentor and mentee, but peer mentoring and leadership can also be structured—as in Dana's case—based upon how a musical style is originally learned.

Each of the four music teachers played an active role in developing student leadership. Dana worked with students on their conducting skills, showing them what hand signals to use to call the next rhythm and how to lead warm-ups, rehearsals, and performances. Kara carefully designed leadership opportunities for older students to help younger students. With the goal of giving all students a voice in the learning process, she also paid close attention to diversity and inclusion; one of her activities had her students teach their classmates a new song that they had selected. Sharon was more informal in her approach: She selected student leaders based on her observations of how students interacted with each other during rehearsals. Vince initially created an orchestra council to encourage student leadership in the orchestra program, but as students eventually assumed more ownership of their learning, he was able to move into the role of facilitator. Student leadership in these examples grew out of an implicit partnership with Dana, Kara, Sharon, or Vince, who shared the responsibility for what went on in their classes and ensembles with their students. As you ponder how Dana, Kara, Sharon, and Vince developed and maintained student leadership in their music programs, think about how you may be able to use any of their strategies with your students.

Despite their individual and unique ways of developing leadership, all four teachers stressed the importance of treating all students as potential leaders, reminding the reader that leadership is a fluid process, where a student at times can take the lead and at other times sit back and be led. An interesting aside about student leadership is noted by Dana, Kara, Sharon, and Vince, where they observe that sometimes the best musicians do not make the best student leaders. Therefore, modeling and then monitoring how students interact with each other are critical in developing student leaders. While leadership also provides opportunities for all students to have a voice in the learning process—as illustrated when Dana and his students selected female student leaders for the samba ensembles—Dana, Kara, Sharon, and Vince all emphasized that learning in music provides multiple chances for everyone to be a leader. These possibilities might include participation in a learning activity in a music class, or leading an ensemble, or demonstrating proper verbal and nonverbal behaviors, or even developing finesse in communicating with the music teacher.

Regardless of the positive outcomes for peer mentoring and student leadership, the process itself was not always easy for Dana, Kara, Sharon, and Vince. Dana noted how peer mentoring is noisy due to the verbal interactions occurring while the students are making music. Kara and Sharon admitted that behavioral issues do occur, and Sharon made the point that not all students react well to mentoring or being mentored. Vince found that student goals for leadership were at times unrealistic, such as students wanting to help lead their peers toward performing repertoire above the skill level of everyone in the orchestra. Despite these issues, when Dana, Kara, Sharon, and Vince noted how quickly and efficiently their students learned from each other, they were once again convinced of the consequential benefits of peer mentoring and student leadership. What the teacher–student partnerships had produced were classrooms and ensembles rich in meaningful learning experiences.

Throughout the book, peer mentoring is linked to student leadership. Based on the stories of these four teachers practicing in the field, peer mentoring and student leadership are *blended* together so that peer mentoring *is* student leadership. Furthermore, it is the music teacher and the student, who together develop opportunities to partner in delivering knowledge and sharing experiences for meaningful learning. Imagine how with your guidance and encouragement, students might become leaders and share the responsibility for explaining musical concepts, modeling good tone, engaging in proper behavior, or even demonstrating their willingness and enthusiasm for learning new knowledge from their peers. Chapter 4 portrayed how student leadership can help increase student participation in learning, how it can help new students become acquainted with program expectations and traditions, how it can support classroom management, and how it can help with team building. Peer mentoring and student leadership can motivate music classes and ensembles to perform beyond their musical objectives when producing some type of musical *product*, and for Dana, Kara, Sharon, and Vince, the *process* of peer mentoring and student leadership remains a most important aspect of learning and plays a major role in developing a community of learners.

Developing a community of learners

Through the process of peer mentoring and student leadership described in Part II, learning expanded beyond musical objectives and ultimately helped establish a community of learners—learners who valued and supported each other in the learning process. For Dana, Kara, Sharon, and Vince, peer mentoring and student leadership played a pivotal role in preparing students to interact with each other in class and rehearsal. Moreover, they predict that peer mentoring and student leadership would prepare students for adult interactions in the future as well. In Dana's samba classes, for example, peer mentoring and student leadership helped students understand that music is not only a high school activity; it can also be a lifelong endeavor. This fact was evidenced by the alumni who return to campus to participate in the samba classes. For Kara, peer mentoring and student leadership helped develop a community of learners—students who supported each other, helped each other increase their knowledge about the subject, and encouraged them to use the skills that Kara considered important for good adult interactions. Sharon expressed a similar viewpoint; for her, peer mentoring and student leadership taught students life skills they could draw upon when working with future colleagues. Vince hoped that peer mentoring and student leadership would provide his students with the skills to be successful and also to continue making music for the rest of their lives. Peer mentoring and student leadership have multiple benefits then. In the moment they help students feel supported and needed, and in the long term, they help students interact with others when they are adults and encourage lifelong participation in music.

Looking forward

As educational professionals continue to find and implement improved, innovative ways to deliver instruction, teaching and learning practices are also recast by this change. Organizations that influence music curricula, like CMP, Arts PROPEL, and Partnership for 21st Century Learning, as well as the National Core Arts Standards, emphasize the importance of student-centered learning. In addition, student-centered learning is a driver of SEL, which influences the curricula and teaching practices in many schools. Furthermore, music teachers in the field use their own approaches to student-centered learning in their school music programs, and at the core of these innovative approaches are peer mentoring and student leadership.

As student-centered learning practices continue to be the focus, music teachers will continue to use peer mentoring, for they recognize it to be an effective instrument for classroom instruction as well as providing a supportive environment for learning. Tangential benefits include preparation of students for future adult interactions as well as nurturing the desire for their lifelong participation in music. Researchers will continue to study peer mentoring and student leadership, and more stories from music teachers will circulate, relating how they connect peer mentoring in school music programs with how musicians mentor each other when learning a musical style, such as was revealed in Dana's story. Through these experiences, music teachers will develop new ways of thinking about peer mentoring and student leadership in a holistic way as they move forward in a *progression* of their ways of using these instructional techniques. Their stories will continue to inspire even deeper connections to learning for both them and their students.

As music education continues to evolve, teachers will discover new ways to co-create brave spaces for learning so that all students are able to contribute their voices to meaningful learning in the music class and ensemble. This book has discussed ways peer mentoring and student leadership provide opportunities for all students to engage in meaningful learning experiences where everyone's voice is valued. Learning that focuses on diversity and inclusion is gaining momentum in school music programs. For example, the Southern Poverty Law Center recently implemented new Social Justice Standards for teaching that address IDJA. As Chapter 2 points out, however, you need to be aware of power relationships that can occur between you and your students and between students themselves when using peer mentoring. You can destabilize these power structures by monitoring student interactions, modeling how to engage in peer mentoring, and continually emphasizing the value of all student voices. As you work with students, you also need to be careful to avoid reaffirming dominant power structures in your role as the music teacher by simply giving permission to marginalized students to engage in peer mentoring. And even though you have the best of intentions, you may end up othering students, where marginalized students are labeled as being deficient in some way. This is where co-creating brave spaces provides a space for learning, where you and your students can not only engage in peer mentoring for elevating comprehension of subject matter but also engage in dialogue to counter prejudice, homophobia, bias, and racism. Through these activities during peer mentoring and student leadership, all students will then have a voice in contributing to meaningful learning in the music class and ensemble.

The *blended progression* of peer mentoring and student leadership, in conjunction with diversity, equity, inclusion, and access, not only establishes a foundation for learning musical objectives but to also go beyond these objectives to provide the cornerstone of a learning community. In a successful community of learners, all student contributions are valued, where they help with creating and participating in exciting learning opportunities. And as these opportunities turn into classroom practice, the ideas of inclusion and engaging in anti-racism communication, for example, become expected. One of the best outcomes is that everyone, even the teacher, becomes a learner. You learn from your students, and they learn from you and from their peers. Learning then becomes transformational as you and your students develop deeper connections to learning about music and also establish stronger connections to each other.

The future of peer mentoring and student leadership, then, is how you and your students co-create learning opportunities so that everyone, including you, elevate their learning in the music classroom. Ultimately, the future of peer mentoring and student leadership is up to you and your students. Working together, you and your learning community can co-create meaningful learning opportunities in your own classes and ensembles for a blended progression of peer mentoring and student leadership, and transform how learning occurs to ensure that all voices are valued in the process.

Appendix
Methods

Methods

The majority of content in Chapters 1–4 is based in research on peer mentoring and student leadership in the fields of music education and education. The quick tips in Chapters 1–4 and the narrative portraits in Chapters 5–8, however, are based on new data collected for this book. In this Appendix, I describe the methods used to generate data for the quick tips and the narrative portraits. Because the narrative portraits required in-depth interviews combined with data analysis, I conducted those interviews first. Once the data were collected, analyzed, and drafted into complete chapters, I then conducted interviews for the quick tips and incorporated those data into Chapters 1–4. To portray how I generated data for the quick tips and narrative portraits, I present the methods procedures in chronological order.

Narrative portraits

I used narrative inquiry as the research design to help me construct the narrative portraits in Chapters 5–8. A primary component of narrative inquiry is telling stories of the participants and sharing their lived experiences for the reader.[1] I sought to tell the stories of the participants by portraying their experiences using peer mentoring and student leadership. Narrative inquiry provided a way for me to not only discover their successes using peer mentoring and student leadership but to also portray the issues they encountered when using these instructional techniques. Through narrative inquiry, then, I not only wanted to portray an in-depth comprehensive portrait of each participant and how they used peer mentoring and student leadership but to also provide a breadth of experiences across Chapters 5–8 with all four of their stories.

In the participants' stories, I sought to discover information that supported and related to key concepts and practices about peer mentoring and student leadership in Chapters 1–4. In addition, narrative inquiry "provides a means to re-conceptualize the ways in which we think about . . .

music education."[2] Thus, I also sought information from the participants that would portray new ways of thinking about peer mentoring and student leadership to not only help music teachers enhance learning in their music classes and ensembles but to also add to the general body of knowledge on research in peer mentoring and student leadership.

Participant selection

I sought participants whom I knew used peer mentoring and student leadership in their teaching and who would also have a lot to say about their experiences. I used purposeful sampling to select the participants. Purposeful sampling provided a way for me to "select information-rich cases"[3] to portray the participants' stories with how they use peer mentoring and student leadership in their music programs. I developed a set of criteria to select participants so their portraits would provide information-rich stories about their experiences with peer mentoring and student leadership. Criteria for selection included race, gender, and geography, in addition to diversity of teaching experiences and grade levels of students. The criteria provided me with an opportunity to select participants for whom I could portray the multi-dimensional ways they used peer mentoring and student leadership.

I contacted potential participants via email and included a consent form along with the interview questions. The consent form included information that described the scope of the book; the interview process and what to expect; and spaces for them to sign their consent to use their real names, teaching positions, and names of their schools. I attached the interview questions so the participants could make a well-informed decision about their participation. In the body of the email, I asked potential participants if they would be interested in participating in an interview for this book and to also let me know if they had any questions. I originally intended to observe these participants in person, but due to the COVID-19 pandemic I ended up focusing solely on conducting interviews. The four participants I contacted all agreed to an interview and consented to using their real names, teaching positions, and locations.

Participants

The participants represent a diverse array of experiences with using peer mentoring and student leadership. Participants included Dana Monteiro, a high school music teacher of samba ensembles at the Frederick Douglass Academy in Harlem, New York; Kara Ireland D'Ambrosio, a TK–eighth-grade general music teacher and choir director on the west side of Bay Area Peninsula, California; Sharon Phipps, a middle school band director in Boxford, Massachusetts; and Vince Cee, a middle school and high school orchestra director at the ISKL, Malaysia. Together, the four participants teach across a broad range of grade levels (TK–12th grade), music classes and ensembles (general music, choir, samba ensembles, band, and orchestra), and geographic location (New York, Massachusetts, California, and Malaysia).

Interviews

I conducted a formal interview of each participant using an open-ended interview protocol. The open-ended protocol included a set of sample interview questions, but it allowed me the flexibility to pursue lines of inquiry and ask additional questions based upon the responses of the participants.[4] I designed the interview questions to help me explore and ultimately construct a comprehensive portrait of how they use peer mentoring and student leadership in their school music programs. I also wanted to explore their musical backgrounds and early experiences with peer mentoring and student leadership to discover how and when they began using these instructional techniques in their teaching. I conducted interviews using Zoom, and they ranged in length from 1.5 to 2 hours. I recorded the interviews using the recording function on Zoom, and I also used my iPhone as a backup audio recording device. Once I had a link to the Zoom recording emailed to me, I forwarded the link to my research assistant, Grace Bybell, at Boston University. Grace transcribed the interviews within two weeks and uploaded them into a shared folder in OneDrive in Microsoft Outlook. I then downloaded the transcripts and begin data analysis.

Data analysis

The first step in data analysis involved focusing on one transcript at a time. I read through the transcript to re-orient myself with the participant's responses, and I began looking for any patterns that reflected peer mentoring and student leadership. I then began to code the data using a system of two-to-four letter codes that aided me with organizing the data.[5] I coded the data directly in the Word document and highlighted codes in the text in red bold font for ease of identification. I used Dewey's framework of sharing knowledge and experiences[6] as a basis for identifying codes (e.g., SK=Sharing Knowledge). During this stage, I revisited the content of Chapters 1–4 to devise additional codes related to peer mentoring (e.g., R=Reflection) to aid with aligning the portraits of the participants with content in Chapters 1–4. During this process, I also coded data that reflected new information to the field of peer mentoring and student leadership (e.g., PM:LL=Peer Mentoring: Lifelong Learning). As I continued to code the data, I began to develop sub-codes within each category of codes (e.g., SI:SL=Student Input: Student Leadership) under the primary code of "L=Leadership." As the data coding progressed, I developed a master code list for each participant. The master code list helped me with organizing the data.[7] I continued to analyze each transcript separately, for I was interested in portraying the uniqueness of each participant's story. When I concluded my first pass through the data and developed a master code list, I went back through the transcript and conducted another sweep through the data to see if any codes were no longer relevant, if there were any contradicting examples, or if any new codes developed. Once I considered the master code list complete, I then reviewed the codes again and began to develop them into themes unique to each participant. Once the themes were developed, I then created an outline and began writing the chapter. I focused on one portrait at a time. Once I had a solid draft of the chapter, I then repeated this process with the next participant.

Reliability

To establish reliability of each chapter, I conducted member checks and peer review. In their interviews, all four of the participants accepted my offer to review a draft of their respective chapter. To conduct the member check, I emailed the chapter to each participant for review. The participants responded within one week to my email request for a member check, and all four of them provided feedback. Feedback ranged from Vince identifying a misspelled word to Dana clarifying some details about his background as a trumpet player, to Kara revising sections of the chapter. Once I implemented the feedback from the participants, I began to write the questions for discussion and reflection at the end of each chapter. I continued to revise each chapter, and during this stage I asked two colleagues of mine to review the chapters as peer reviewers. I tasked them with making sure the writing was engaging, that ideas flowed well from one to the next, and that the writing aligned with narrative inquiry. They provided minor suggestions that I incorporated into subsequent drafts of each chapter.

Quick tips

The quick tips were designed to help "bring to life" the content in Chapters 1–4 to make the information more relevant and easily accessible for in-service and preservice music teachers. Similar to the narrative portraits, I used narrative inquiry as the basis for conducting interviews for the quick tips. With these interviews, however, my goal was not to share stories of the lived experiences of the participants but rather portray brief examples of helpful advice for in-service and preservice music teachers to illuminate potential ways to use peer mentoring and student leadership in school music programs.

Appendix: Methods

Participant selection

While I conducted interviews for the narrative portraits, I began to select participants for the quick tips found in Chapters 1–4. I utilized snowball sampling to select participants.[8] Snowball sampling is a process where a potential participant is asked about peer mentoring, who then recommends other participants, who then recommends additional participants.[9] Criteria for selection included music teachers who used peer mentoring and student leadership, geographic location, and who taught in K–12 grade levels with a variety of music classes and ensembles. I also sought diversity in terms of race, ethnicity, gender, and sexual identity. The criteria aided me with selecting participants who provided a comprehensive portrait of peer mentoring and student leadership in K–12 music education. I began this process by contacting a couple of music teachers I knew who used peer mentoring. When doing so, I asked them if they knew music teachers who used peer mentoring as well. They emailed their peers, gave them my email address, and told them to email me if interested. I received several responses, and I continued to email music teachers I knew who used peer mentoring. When I emailed the music teachers, I included a consent form that explained what the book was about and information about the interview process. I also included the interview questions, which were a different set of questions from the ones used for the narrative portraits.

Participants

Ultimately, ten music teachers agreed to be interviewed for this book project and consented to using their real names, teaching positions, and locations. They included Esteban Adame, Band Director, Artesia High School, Lakewood, CA; Tiffany Unarce Barry, former Music Teacher at Steindorf K–8 STEAM School, San Jose, CA, and now current Professor of Music Education at San Jose State University, San Jose, CA; David Cosby, Department Chair of Music, Besant Hill School, Ojai, CA; Troy Davis, former Band and Jazz Band Director at Aragon High School, San Mateo, CA, and now Director of Instrumental Music and Jazz Studies at West Valley College, Saratoga, CA; Gary Gillett, retired Band Director at Sentinel High School, Missoula, MT; Warren Gramm, former Music Teacher in Jersey City Public Schools, NJ, and now current Assistant Professor of Music Education at Lebanon Valley College, Annville, PA; Helene Grotans, Band, Orchestra, and Choir Director at Borel Middle School, San Mateo, CA; Terri Knight, TK through fifth-grade general music, band, and orchestra at Greenbrook Elementary and Twin Creeks Elementary, San Ramon Valley Unified School District, CA; Allison Lacasse, Band Director, Belmont High School, Belmont, MA; and Lieven Smart, Music Teacher Grades 6–8 at Junction Avenue K–8 School, Livermore, CA.

Interviews

Although I used a different set of interview questions for this group of participants, the protocols were similar to the procedures I used for interviewing participants for the narrative portraits. I conducted a formal interview of each participant using an open-ended interview protocol. The open-ended protocol included a set of sample interview questions, but it also allowed me the flexibility to pursue lines of inquiry and ask additional questions based upon the responses of the participants.[10] I designed the interview questions to reflect the research on peer mentoring and student leadership used to construct Chapters 1–4 so that I could provide real-life examples to supplement the content in these chapters. I sought to explore how each participant used peer mentoring and student leadership in their music programs. Interviews ranged from 30 minutes to one hour and occurred via Zoom. I recorded the interviews using the recording function on Zoom and also used my iPhone as a backup audio recording device. Once I had a link to the Zoom recording emailed to me, I forwarded the link to my research assistant, Grace Bybell, at Boston University. Grace transcribed the interviews within one month and uploaded them into a shared folder in OneDrive in Microsoft Outlook. I then downloaded the transcripts and began data analysis.

Data analysis

I read the transcripts to re-orient myself with what the participants said in their interviews. While doing so, I looked for statements that related to content in Chapters 1–4. I extracted these statements out of the interview transcripts and created a separate Word document. Once I compiled all the potential quick tips together in the Word document, I then read through them again to determine which quotes were the most suitable for inclusion; I sought quotes that most directly related to the content in Chapters 1–4. To aid with this endeavor, I created a chart of how many quotes from each participant were being considered and in which chapter I was thinking of placing them. In an effort to use a similar amount of quotes from each participant, I trimmed down the number of quotes until I settled on 26 quick tips from ten participants in Chapters 1–4. During this process, I conducted minor edits for ease of reading and grammatical structure.

Reliability

Once I selected which quick tips I would include in the book, I emailed them as an attachment in a Word document to the respective participants who reviewed their quick tips for accuracy. Participants responded quickly and provided suggestions, including edits for grammar, sentence structure, and overall clarity of the quote. In some instances, I sent the revised quick tips back for additional review to make sure the participant was comfortable with it. Once the participants were satisfied with their quick tips, I then inserted them into the book.

Notes

1. Jean D. Clandinin, "Embodied Narrative Inquiry: A Methodology of Connection," *Research Studies in Music Education* 27, no. 1 (2006): 44–54, https://doi.org/10.1177/1321103X0602700110301.
2. Margaret S. Barrett and Sandra Stauffer, "Introduction," in *Narrative Inquiry in Music Education: Troubling Certainty*, ed. Margaret Barrett and Sandra Stauffer (New York: Springer, 2009), 1.
3. Michael Q. Patton, *Qualitative Research and Evaluation Methods* (Thousand Oaks, CA: SAGE, 2002), 42.
4. John W. Creswell and Cheryl N. Poth, *Qualitative Inquiry and Research Design: Choosing Among Five Traditions* (Thousand Oaks, CA: SAGE), 2017.
5. Corrine Glesne, *Becoming Qualitative Researchers: An Introduction* (Upper Saddle River, NJ: Pearson, 2016).
6. John Dewey, *Experience and Education* (New York: Collier, 1938).
7. Glesne, *Qualitative Researchers*.
8. Creswell and Poth, *Qualitative Inquiry*.
9. Patton, *Qualitative Research*.
10. Creswell and Poth, *Qualitative Inquiry*.

Bibliography

Abrahams, Frank. "The Application of Critical Pedagogy to Music Teaching and Learning: A Literature Review," *Update: Applications of Research in Music Education* 23, no. 2 (2005): 12–22. https://doi.org/10.1177/87551233050230020103.

Aderibigbe, Semiyu, Djonde Frega Antiado, and Annaliza Sta Anna. "Issues in Peer Mentoring for Undergraduate Students in a Private University in the United Arab Emirates," *International Journal of Evidence Based Coaching and Mentoring* 13, no. 2 (2015): 65–80. https://radar.brookes.ac.uk/radar/items/1641d9e8-3d45-424b-8f50-6b0096075df0/1/.

Alexander, Lucille, and Laura G. Dorow. "Peer Tutoring Effects on the Music Performance of Tutors and Tutees in Beginning Band Classes," *Journal of Research in Music Education* 31, no. 1 (1983): 33–47. https://doi.org/10.2307/3345108.

Allen, Scott J., and Nathan S. Hartman. "Sources of Learning in Student Leadership Development Programming," *Journal of Leadership Studies* 3, no. 3 (2009): 6–16. https://doi:10.1002/jls.20119.

Allen, Tammy, Stacy McManus, and Joyce Russell. "Newcomer Socialization and Stress: Formal Relationships as a Source of Support," *Journal of Vocational Behavior* 54 (1999): 453–470. https://doi.org/10.1006/jvbe.1998.1674.

Arao, Brian, and Kristi Clemens. "From Safe Spaces to Brave Spaces: A New Way to Frame Dialogue Around Diversity and Social Justice." In *The Art of Effective Facilitation: Reflections from Social Justice Educators*, edited Lisa M. Landreman, 135–150. Sterling: Stylus Publishing, 2013.

Bandura, Albert. "Social Cognitive Theory." In *Annals of Child Development*, edited by Ross Vasta, 1–60. Greenwich, CT: JAI Press, 1989.

Barrett, Margaret S., and Sandra Stauffer. "Introduction." In *Narrative Inquiry in Music Education: Troubling Certainty*, edited by Margaret Barrett and Sandra Stauffer, 1–6. New York: Springer, 2009.

Bierema, Laura, and Sharan B. Merriam. "E-Mentoring: Using Computer Mediated Communication to Enhance the Mentoring Process," *Innovative Higher Education* 26, no. 3 (2002): 211–228. https://link.springer.com/content/pdf/10.1023/A:1017921023103.pdf.

Björck, Cecilia. "A Music Room of One's Own: Discursive Constructions of Girls-Only Spaces for Learning Popular Music," *Girlhood Studies* 6, no. 2 (2013): 11–29. https://doi.org/10.3167/ghs.2013.060203.

Boat, Mary B., Laurie A. Dinnebeil, and Youlmi Bae. "Individualizing Instruction in Preschool Classrooms," *Dimensions of Early Childhood* 38, no. 1 (2010):

3–11. www.jcsicsa.ir/article_85708_66c5d66c5a0798df29d8296d54c273e9.pdf.

Borrero, Noah, Christine Yeh, Crivir Cruz, and Jolene Suda. "School as a Context for "Othering" Youth and Promoting Cultural Assets," *Teachers College Record* 114, no. 2 (2012): 1–37. https://doi.pdf/10.1177/016146811211400207.

Boud, David. "Using Journal Writing to Enhance Reflective Practice," *New Directions for Adult and Continuing Education* 2001, no. 90 (2001): 9–17. https://doi.org/10.1002/ace.16.

Bozeman, Barry, and Mary Kay Feeney. "Toward a Useful Theory of Mentoring: A Conceptual Analysis and Critique," *Administration and Society* 39, no. 6 (2007): 719–739. https://doi.org/10.1177/0095399707304119.

Bradley, Deborah. "The Sounds of Silence: Talking Race in Music Education," *Action, Criticism, and Theory for Music Education* 6, no. 4 (2007): 132–162. http://act.maydaygroup.org/articles/Bradley6_4.pdf.

Bradley, Deborah. "Hidden in Plain Sight: Race and Racism in Music Education." In *The Oxford Handbook of Social Justice and Music Education*, edited by Cathy Benedict, Patrick Schmidt, Gary Spruce, and Paul Woodford, 190–203. New York: Oxford University Press, 2015.

Bruffee, Kenneth. "Sharing Our Toys: Cooperative Learning Versus Collaborative Learning," *Change: The Magazine of Higher Learning* 27, no. 1 (1995): 12–18. www.jstor.org/stable/40165162.

Byrne, Kathryn. "The Give and Take of Peer Review: Utilizing Modeling and Imitation." PhD dissertation, Kent State University, 2015. https://rave.ohiolink.edu/etdc/view?acc_num=kent1438036070.

Canales, Mary. "Othering: Toward an Understanding of Difference," *Advances in Nursing Science* 22, no. 4 (2000): 16–31. https://journals.lww.com/advances-innursingscience/Fulltext/2000/06000/Othering_Toward_an_Understanding_of_Difference.3.aspx.

Carter, Erik W., Jennifer Asmus, Colleen K. Moss, Molly Cooney, Katie Weir, Lori Vincent, Tiffany Born, Julia Hochman, Kristen Bottema-Beutel, and Ethan Fesperman. "Peer Network Strategies to Foster Social Connections among Adolescents with and without Severe Disabilities," *Exceptional Children* 46, no. 2 (2013): 51–59. https://doi.org/10.1177/004005991304600206.

Cavallaro, Francesco, and Kenneth Tan. "Computer-Mediated Peer-to-Peer Mentoring," *Association for the Advancement of Computing in Education Journal* 14, no. 2 (2006): 129–138. www.learntechlib.org/primary/p/6219/.

Cawley, John, Linda Cisek-Gillman, Rob Roberts, Carolyn Cocotas, Tieshka Smith-Cook, Michelle Bouchard, and Mehmet Oz. "Effect of HealthCorps, a High School Peer Mentoring Program, on Youth Diet and Physical Activity," *Childhood Obesity* 7, no. 5 (2011): 364–371. https://doi.org/10.1089/chi.2011.0022.

Cayari, Christopher. "Demystifying Trans*+ Voice Education: The Transgender Singing Voice Conference," *International Journal of Music Education* 37, no. 1 (2019): 118–131. https://doi.org/10.1177/0255761418814577.

Cee, Vincent. "Christopher Small and Music Education, 1977–2007." PhD dissertation, University of Massachusetts Amherst, 2008. ProQuest (AAT3336978).

Chao, Georgia T., Howard J. Klein, and Philip D. Gardner. "Organizational Socialization: Its Content and Consequences," *Journal of Applied Psychology* 79, no. 5 (1994): 730–743. https://doi.10.1037/0021-9010.79.5.730.

Chavous, Tabbye, Derborah Rivas-Drake, Ciara Smalls, Tiffany Griffin, and Courtney Cogburn. "Gender Matters, Too: The Influences of School Racial Discrimination and Racial Identity on Academic Engagement Outcomes among African American Adolescents," *Developmental Psychology* 44, no. 3 (2008): 637–654. https://doi.org/10.1037/0012-1649.44.3.637.

Clandinin, Jean D. "Embodied Narrative Inquiry: A Methodology of Connection," *Research Studies in Music Education* 27, no. 1 (2006): 44–54. https://doi.org/10.1177/1321103X0602700110301.

Coeyman, Barbara. "Applications of Feminist Pedagogy to the College Music Major Curriculum: An Introduction to Issues," *College Music Symposium* 36 (1996): 73–90. www.jstor.org/stable/40374285.

Colvin, Janet W., and Marinda Ashman. "Roles, Risks, and Benefits of Peer Mentoring Relationships in Higher Education," *Mentoring & Tutoring: Partnership in Learning* 18, no. 2 (2010): 121–134. https://doi.org/10.1080/13611261003678879.

Coppock, Vicki. "Children as Peer Researchers: Reflections on a Journey of Mutual Discovery," *Children & Society* 25, no. 6 (2001): 435–446. https://doi.org/10.1111/j.1099-0860.2010.00296.x.

Corbitt, Benjamin J. "A Qualitative Exploration of Schools with Gay-Straight Alliances as Learning Environments for LGBTQ Students." PhD dissertation, California State University, Long Beach, 2016. ProQuest (AAT10076450).

Coyle, Daniel. *The Culture Code: The Secrets of Highly Successful Groups*. New York: Bantam, 2018.

Creswell, John W., and Cheryl N. Poth. *Qualitative Inquiry and Research Design: Choosing Among Five Traditions*. Thousand Oaks, CA: SAGE, 2017.

Crozier, Gill, Penny Jane Burke, and Louise Archer. "Peer Relations in Higher Education: Raced, Classed and Gendered Constructions and Othering," *Whiteness and Education* 1, no. 1 (2016): 39–53. http://dx.doi.org/10.1080/23793406.2016.1164746.

D'Ambrosio, Kara Elizabeth Ireland. "The California Music Project Teacher Training Program as an Intervention in Poverty and Income Equality." DMA dissertation, Boston University, 2015. ProQuest (AAT3686092).

d'Arripe-Longueville, Fabiennne, and Christophe Gernigon. "Peer-Assisted Learning in the Physical Activity Domain: Dyad Type and Gender Differences," *Journal of Sport & Exercise Psychology* 24, no. 3 (2002): 219–238. https://doi.org/10.1123/jsep.24.3.219.

Darrow, Alice-Ann, Pamela Gibbs, and Sarah Wedel. "Use of Classwide Peer Tutoring in the General Music Classroom," *Update: Applications of Research in Music Education* 24, no. 1 (2005): 15–26. https://doi.org/10.1177/87551233050240010103.

Dennison, Susan. "A Win-Win Peer Mentoring and Tutoring Program: A Collaborative Model," *The Journal of Primary Prevention* 20, no. 3 (2000): 161–174. https://doi.org/10.1023/A:1021385817106.

Dewey, John. *Experience and Education*. New York: Collier, 1938.

Doke, David. "Collaborative Learning among High School Students in an Alternative Styles Strings Ensemble." DMA dissertation, Boston University, 2020. ProQuest (AAT27955823).

Durst, Russel K. *Collision Course: Conflict, Negotiation, and Learning in College Composition*. Urbana, IL: National Council of Teachers of English, 1999.

Edgar, Scott N. *Music Education and Social Emotional Learning: The Heart of Teaching Music*. Chicago, IL: GIA Publications, 2017.

Ensergueix, Pierre J., and Lucille Lafont. "Reciprocal Peer Tutoring in a Physical Education Setting: Influence of Peer Tutor Training and Gender on Motor Performance and Self-Efficacy Outcomes," *European Journal of Psychology of Education* 25, no. 2 (2010): 222–242. https://doi.org/10.1007/s10212-009-0010-0.

Evans, Sarah, Katie Davis, Abigail Evans, Julie Ann Campbell, David Randall, Kodlee Yin, and Cecilia Aragon. "More Than Peer Production: Fanfiction Communities as Sites of Distributed Mentoring." In *Proceedings of the 2017 ACM Conference on Computer Supported Cooperative Work and Social Computing*, 259–272. https://doi.org/10.1145/2998181.2998342.

Fay, Kaitlyn A. "In Search of Effective Jazz Education: An Analysis and Comparison of Pedagogical Methods Employed by Directors of Successful High School Jazz Ensembles." PhD dissertation, William Patterson University, 2013. ProQuest (AAT1538595).

Feldhusen, John F., and Mary K. Pleiss. "Leadership: A Synthesis of Social Skills, Creativity, and Historical Ability?" *Roper Review* 16, no. 4 (1994): 292–293. https://doi.org/10.1080/02783199409553602.

Fernández-Barros, Andrea, David Duran, and Laia Viladot. "Peer Tutoring in Music Education: A Literature Review," *International Journal of Music Education*, online first (2022): 1–12. https://doi.org/10.1177/02557614221087761.

Fink, L. Dee. *Creating Significant Learning Experiences: An Integrated Approach to Designing College Courses*. San Francisco, CA: Jossey-Bass, 2013.

Fodor, David B. "Critical Moments of Change: A Study of the Social and Musical Interactions of Precollegiate Jazz Combos." PhD dissertation, Northwestern University, 1998. ProQuest (AAT9913792).

Frost, David, and Amanda Roberts. "Student Leadership, Participation and Democracy," *Leading and Managing* 17, no. 2 (2011): 66–84. https://search.informit.org/doi/10.3316/ielapa.318017162668709.

Glesne, Corrine. *Becoming Qualitative Researchers: An Introduction*. Upper Saddle River, NJ: Pearson, 2016.

Goodrich, Andrew. "Peer Mentoring in a High School Jazz Ensemble," *Journal of Research in Music Education* 55, no. 2 (2007): 94–114. https://doi.org/10.1177/002242940705500202.

Goodrich, Andrew. "Utilizing Elements of the Historic Jazz Culture in a High School Setting," *Bulletin of the Council for Research in Music Education* 175 (2008): 11–30. www.jstor.org/stable/40319410.

Goodrich, Andrew. "Peer Mentoring in a University Jazz Ensemble," *Visions of Research in Music Education* 28 (2016). https://opencommons.uconn.edu/vrme/vol28/iss1/7/.

Goodrich, Andrew. "Peer Mentoring and Peer Tutoring Among K-12 Students: A Literature Review," *Update: Applications of Research in Music Education* 36, no. 2 (2018): 13–21. https://doi.org/10.1177/8755123317708765.

Goodrich, Andrew. "The Social Language of Jazz." In *Teaching School Jazz: Perspectives, Principles and Strategies*, edited by Mike Titlebaum and Chad West. New York: Oxford University Press, 2019.

Goodrich, Andrew. "Counterpoint in the Music Classroom: Creating an Environment of Resilience with Peer Mentoring and LGBTQIA+ Students," *International Journal of Music Education* 38, no. 4 (2020): 582–592. https://doi.org/10.1177/0255761420949373.

Goodrich, Andrew. "Peer Mentoring in an Extracurricular Music Class," *International Journal of Music Education* 39, no. 4 (2021a): 410–423. http://doi:10.1177/0255761420988922.

Goodrich, Andrew. "Online Peer Mentoring and Remote Learning," *Music Education Research* 23, no. 2 (2021b): 256–269. https://doi.10.1080/14613808.2021.1898575.

Goodrich, Andrew. "Valuing Racialized Student Voices: Transforming Learning Through Peer Mentoring," *Action, Criticism, and Theory for Music Education* 21, no. 1 (2021c): 142–171. https://doi:10.22176/act21.2.142.

Goodrich, Andrew. "Developing Trust and Empathy Through Peer Mentoring in the Music Classroom." In *The Oxford Handbook of Compassion and Care in Music Education*, edited by Karin S. Hendricks. New York: Oxford University Press, 2023.

Goodrich, Andrew, Elizabeth Bucura, and Sandra Stauffer. "Peer Mentoring in a University Music Methods Class," *Journal of Music Teacher Education* 27, no. 2 (2018): 1–16. https://doi.org/10.1177/1057083717731057.

Goodrich, Andrew, Jon Kracht, Josh McDonald, and Colin Sapp. "Comentoring in a University Jazz Ensemble," *Visions of Research in Music Education* 25 (2014). https://www-usr.rider.edu/~vrme/v25n1/visions/Goodrich_Comentoring_University_Jazz_Ensemble.

Gramm, Warren. "Peer Mentoring in a Modern Band." DMA dissertation, Boston University, 2021. ProQuest (AAT283117250).

Green, Lucy. *How Popular Musicians Learn: A Way Ahead for Music Education*. Burlington, VT: Ashgate, 2002.

Green, Lucy. *Music, Informal Learning, and the School: A New Classroom Pedagogy*. Burlington, VT: Ashgate, 2008.

Gustafson, Ruth. *Race and Curriculum: Music in Childhood Education*. New York: Macmillan, 2009.

Hallinger, Philip, and Ronald H. Heck. "Leadership for Learning: Does Collaborative Leadership Make a Difference in School Improvement?" *Educational Management* 38, no. 6 (2010): 654–678. https://doi:10.1177/1741143210379060.

Hansen, Dee, and Leslie A. Imse. "Student-Centered Classrooms: Past Initiatives, Future Practices," *Music Educators Journal* 103, no. 2 (2016): 20–26. http://doi:10.1177/0027432116671785.

Hansman, Catherine. "Diversity and Power in Mentoring Relationships." In *Critical Perspectives on Mentoring: Trends and Issues*, edited by Catherine Hansman, 39–48. Columbus, OH: ERIC Clearinghouse on Adult, Career, and Vocational Education, Center of Education and Training for Employment, College of Education, The Ohio State University, 2002.

Hardcastle, Beverly. "Spiritual Connections: Protégés' Reactions on Significant Mentorships," *Theory into Practice* 27, no. 3 (1988): 201–208. https://doi.org/10.1080/00405848809543352.

Harvey, Michael, Nancy McIntyre, Joyce T. Heames, and Miriam Moeller. "Mentoring Global Female Managers in the Global Marketplace: Traditional, Reverse, and Reciprocal Mentoring," *International Journal of Human Resource Management* 20, no. 6 (2009): 1344–1361. https://doi:10.1080/09585190902909863.

Hash, Phillip M. "Remote Learning in School Bands During the COVID-19 Shutdown," *Journal of Research in Music Education* 68, no. 4 (2021): 381–397. http://doi:10.1177/0022429420967008.

Hay, Ian, and Neil Dempster. "Student Leadership Development Through General Classroom Activities," Paper presented at Educating: Weaving Research into

Practice, Queensland, Australia, 2004. Queensland: Griffith University. https://research-repository.griffith.edu.au/bitstream/handle/10072/2080/25690_1.pdf.

Hebert, David. "Music Competition, Cooperation, and Community: An Ethnography of a Japanese School Band." PhD dissertation, University of Washington, 2005. ProQuest (AAT3163382).

Hendricks, Karin S. *Compassionate Music Teaching: A Framework for Motivation and Engagement in the 21st Century.* Lanham, MD: Rowman & Littlefield, 2018.

Hendricks, Karin S., and June Boyce-Tillman. *Queering Freedom: Music, Identity, and Spirituality.* Bern: Peter Lang, 2018.

Hendricks, Karin S., and Dorothy. "Negotiating Communities of Practice in Music Education: Dorothy's Narrative." In *Marginalized Voices in Music Education*, edited by Brent Talbot, 65–79. New York: Routledge, 2018.

Hendricks, Karin S., and Gary E. McPherson. "Reconsidering Musical Ability Development Through the Lens of Diversity and Bias." In *The Oxford Handbook of Compassion and Care in Music Education*, edited by Karin S. Hendricks. New York: Oxford University Press, 2023.

Hess, Juliet. "Equity and Music Education. Euphemisms, Terminal Naivety, and Whiteness." *Action, Criticism, and Theory for Music Education* 16, no. 3 (2017): 15–47. http://doi:10.22176/act16.3.15.

Hess, Juliet. *Music Education for Social Change: Constructing an Activist Music Education.* New York: Routledge, 2019.

Higa, Darrel, Marilyn J. Hoppe, Taryn Lindhorst, Shawn Mincer, Blair Beadnell, Diane M. Morrison, Elizabeth A. Wells, Avry Todd, and Sarah Mountz. "Negative and Positive Factors Associated with the Well-Being of Lesbian, Gay, Bisexual, Transgender, Queer, and Questioning (LGBTQ) Youth," *Youth & Society* 46, no. 5 (2014): 663–687. https://doi.org/10.1177/0044118X12449630.

Hill, Shirley, Brian Gay, and Keith Topping. "Peer-Assisted Learning Beyond School." In *Peer Assisted Learning*, edited by Keith Topping and Stewart Ehly, 291–311. New York: Routledge, 1998.

Hobson, Andrew J. "Fostering Face-to-Face Mentoring and Coaching." In *The Sage Handbook of Mentoring and Coaching in Education*, edited by Sarah Fletcher and Carol Mullen, 59–73. Thousand Oaks, CA: SAGE, 2012.

hooks, bell. *Teaching to Transgress.* New York: Routledge, 2014.

Hoover, Grant. "LGBT Leadership Development: Uniting LGBT and Leadership Scholarship to Determine Best Practices," *The Vermont Connection* 30, no. 4 (2009): 32–41. https://scholarworks.uvm.edu/tvc/vol30/iss1/4.

Howe, Christine. *Peer Groups and Children's Development* (Vol. 14). Hoboken, NJ: John Wiley & Sons, 2009.

Jellison, Judith A. *Including Everyone: Creating Music Classrooms Where All Children Learn.* New York: Oxford University Press, 2015.

Jellison, Judith A., Laura Brown, and Ellary Draper. "Peer-Assisted Learning and Interactions in Inclusive Music Classrooms: Benefits, Research, and Applications," *General Music Today* 28, no. 3 (2015): 18–22. https://doi.org/10.1177/1048371314565456.

Jellison, Judith A., and Donald M. Taylor. "Attitudes Toward Inclusion and Students with Disability: A Review of Three Decades of Music Research," *Bulletin of the Council for Research in Music Education*, no. 172 (2007): 9–23. www.jstor.org/stable/40319362.

Johnson, David, and Roger T. Johnson. "Making Cooperative Learning Work," *Theory into Practice* 38, no. 2 (1999): 67–73. https://doi.10.1080/00405849909543834.

Johnson, David, and Roger T. Johnson. "Essential Components of Peace Education," *Theory into Practice* 44, no. 4 (2005): 280–292. https://doi.10.1207/s1543042tip4404_2.

Johnson, Erik A. "The Effect of Peer-Based Instruction on Rhythm Reading Achievement," *Contributions to Music Education* 38, no. 2 (2011): 43–60. www.jstor.org/stable/24127190.

Johnson, Erik A. "Peer Teaching in the Secondary Music Ensemble," *Journal of Education Training Studies* 3, no. 5 (2015): 35–42. https://doi.org/10.11114/jets.v3i5.906.

Jonassen, D. H., and Johannes Strobel. "Modeling for Meaningful Learning." In *Engaged Learning with Emerging Technologies*, edited by David Hung and Myint Swe Khine, 1–27. Dordrecht: Springer, 2006.

Jones, Lisa, Charlotte Dean, Amy Dunhill, Max A. Hope, and Patricia A. Shaw. "'We Are the Same as Everyone Else Just with a Different and Unique Backstory'": Identity, Belonging, and 'Othering' within Education for Young People Who Are 'Looked After," *Children & Society* 34 (2020): 492–506. https://doi:10.1111/chso.12382.

Kaplan, Phyllis R., and Sandra Stauffer. *Cooperative Learning in Music*. Reston, VA: MENC, The National Association for Music Education, 1994.

Karcher, Michael J. "The Cross-Age Mentoring Program: A Developmental Intervention for Promoting Students' Connectedness across Grade Levels," *Professional School Counseling* 2 (2008): 137–143. https://doi/pdf/10.1177/2156759X0801200208.

Karcher, Michael J., Alice Davidson, Jean Rhodes, and Carla Herrera. "Pygmalion in the Program: The Role of Teenage Peer Mentors' Attitudes in Shaping Their Mentees' Outcomes," *Applied Developmental Science* 14, no. 4 (2010): 212–227. https://doi.org/10.1080/10888691.2010.516188.

Karcher, Michael J., Gabriel Kuperminc, Sharon Portwood, Cynthia Sipe, and Andrea Taylor. "Mentoring Programs: A Framework to Inform Program Development, Research, and Evaluation," *Journal of Community Psychology* 34, no. 6 (2006): 709–725. https://doi.org/10.1002/jcop.20125.

Kendi, Ibrim X. *How to Be an Anti-Racist*. New York: Penguin Random House, 2019.

Kiersch, Christa, and Janet Peters. "Leadership from the Inside Out: Student Leadership Development within Authentic Leadership and Servant Leadership Frameworks," *Journal of Leadership Education* 16, no. 1 (2017): 148–168. https://doi.10.12806/V16/I1/T4.

Kinghorn, Janice. "The New Digital Divide: Peer Collaboration as a Bridge," *Association for University Regional Campuses of Ohio Journal* 20, no. 6 (2014): 24–31. https://aurco.org/Journals/AURCO_Journal_2014/Digital_Divide_Rye-Kinghorn_AURCO_Vol20_2014.pdf.

Kivunja, Charles. "Innovative Methodologies for 21st Century Learning, Teaching and Assessment: A Convenience Sampling Investigation into the Use of Social Media Technologies in Higher Education," *International Journal of Higher Education* 4, no. 2 (2015): 1–26. https://doi.org/10.5430/ijhe.v4n2p1.

Kouzes, James M., and Barry Z. Posner. *The Student Leadership Challenge: Five Practices for Becoming an Exemplary Leader*. Hoboken, NJ: John Wiley & Sons, 2018.

Kraiger, Kurt. "Transforming Our Models of Learning and Development: Web-Based Instruction as Enabler of Third-Generation Instruction," *Industrial and Organizational Psychology* 1 (2008): 454–467. https://doi.org/10.1111/j.1754-9426/08.

Lawrence-Brown, Diana. "Differentiated Instruction: Inclusive Strategies for Standards-Based Learning That Benefit the Whole Class," *American Secondary Education* 32, no. 3 (2004): 34–62. www.jstor.org/stable/41064522.

Leppisaari, Irja. "Exploring Emerging Mentoring Practices in New Ecosystems of Learning in Finland," *International Association for Development of the Information Society* (2019): 97–108. https://files.eric.ed.gov/fulltext/ED601177.pdf.

Liebowitz, Jay, and Thomas Beckman. *Knowledge Organizations: What Every Manager Should Know*. Boca Raton, FL: St. Lucie Press, 1998.

Lindwall, Jennifer. "Will I Be Able to Understand My Mentee? Examining the Potential Risk of the Dominant Culture Mentoring Minority Youth," *Journal of Youth Development* 12, no. 1 (2017): 1–20. https://doi.org/10.5195/jyd.2017.485.

Lucas, Katharina F. "The Social Construction of Mentoring Roles," *Mentoring & Tutoring: Partnership in Learning* 9, no. 1 (2001): 23–47. https://doi.org/10.1080/13611260120046665.

Madsen, Clifford K. "Music Teacher Education Students as Cross-Age Reading Tutors in an After-School Setting," *Journal of Music Teacher Education* 20, no. 2 (2011): 40–54. https://doi.org/10.1177/1057083710371441.

Madsen, Clifford K., David S. Smith, and Charles C. Feeman, Jr. "The Use of Music in Cross-Age Tutoring within Special Education Settings," *Journal of Music Therapy* 25, no. 3 (1988): 135–144. https://doi.10.1093/jmt/25.3.135.

Marshal, Michael P., Laura J. Dietz, Mark S. Friedman, Ron Stall, Helen A. Smith, James McGinley, Brian C. Thoma, Pamela J. Murray, Anthony R. D'Augelli, and David A. Brent. "Suicidality and Depression Disparities between Sexual Minority and Heterosexual Youth: A Meta-Analytic Review," *Journal of Adolescent Health* 49, no. 2 (2011): 115–123. https://doi.org/10.1016/j.jadohealth.2011.02.005.

Mayer, Richard. "Rote Versus Meaningful Learning," *Theory into Practice* 41, no. 4 (2002): 226–232. https://doi.org/10.1207/s15430421tip4104_4.

McCarthy, Josh. "International Design Collaboration and Mentoring for Tertiary Students through Facebook," *Australasian Journal of Educational Technology* 28, no. 5 (2012): 755–775. https://doi.org/10.14742/aejt.1383.

McGregor, Jane. "Recognizing Student Leadership: Schools and Networks as Sites of Opportunity," *Improving Schools* 10, no. 1 (2007): 86–101. https://doi:10.1177/1365480207073725.

Miksza, Peter. "The Future of Music Education: Continuing the Dialogue about Curricular Reform," *Music Educators Journal* 99, no. 4 (2013): 45–50. https://doi.org/10.1177/0027432113476305.

Miller, Alexander R. "Learning and Leading: Transformational Learning Experiences among College Student Peer Leaders." EdD dissertation, Northern Illinois University, 2016. https://commons.lib.niu.edu/handle/10843/21078.

Miller, Hugh, and Mark Griffiths. "E-Mentoring." In *The Handbook of Youth Mentoring*, edited by David Dubois and Michael J. Karcher, 300–313. Thousand Oaks, CA: SAGE, 2005.

Monteiro, Dana. "Samba: The Sense of Community in Participatory Music." DMA dissertation, Boston University, 2016. ProQuest (AAT10193022).

Mullen, Carol A. *Mentorship Primer.* New York: Peter Lang, 2005.
Murphy, Heather. "Improving the Lives of Students, Gay and Straight Alike: Gay-Straight Alliances and the Role of School Psychologists," *Psychology in the Schools* 49, no. 9 (2012): 883–891. https://doi.org/10.1002/pits.21643.
"National Core Arts Standards," 2014. www.nationalartsstandards.org.
Navalka, Chandni, James N. Levitt, Shawn Johnson, and Sharon Farrell. "Putting Collaborative Leadership into Practice," *Parks Stewardship Forum* 37, no. 2 (2021): 316–324. https://doi.org/10.5070/P537253237.
Nichols, Jeananne. "Rie's Story, Ryan's Journey: Music in the Life of a Transgender Student," *Journal of Research in Music Education* 61, no. 3 (2013): 262–279. https://doi.org/10.1177/0022429413498259.
Novak, Joseph D. "Meaningful Learning: The Essential Factor for Conceptual Change in Limited or Inappropriate Propositional Hierarchies Leading to Empowerment of Learners," *Science Education* 86, no. 4 (2002): 548–571. https://doi.org/10.1002/sce.10032.
Owen, Julie. "Transforming Leadership Development for Significant Learning," *New Directions for Student Leadership* 145 (2015): 7–17. https://doi.org/10.1002/yd.20120.
Palkki, Joshua. " 'My Voice Speaks for Itself:' The Experiences of Three Transgender Students in Secondary School Choral Programs." PhD dissertation, Michigan State University, 2016. ProQuest (AAT10141543).
Patton, Michael Q. *Qualitative Research and Evaluation Methods.* Thousand Oaks, CA: SAGE, 2002.
Pereira, Nádia Salgado, and Alexandra Marques-Pinto. "Including Educational Dance in an After-School Socio-Emotional Learning Program Significantly Improves Pupils' Self-Management and Relationship Skills? A Quasi-Experimental Study," *The Arts in Psychotherapy* 53 (2017): 36–43. https://doi.org/10.1016/j.aip.2017.01.004.
Posner, Barry Z. "Effectively Measuring Student Leadership," *Administrative Sciences* 2, no. 4 (2012): 221–234. https://doi.10.3390/admsci2040221.
Pretti-Frontczak, Kristi, and Dianne Bricker. *An Activity-Based Approach to Early Intervention.* Baltimore, MD: Brookes Publishing, 2004.
Punie, Yves, and Kirsti Ala-Mutka. "Future Learning Spaces: New Ways of Learning and New Digital Skills to Learn," *Nordic Journal of Digital Literacy* 2, no. 4 (2007): 210–225. https://doi.org/10.18261/ISSN1891-943X-2007-04-02.
Rhodes, Christopher, and Mark Brundrett. "Leadership for Learning." In *The Principles of Educational Leadership and Management*, edited by Tony Bush, David Middlewood, and Les Bell, 153–175. Thousand Oaks, CA: SAGE, 2010.
Richardson, Keith D. "How High School Band Directors Learn Leadership: The Journey to Transformational Leadership and Autonomous Student Leaders." DMA dissertation, Boston University, 2022. ProQuest (AAT28776378).
Riese, Hanne, Akylina Samara, and Sølvi Lillejord. "Peer Relations in Peer Learning," *International Journal of Qualitative Studies in Education* 25, no. 2 (2012): 601–624. http://dx.doi.org/10/1080/09518398.2011.605078.
Rossetti, Zachary S. " 'That's How We Do It': Friendship Work between High School Students with and without Autism or Developmental Delay," *Research & Practice for Persons with Severe Disabilities* 36, nos. 1–2 (2011): 23–33. https://doi.org/10.2511/rpsd.36.1-2.23.
Rush, Scott. *Habits of a Successful Band Director: Pitfalls and Solutions.* Chicago, IL: GIA Publications, 2006.

Ryan, Caitlin, Stephen T. Russell, David Huebner, Rafael M. Diaz, and Jorge Sanchez. "Family Rejection as a Predictor of Negative Health Outcomes in White and Latino Lesbian, Gay, and Bisexual Young Adults," *Pediatrics* 123, no. 1 (2009): 346–352. https://doi.org/10.1542/peds.2007-3524.

Salavuo, Miikka. "Social Media as an Opportunity for Pedagogical Change in Music Education," *Journal of Music Education and Technology* 1, nos. 2–3 (2008): 121–136. https://doi:10.1386/jmte.1.2.

Sawyer, Richard D. "Mentoring but Not Being Mentored: Improving Student—Student Mentoring Programs to Attract Urban Youth to Teaching," *Education* 36, no. 1 (2001): 39–59. https://doi.org/10.1177/0042085901361004.

Schön, Donald A. *Educating the Reflective Practitioner: Toward a New Design for Teaching and Learning in the Professions.* San Francisco, CA: Jossey Bass, 1987.

Schul, James E. "Revisiting an Old Friend: The Practice and Promise of Cooperative Learning for the Twenty-First Century," *The Social Studies* 102, no. 2 (2011): 88–93. https://doi:10.1080/00377996.2010.509370.

Scruggs, Bernadette Butler. "Learning Outcomes in Two Divergent Middle School String Orchestra Classroom Environments: A Comparison of a Learner-Centered and a Teacher-Centered Approach." PhD dissertation, Georgia State University, 2009. ProQuest (AAT3371516).

Sensoy, Özlem, and Robin DiAngelo. *Is Everyone Really Equal? An Introduction to Key Concepts in Social Justice Education.* New York: Teachers College Press, 2017.

Sharan, Yael. "Meaningful Learning in the Co-Operative Classroom," *International Journal of Primary, Elementary, and Early Years of Education* 43, no. 1 (2015): 83–94. https://doi.org/10.1080/03004279.2015.961723.

Shields, Christina. "Music Education and Mentoring as Intervention for at-Risk Urban Adolescents: Their Self-Perceptions, Opinions, and Attitudes," *Journal of Research in Music Education* 49, no. 3 (2001): 273–286. https://doi.org/10.2307/3345712.

Shotton, Heather, Star Oosahwe, and Rosa Cintrón. "Stories of Success: Experiences of American Indian Students in a Peer-Mentoring Retention Program," *Review of Higher Education* 31, no. 1 (2007): 81–107. https://doi.org/10.1353/rhe.2007.0060.

Shpigelman, Carmit-Noa, Patrice Weiss, and Shunit Reiter. "E-Mentoring for All," *Computers in Human Behavior* 25 (2009): 919–928. https://doi:10.1016/j.chb.2009.03.007.

Single, Peg Boyle, and Richard M. Single. "E-Mentoring for Social Equity: Review of Research to Inform Program Development." *Mentoring and Tutoring: Partnership in Learning* 13, no. 2 (2005): 301–320. https://doi:10.1080/13611260500107481.

Smith, Elizabeth. "The Role of Tacit and Explicit Knowledge in the Workplace," *Journal of Knowledge Management* 5, no. 4 (2001): 311–321. https://doi.org/10.1108/13673270110411733.

"Social Justice Issues." *Southern Poverty Law Center.* Accessed January 16, 2021. http://tolerance.org/frameworks/social-justice-standards.

Spigelman, Candace. "Reconstructing Authority: Negotiating Power in Democratic Learning Sites," *Composition Studies* 29, no. 1 (2001): 27–49. www.jstor.org/stable/43501474.

Stader, David L. "Lifeworld and System: Promoting Respect and Responsibility in High School," *Journal of School Improvement* 2, no. 2 (2001): 11–15. https://eric.ed.gov/?id=EJ637703.
Stevens, Richard A. "Understanding Gay Identity Development within the College Environment," *Journal of College Student Development* 45, no. 2 (2004): 185–206. https://doi.org/10.1353/csd.2004.0028.
Stoeger, Heidrun, Manuel Hopp, and Albert Ziegler. "Online Mentoring as an Extracurricular Measure to Encourage Talented Girls in STEM (Science, Technology, Engineering, and Mathematics): An Empirical Study of One-on-One Versus Group Mentoring," *Gifted Child Quarterly* 61, no. 3 (2017): 239–249. https://doi.org/10/1177/ 0016986217702215.
Stoszkowski, John Robert, Liam McCarthy, and Joana Fonseca. "Online Peer Mentoring and Collaborative Reflection: A Cross-Institutional Project in Sports Coaching," *Journal of Perspectives in Applied Academic Practice* 5, no. 3 (2017): 118–121. https://clok.uclan.ac.uk/19860/.
Strand, Katherine. "Nurturing Young Composers: Exploring the Relationship between Instruction and Transfer in 9–12 Year-Old Students," *Bulletin of the Council for Research in Music Education* 165 (2005): 17–36. www.jstor.org/stable/40319268.
Swap, Walter, Dorothy Leonard, Mimi Shields, and Lisa Abrams. "Using Mentoring and Storytelling to Transfer Knowledge in the Workplace," *Journal of Management Information Systems* 18, no. 1 (2001): 95–114. https://doi.org/1 0.1080/07421222.2001.11045668.
Tabuenca, Bernardo, Dominique Verpoorten, Stefaan Ternier, Wim Westera, and Marcus Specht. "Fostering Reflective Practice with Mobile Technologies." In *Proceedings of the 2nd Workshop on Awareness and Reflection in Technology Enhanced Learning*, Technical University of Aachen (RWTH) (2012): 87–100. http://hdl.handle.net/2268/151980.
Talbot, Brent C. "Introduction." In *Marginalized Voices in Music Education*, edited by Brent Talbot, 1–12. New York: Routledge, 2018.
Taylor, Catherine, and Tracey Peter. *Every Class in Every School: Final Report on the First National Climate Survey on Homophobia, Biphobia, and Transphobia in Canadian Schools*. Toronto, ON: Egale Canada Human Rights Trust, 2011.
Taylor, Jeff. "Peer Mentoring within the Middle and High School Music Department of the International School of Kuala Lumpur: A Case Study." DMA dissertation, Boston University, 2016. ProQuest (AAT10135020).
Terrion, Jenepher L., and Ruth Philion. "The Electronic Journal as Reflection-on-Action: A Qualitative Analysis of Communication and Learning in a Peer Mentoring Program," *Studies on Higher Education* 33, no. 5 (2008): 583–597. https://doi.org/10.1080/03075070802373073.
Thies, Tamara T. "Student Leaders as Change Agents: Benefits Emerging from a Curricular Change," *Visions of Research in Music Education* 23 (2013): 1–25. https://opencommons.uconn.edu/vrme/vol23/iss1/4/.
Thomas, Kecia M., Changya Hu, Amanda G. Gewin, Kecia Bingham, and Nancy Yanchus. "The Roles of Protégé Race, Gender, and Proactive Socialization Attempts on Peer Mentoring," *Advances in Developing Human Resources* 7, no. 4 (2005): 540–555. https://doi/pdf/10.1177/1523422305279681.

Thomson, Pat. "Understanding, Evaluating, and Assessing What Students Learn from Leadership Activities: Student Research in Woodlea Primary," *Management in Education* 26, no. 3 (2012): 96–103. https://doi.10.1177/0892020612445677.

Tingson-Gatuz, Connie. "Mentoring the Leader: The Role of Peer Mentoring in the Leadership Development of Students-of-Color in Higher Education." PhD dissertation, Michigan State University, 2009. ProQuest (AAT3381412).

Tomlinson, Carol Ann, and Layne Kalbfleisch. "Teach Me, Teach My Brain: A Call for Differentiated Classrooms," *Educational Leadership* 56, no. 3 (1998): 52–55. https://eric.ed.gov/?id=EJ575232.

Topping, Keith J. *The Peer Tutoring Handbook: Promoting Co-operative Learning*. Cambridge, MA: Brookline Books, 1988.

Topping, Keith J. "Trends in Peer Learning," *Educational Psychology* 25, no. 6 (2005): 631–645. https://doi.10.1080/01443410500345172.

Topping, Keith J., and Stewart Ehly. "Introduction to Peer Assisted Learning." In *Peer-Assisted Learning*, edited by Keith Topping and Stewart Ehly, 1–25. New York: Routledge, 1998.

Topping, Keith J., and Stewart Ehly. "Peer Assisted Learning: A Framework for Consultation," *Journal of Educational and Psychological Consultation* 12, no. 2 (2001): 113–132. https://doi.org/10.1207/S1532768XJEPC1202_03.

Ungar, Michael. "Resilience across Cultures," *British Journal of Social Work* 38, no. 2 (2008): 218–235. https://doi.org/10.1093/bjsw/bcl343.

Ungar, Michael. "The Social Ecology of Resilience: Addressing Contextual and Cultural Ambiguity of a Nascent Construct," *American Journal of Orthopsychiatry* 81, no. 1 (2011): 1–17. https://doi.org/10.1111/j.1939-0025.2010.01067.x.

Valori, Antoni B. "Meaningful Learning in Practice," *Journal of Education and Human Development* 3, no. 4 (2014): 199–209. https://dx.doi.org/10.15640/jehd.v3n4a18.

Van Weelden, Kimberly, Julia Heath-Reynolds, and Scott Lehman. "The Effect of a Peer Mentorship Program on Perceptions of Success in Choral Ensembles: Pairing Students with and without Disabilities," *Update: Applications of Research in Music Education* 35, no. 1 (2016): 1–7. https://doi:10.1177/8755123316675480.

Vygotsky, Lev. *Mind in Society: The Development of Higher Psychological Processes*. Cambridge, MA: Harvard University Press, 1978.

Webb, Richard S. "An Exploration of Three Peer Tutoring Cases in the School Orchestra Program," *Bulletin of the Council for Research in Music Education*, no. 203 (2015): 63–80. www.jstor.org/stable/10.5406/bulcouresmusedu.203.0063.

Webster, Peter R. "Construction of Musical Learning." In *Strategies. Vol. 1 of MENC Handbook of Research on Music Learning*, edited by Richard Colwell and Peter Webster, 35–83. New York: Oxford University Press, 2011.

Weidner, B. N. "Developing Musical Independence in a High School Band," *Bulletin of the Council for Research in Music Education* 205 (2015): 71–86. www.jstor.org/stable/10.5406/bulcouresmusedu.205.0071.

Weidner, B. N. "A Grounded Theory of Musical Independence in the Concert Band," *Journal of Research in Music Education* 68, no. 1 (2020): 53–77. https://doi:10.1177/0022429419897616.

Wheatley, M. *Leadership and the New Science: Learning about Organization from an Orderly Universe*. San Francisco, CA: Berrett-Koehler Publishers, 1994.

Wiggins, J. "Constructivism, Policy, and Arts Education: Synthesis and Discussion," *Arts Education Policy Review* 116 (2015): 155–159. https://doi:10.1080/10632913.2015.1038674.

Wiggins, Jackie H. *Teaching for Musical Understanding*. Rochester, MI: Center for Applied Research in Musical Understanding, 2009.
Woody, Robert H. "Popular Music in School: Remixing the Issues," *Music Educators Journal* 93, no. 4 (2007): 32–37. https://doi.org/10.1177/002743210709300415.
Young, Raymond W., and Carl M. Cates. "Emotional and Directive Listening in Peer Mentoring," *International Journal of Listening* 18, no. 1 (2004): 21–33. https://doi.org/10.1080/10904018.2004.10499060.

Index

active learning 20, 90
Adame, Esteban 29, 55, 192
advanced mentors 92
alumni leadership in samba class 122–124, 129–130
application, as category of learning in development of student leadership 95
Armstrong, Louis 125
asynchronous learning in online peer mentoring 69, 70
authenticity 92, 180
authentic leadership 92–93
autistic student, as mentee 159

band classes *see* Phipps, Sharon
behavior, modeling in peer mentoring 49, 117, 161
Bell, Andrew 26
Best Buddies program 158–159
blended progression of peer mentoring and student leadership 182–185
brave spaces: co-creation in general music class 144; future co-creation of 186–187; music teacher's creation of 41–44; and preparation of student leaders 95
Brown v. Board of Education of Topeka 24
"Buddies" school program 135–136, 144
Buffett, Warren 171
bullying of LGBTQ+ students 43
Bybell, Grace 190, 193

caring, as category of learning in development of student leadership 95–96
Cee, Vince 7, 164–181, 189; background of 164–170; eating together as family 172–173, 179; lifelong participation in music 178; orchestra council 167, 172, 174–175, 179; refinement of teaching ideas 167–168; reflection 179–181; student identity 177–178; student initiative with learning 168–169; student leadership *see* student leadership, in orchestra program; student reflection 176–177; summary of blended progression 182–185
chamber music program 155–156
class, ensemble, and family 172–173
classroom management 117, 128, 136, 144
collaborative leadership 97
collaborative learning 25–26
co-mentoring 23, 67–68
community of learners 83, 84, 185
community samba ensembles 123
comprehensiveness 66
concrete objects, as component of learning 83
constructivism 20
cooperative learning 24–25
Cosby, David 21, 48, 54, 66, 192
critical thinking 21
cross-age mentoring 22–23; in general music class 140–141, 145; in samba class 130; similarities with fixed role of students 67
Culture Code, The 173
cultures, at U.S. Embassy school 170

D'Ambrosio, Kara Ireland 6–7, 132–147, 189; background of 132–135; early experiences using peer mentoring 135–136; modeling and monitoring peer mentoring

145–146; peer mentoring for May Day Dances 136–137; preparation of students for peer mentoring 137–142; reflection 142–146; rotating peer mentoring roles 141–142; sharing knowledge 143–144; structuring peer mentoring 145; student initiative 140–141; student interactions 138–140; summary of blended progression 182–185; using school resources for peer mentoring 144–145
Davis, Troy 22, 42, 72, 96, 192
decentralized learning 21
decision-making skills 21
Dewey, John 20, 23
differentiated instruction 54–55; in samba 128, 129; similarities with fixed role of students 67
digital mentoring 69
disabilities: defined 40
disabilities, students with: in brave spaces 41–42; in middle school band class 158–159, 162; preparation of peer mentoring for 42
diversity 4; and inclusion in general music class 139; and inclusion in samba class 118–119; of students, and preparation of student leaders 95
diversity, equity, inclusion, and access 35, 40, 46, 187
Down syndrome student, as mentee 158–159

Ehly, Stewart 27
e-mentoring 69
emotional tri-fold assessments 137, 143
empathy 86, 98
engagement in peer mentoring, levels of 68–69
Evander Childs High School, New York 109–111
Excellence Without a Soul (Lewis) 171
exit ticket surveys 137–138, 143–144
explicit knowledge 29

facilitator, teacher as 114–115, 124–125
feedback, modeling of 50, 51
fishbowl activity 138
fixed role of students in peer mentoring 66–67, 76
foundational knowledge 28
fourth-grade music class 80–83
Frederick Douglass Academy, Harlem, New York 109, 111
friendships, from socializing 83

Gardner, Mr., youth orchestra 63–65
general music teaching *see* D'Ambrosio, Kara Ireland
Gillett, Gary 56, 192
goals *see* objectives for learning
Gordon, Ed 150
Gramm, Warren 49, 90, 192
Grotans, Helene 28, 43, 48, 192

handbook on peer mentoring, written by students 158
hierarchical peer mentoring 22–23; fixed role of students 67
high-level engagement in peer mentoring 68–69
history of music program: as dimensional trait in socializing 87
humor, in learning 84, 98

identity, diversity, justice, and action (IDJA) 4, 186
imitation 88, 89
inclusion in brave spaces 41–42
individualized instruction 53–54
instruction options for peer mentoring 53–55; differentiated instruction 54–55; individualized instruction 53–54
integration, as category of learning in development of student leadership 95
integrity, energy, and smarts 171
interactions between students during peer mentoring 87–89; in general music classes 138–140; imitation 88, 89; modeling 88–89; nonverbal interactions 87, 88–89; verbal interactions 87–88
interdependence 26
interruptions, peer pressure, sarcasm, and disparate abilities 85–86, 98
intersubjectivity 26
inward leadership 92
ISKL, Kuala Lumpur, Malaysia 164, 169–170, 173

Jackson, Mrs., jazz ensemble 17–19
jazz and peer mentoring 125
jazz ensemble 17–19
jazz improvisation 72
Jellison, Judith 42
journaling by students 50, 74

key signatures, understanding 52
Knight, Terri 85, 192
knowledge: as category of learning in development of student leadership 95; sharing, in general music classes 143–144
knowledge, nature of 27–30; explicit knowledge 29; foundational knowledge 28; non-foundational knowledge 28; prior knowledge 65–66; socializing 27–28; tacit knowledge 29
K-Pop music 139–140

LABBB program 159, 163n2
Lacasse, Allison 75, 84, 93, 192
language: as component of learning 83; as dimensional trait in socializing 87
lateral mentoring 44, 92
leadership: for musical reasons 91; for nonmusical reasons 91; sharing with students 96–97; by students *see* student leadership
leadership training academy 96
lead mentors 92
learning: categories of, as basis for development of student leaders 95–96; components of 83–84; creation of supportive environments *see* music teacher's creation of supportive learning environment
learning how to learn, as category of learning in development of student leadership 96
Lewis, Harry R. 171
LGBTQ+ students: brave spaces for 43; defined 40
low-level engagement in peer mentoring 68

macrostructures, in power structure 44–45
marginalized students: co-creation of brave spaces for 4–5; in general music class 144; as leaders in samba 127; meaningful learning with 44; power relationships and othering students 35, 45–46, 186–187; and preparation of student leaders 95
May Day Dances 136–137, 145
meaningful learning: as foundation of peer mentoring 20–22; introduction to 3–4; with marginalized students 44
memory, group and institutional 122–123, 129–130
mentees: meeting with 48–51; preparation of 152–153; selection of 47–48
Mentor, ancient Greek 20
mentoring: history of 20; of other music teachers 123–124
mentors: lead and advanced 92; meeting with 48–51; preparation of 152–153; selection of 47–48
microstructures, in power structure 44–45
middle school band classes *see* Phipps, Sharon
mid-level engagement in peer mentoring 68
minoritized students: brave spaces for 4, 44; defined 40; *see also* marginalized students
misinformation: teacher's role in student sharing 39, 71
modeling, as nonverbal interaction 88–89
modeling feedback 50, 51
modeling peer mentoring 51–52, 183; in general music class 145–146; and imitation in samba 127–130
monitoring of peer mentors and mentees 49, 71, 145–146, 156–157
Monteiro, Dana 6, 109–131, 189; alumni leadership 122–124, 129–130; background of 109–115; discovery of samba 112–113; genesis of student leadership and peer mentoring 113–114; peer mentoring and samba 115, 125–126; reflection 124–130; student leadership 115–124; *see also* student leadership, in samba class; summary of blended progression 182–185; teacher as facilitator 114–115, 124–125
more-knowledgeable other (MKO) 26

Morris Elementary School, Pacific Northwest 80
music teacher, role of 35–62; instruction options for peer mentoring 53–55; leadership, sharing with students 96–97; reflection 56–57; snapshot: summer choir meeting 36–38; with socializing 86; teacher authority 55–56; verbal mentoring 55
music teacher's construction of peer mentoring system 46–53, 52–53; meeting with mentors and mentees 48–51; modeling feedback 50, 51; modeling peer mentoring 51–52; monitoring peer mentoring 49; selection of mentors and mentees 47–48
music teacher's creation of supportive learning environment 38–46; co-creation of brave spaces for learning 41–44; diversity, equity, inclusion, and access 40, 46; othering students 45–46; power relationships 44–45
mutuality 66

narrative inquiry 188, 191
narrative portraits, methods of research for 188–191
non-binary students, peer mentoring with 43
non-foundational knowledge 28
nonhierarchical peer mentoring 23; reciprocal role of students 23
nonverbal interactions 87, 88–89

objectives for learning: setting daily mentoring objectives in band class 154–155, 162; student co-creation of 49, 70, 144
Oliver, Joe "King" 125
online peer mentoring 69–71; asynchronous and synchronous learning 69; engaging with peers at other institutions 70; issues with online access 71; and learning 70–71; resources beyond the music classroom 70
orchestra program *see* Cee, Vince
Orff Schulwerk 38
othering students 45–46, 187
outward leadership 92

pairing students, strong-weak next to each other 155
pair/share 137
peer-assisted learning 27
peer mentoring: about 1–2; levels of engagement in 68–69; for lifelong participation in music 178; for nonmusical reasons 22; online *see* online peer mentoring; outside of school 72; setting objectives 154–155, 162; types of student roles (fixed and reciprocal) 66–68, 76
peer mentoring, foundations of 20–24; characteristics of 22–24; decentralized learning 21; meaningful learning 20–22
peer mentoring, instruction options 53–55; differentiated instruction 54–55; individualized instruction 53–54
peer mentoring and sharing knowledge 17–34; foundations of peer mentoring 20–24; nature of knowledge 27–30; reflection 30–31; snapshot: jazz ensemble 17–19; student-centered learning, other types of 24–27
peer mentoring system *see* music teacher's construction of peer mentoring system
peer pressure 85–86, 93, 98
peer tutoring 26–27
performance proficiency: as dimensional trait in socializing 87
Phipps, Sharon 7, 148–163, 189; background of 148–151; monitoring of peer mentoring 156–157; pairing students together 155–156; philosophy of peer mentoring 151–152; preparation of mentors and mentees 152–153, 160–162; reflection 160–163; setting objectives 154–155, 162; student initiative and leadership 157–158, 162–163; students with disabilities 158–159; summary of blended progression 182–185
popular music, and peer mentoring 126
power relationships: in creation of supportive learning environment 44–45; as dimensional trait in socializing 87

Index

preparation of student directors in samba class 119–120, 126–127
preparation of student leaders 93, 94–97
problem-solving skills 20–21
procedures, as component of learning 83

quick tips, methods of research for 191–194

racism, and brave spaces for minoritized students 44
Ramirez, Mr., fourth-grade music class 80–83
recess monitors 136, 144
reciprocal role of students in peer mentoring 66, 67–68, 76
reflection-in-action 73–74, 177, 180
reflection-on-action 73–74, 177, 180
relationships among students, building through socializing 85
remote learning environments 69, 76
research methods: for narrative portraits 188–191; for quick tips 191–194
resilience for LGBTQ+ students 43
respect 172
responsibility, shared 92
Rideout, Roger 167
Roseman, Ronald 150

safe spaces for learning 41; *see also* brave spaces
samba *see* Monteiro, Dana
sampling: purposeful 189; snowball 192
San Pedro, Mrs., summer choir meeting 36–38, 47, 54
sarcasm 85, 93, 98
scaffolding 21
"scramble" tactic 153
SEL (social-emotional learning): environment for inclusive learning in brave spaces 41–42; in general music classes 137, 138, 141–142; student-centered learning as driver of 1, 186
servant leadership 93, 175, 179–180
shared leadership 97
shared responsibility 92
Shelby High School, California 36
Small, Christopher 167, 177
Smart, Lieven 51, 71, 192

social-emotional learning (SEL) *see* SEL (social-emotional learning)
social-emotional tri-fold assessments 137, 143
socializing 80–90, 97–105; benefits of 84–85; as building blocks of leadership 89–90; *see also* student leadership; building community 84; building relationships 85; dimensional traits of 86–87; interactions: verbal and nonverbal 87–89; interruptions, peer pressure, sarcasm, and disparate abilities 85–86, 98; as knowledge transfer 27–28; reflection 98–99; role of music teacher 86; snapshot: fourth-grade music class 80–83; as springboard for student interaction in peer mentoring 83–87
Social Justice Standards 4, 186
Southern Poverty Law Center 4, 186
String Fling 176, 180
student, role of 63–79; fixed role in peer mentoring 66–67, 76; levels of engagement in peer mentoring 68–69; online peer mentoring 69–71; *see also* online peer mentoring; peer mentoring outside of school 72; prior knowledge in peer knowledge exchange 65–66; reciprocal role in peer mentoring 66, 67–68, 76; reflection 75–76; snapshot: youth orchestra 63–65; student reflection 72–75; students learning from their peers 66
student-centered learning 1–2, 24–27; collaborative learning 25–26; cooperative learning 24–25; as driver of SEL 1, 186; peer-assisted learning 27; peer tutoring 26–27
student directors 118; leading warm-ups and the samba class 120–122; preparation of 119–120, 126–127
student identity 177–178
student initiative 140–141, 157–158, 162–163, 168–169
student leadership 80, 89–105; effective traits of 91–94; introduction to 2–3; preparation of student leaders 93, 94–97; reflection 98–99; snapshot: fourth-grade music class 80–83; socializing as building blocks of 89–91; *see also* socializing

student leadership, in middle school band 152–153, 157–158, 160–162
student leadership, in orchestra program 170–178; creating opportunities for 179–180; development of 166–167; expansion of 175–176; qualities of effective 171–172; and reflection 180–181
student leadership, in samba class 115–124; diversity and inclusion 118–119, 127; genesis of peer mentoring 113–114; strength in numbers 116–117; student directors 118; student directors, preparation of 119–120, 126–127; student directors leading warm-ups and the samba class 120–122; students modeling behavior and commitment 117–118, 127–130
student reflection 72–75, 176–177; importance of 50; reflection-in-action 73–74, 177, 180; reflection-on-action 73–74, 177, 180; types of reflection 73
student roles in peer mentoring 66–68; fixed role 66–67, 76; reciprocal role 66, 67–68, 76
students with disabilities *see* disabilities, students with
Sunbeam High School 17
synchronous learning in online peer mentoring 69, 70

tacit knowledge 29
teacher authority 55–56
teachers *see* music teacher, role of
teaching: compared with mentoring 23; and peer mentoring *see* music teacher, role of
teaching stations, and rotating peer mentoring roles 141–142, 145
This American Life 168
Topping, Keith 27
transitional kindergarten (TK) 137
trust 86, 98
typically developing students: in brave spaces 41; defined 40; peer mentoring of students with disabilities in band class 158–159; preparation of peer mentoring for 42

Unarce Barry, Tiffany 38, 50, 95, 192
underrepresented minorities 40; *see also* marginalized students
U.S. Embassy school 169–170

valuing the human dimensions of learning, as category of learning in development of student leadership 95
verbal interactions 87–88
verbal mentoring 55
vulnerability 92, 95, 180
Vygotsky, Lev 25, 88

Youth Orchestra 63–65
YouTube videos, created by student 158

zone of proximal development 26

For Product Safety Concerns and Information please contact our EU
representative GPSR@taylorandfrancis.com
Taylor & Francis Verlag GmbH, Kaufingerstraße 24, 80331 München, Germany

www.ingramcontent.com/pod-product-compliance
Lightning Source LLC
Chambersburg PA
CBHW061347300426
44116CB00011B/2023